RECONSTRUCTING THE
COMMON GOOD IN EDUCATION

RECONSTRUCTING THE COMMON GOOD IN EDUCATION

COPING WITH INTRACTABLE AMERICAN DILEMMAS

Edited by
Larry Cuban and Dorothy Shipps

Stanford University Press
Stanford, California

Stanford University Press
Stanford, California
© 2000 by the Board of Trustees of the
Leland Stanford Junior University

Printed in the United States of America
CIP data appear at the end of the book

For David B. Tyack,
outstanding scholar, gifted teacher,
and dear friend

ACKNOWLEDGMENTS

A conversation triggered this volume. It took place in April 1996 between Dorothy Shipps and Larry Cuban in New York City at the annual meeting of the American Educational Research Association. Dorothy suggested that former students find some way of honoring David Tyack, who had just announced that he would retire from Stanford in 2000. Within an hour we had sketched out some possibilities, one of which was a volume of essays drawing from the ideas that David had written about and taught in a career extending from Harvard through Reed College, the University of Illinois, and, since 1969, Stanford University.

Within a few weeks, we compiled a list of David's former students and colleagues, drafted a letter, and enlisted Elisabeth Hansot, his frequent co-author (and wife), in the plan to edit a volume of original essays on the theme of the common good in education. This core notion had inspired not only David's scholarly work for four decades but also those of us who have been his students, colleagues, and friends.

The response from the 25 scholars we contacted was overwhelmingly positive. We began the long winnowing process of figuring out the themes of the volume, determining which writers found the theme congenial and convenient for their schedules in the months ahead, and, of course, seeking a publisher.

For the co-editors, the journey from conversation to published book has been filled with occasional potholes and a few zigzags but has nonetheless arrived at its destination intact. We not only continue to speak to one another but have come to be colleagues full of admiration and affection for each other.

We wish to acknowledge first with much fondness and respect our co-authors, who were prompt with their drafts and tolerant of our editorial peskiness. They have contributed to a volume that honors David's legacy as a historian of education while raising and elaborating important issues at the core of a democratic society committed to public schooling.

Along the way, several individuals contributed ideas that refined our focus and greatly improved this volume. John Meyer and Dan Perlstein gave us new, and quite different, perspectives when the central theme seemed to be pulling in several directions. John Rury and an anonymous reviewer of the manuscript helped with the final conceptual organization of the volume. We thank them all.

At Stanford University Press, we thank the director, Norris Pope, and acquisitions editor Laura Comay. They saw the importance of the intellectual content of this volume to scholars, policy makers, and informed citizens who are deeply concerned about the increasing constriction of the purposes of public schooling. They adopted our call to reinvigorate discussion about education's public purposes at a time when individual interests seem more prized. We also express our appreciation to our production editor Nathan MacBrien, Julia Zafferano, and Janet Gardiner, who shepherded the volume to publication.

Finally, we thank Marla Ucelli at the Rockefeller Foundation for a grant that accelerated publication and publicized the book to an audience beyond scholars. She saw the link between a revitalized expression of the common good in education and the lives of poor and marginalized Americans.

None of this, of course, would have occurred without David Tyack, who has been to all of us a generous, humane teacher, scholar, and friend.

L.C. and D.S.

CONTENTS

CONTRIBUTORS

LARRY CUBAN, a former high school teacher of history and school superintendent, has taught at Stanford University since 1981. His most recent book is *How Scholars Trumped Teachers: Change Without Reform in University Curriculum, Teaching, and Research, 1890–1990* (1999).

RUBÉN DONATO is Associate Professor and Chair of Educational Foundations, Policy and Practice in the School of Education at the University of Colorado at Boulder. His research focuses on the history of American education in general and the history of Mexican American education in particular. He has written on the history of Mexican Americans during the civil rights era, Hispano education, and how educational reform movements have affected Latinos in the Southwest.

PATRICIA ALBJERG GRAHAM is Charles Warren Professor of the History of American Education at the Harvard Graduate School of Education and president of the Spencer Foundation, which supports research on education.

ELISABETH HANSOT teaches at Stanford University's political science department and is a frequent co-author with David Tyack, including *Managers of Virtue: Public School Leadership in America, 1820–1980* (1982); *Public Schools in Hard Times: The Great Depression and Recent Years* (1984); and *Learning Together: A History of Coeducation in American Public Schools* (1990). She has also written on utopias, gender, and humor in organizations.

HARVEY KANTOR is Professor of Education at the University of Utah, where he teaches the history of education and social policy. His current research interests focus on the history of race, poverty, and federal education policy since World War II.

MICHAEL B. KATZ is Sheldon and Lucy Hackney Professor of History at the University of Pennsylvania. He has written on the history of American education, of nineteenth-century social structure and family organization, and of poverty and social welfare.

DAVID F. LABAREE is a professor in the Department of Teacher Education at Michigan State University, where he coordinates the doctoral program in Curriculum, Teaching, and Educational Policy. His work focuses on the historical sociology of American education, resulting in two books, *The Making of an American High School* (1988) and *How to Succeed in School Without Really Learning* (1997). He is currently writing a book about the distinctive nature of education schools in the United States.

ROBERT LOWE is a professor of education at Marquette University. He is currently working on a historical study of teachers in Milwaukee.

JOHN MEYER is Professor of Sociology (and, by courtesy, Education) at Stanford University. He has been involved for many years in the field of comparative education, with historical and cross-national research on the curriculum, enrollment expansion, organizational structures, and linkages between education and the political system.

TED MITCHELL began his career as an educational historian in an undergraduate seminar taught by David Tyack. That experience started a long, happy colleagueship and friendship that continues today. After obtaining his Ph.D. from Stanford under David Tyack's mentorship, Mitchell taught at Dartmouth College and the University of California at Los Angeles. He currently serves as president of Occidental College.

DANIEL PERLSTEIN teaches history and policy at the University of California at Berkeley Graduate School of Education. His research focuses on the interaction of democratic aspirations and social inequalities in the politics and practices of American education. His writings include *Justice, Justice: School Politics and the Eclipse of Liberalism* (2000).

WILLIAM J. REESE is Professor of Educational Policy Studies and of History at the University of Wisconsin-Madison. He is the former editor of

History of Education Quarterly, and his books include *The Origins of the American High School* (1995).

DOROTHY SHIPPS teaches and conducts policy research on the improvement of urban school systems and the role of business and other political actors in education at Teachers College, Columbia University. She has most recently written on the case of the Chicago Public Schools.

Foreword

Patricia Albjerg Graham

The impetus for this volume is David B. Tyack, whose life and work actively continue, I am happy to report, but whose retirement from the Vida Jacks Professorship of Education at Stanford University will occur in September 2000, after 31 years of service there. Anticipating that occasion prompted a group of colleagues, many of whom were his former students and all of whom have learned immensely from him, to gather their wits and their research interests to prepare essays in his honor. As editors Larry Cuban and Dorothy Shipps observe, each chapter is related to ideas that have long underlain Tyack's work. These issues were evident when he wrote his senior thesis at Harvard College about Cape Verdeans' educational experiences in the United States. The themes are expressed in the title of this book, *Reconstructing the Common Good in Education: Coping with Intractable American Dilemmas.*

Concern with education's commitment to the common good has permeated Tyack's work, from his early discussions of the role of education in the formation of early U.S. national identity to his current essays on the purposes of education at the end of the twentieth century. A fundamental question has been whether inevitable conflicts occur between education that is organized to benefit the society and education that is intended to provide maximum benefit to an individual or selected groups of individuals. The tension between two obviously valuable goals—the benefit to society and the benefit to the individual—forms the central theme of this volume.

Many of the authors, like Tyack himself, are historians, and they trace changes in national expectations for education at different periods in our history and different regions of our nation. Others focus on the lives of individuals whom educators must reach if learning is to occur and the common good to be realized. Still others discuss the structures and institutions of education and the societal forces buffeting them.

All recognize the American goal of individual advancement through education, one particularly cherished as a universal standard by the portion of the population to whom it most applied: white males. The broader needs for education, however, that would enhance the society as a whole rather than simply those already privileged by race, gender, and disposition constitute much of the work of this volume. How to build a constituency for these needs and then how to manage the organizational effort to provide the education and concomitant social benefit form the essence of Tyack's own scholarship. Perhaps this concern is best captured and expressed in the essay contributed to this volume by his wife and frequent scholarly collaborator, Elisabeth Hansot, "Civic Friendship: An Aristotelian Perspective," in which she sets forth Aristotle's argument that institutions, such as educational systems, rely on the existence of "civic friendship" to sustain their endeavors.

The phrase "civic friendship" captures Tyack's work and life. He is rare among prolific scholars in his willingness to participate avidly with others in talks, walks, bicycle rides, kayak excursions, and other, preferably outdoor and energetic activities. While the calories are being burned, similar intensity occurs in the conversation around issues of social justice, community, and education. Tactful and generous references are made to others' work as well as insightful suggestions for its improvement. Ideally these discussions take place in a setting of remarkable natural beauty, often in the hills or at the ocean near his Stanford home, but they can also occur on treks through city streets, particularly at times of national conferences, when the need for more intense conversation than that afforded by professional meetings overcomes him and his fortunate friend.

The result of these talks, walks, and subsequent correspondence is a group of lucky educators, some of whom were his students but all of whom value him as a teacher and as a friend. In their "civic friendship," they sustain and advance the ideals of "reconstructing the common good" that this volume represents. David B. Tyack has left us a formidable legacy.

RECONSTRUCTING THE
COMMON GOOD IN EDUCATION

INTRODUCTION

Larry Cuban and Dorothy Shipps

School reform has given pundits, policy makers, and academics full-time work for the past half-century. Highly touted reforms have repeatedly washed over public schools, leaving in their wake the debris of once-heralded programs and public disappointment. Reformers have advocated using schools to solve major social ills, such as poverty and racial oppression, and to prevent drug abuse, teenage pregnancy, and crime. Program after program was established and, within a few years, under the shadow of criticism, dismantled.

In virtually every instance in this century, decision makers and school administrators have reacted to reformers' demands by adopting new policies and implementing new programs. Eventually, however, educators, taxpayers, and parents have become frustrated by the gap between their grand expectations and the niggling results. Public schools, it would seem, have been crude and inefficient tools for solving major societal problems. Nonetheless, amid disappointing results, reformers have persisted with almost religious fervor.

Since the early 1980s, a new generation of school reformers has been intent upon solving the nation's economic problems. An economic justification for public schools—helping the nation compete in a global economy while providing marketable skills to students entering a workplace anchored in an information age—has overwhelmed other popular purposes for tax-supported public schools. For almost two centuries, Americans expected that their public schools—the *common* school as it was initially called—would build citizens, cultivate the moral and social development of individual students, and bind diverse groups into one nation. Now, as public schools are being asked to build the human capital that many believe is essential to maintain economic primacy, other historic purposes appear to be distractions.

Reduced to the dichotomy of private vs. public interests, recent reform proposals have called for more individual parental choice through government-funded vouchers to send children to private schools, independent charter schools, and public schools contracted out to private entrepreneurs. Advocates of choice often see schooling as another consumer commodity. Moreover, private sector management has become the model for public school systems as school and district activities are "downsized," "restructured," and "outsourced." School buses, lunchrooms, and stadiums sport advertisements. Corporate logos dot school corridors. Critics ask, is everything that is public for sale? Is being a good citizen only about being a consumer making individual choices among products? What about the common good the founders of tax-supported public schools so fervently sought?

This tension between public and private, between cultivating the common good and serving individual interests, is one of many conflicts deeply embedded in the institution of public schools and the subject of this book. In the founding of American public schools almost two centuries ago, multiple and conflicting purposes took root, justified on the grounds that both the nation as a whole and individual Americans would prosper as a result.

In the nineteenth century, antebellum school reformers such as Horace Mann and postbellum ones such as William T. Harris believed that publicly funded, locally controlled schools open to all children would promote the common good and improve society. Through universal public schooling, children of the nation would learn the essential knowledge of the past and present to prepare for their future responsibilities. These reformers assumed that public schools were carriers of common democratic values ensuring the survival of the Republic and stability of the social order. Education and the public good were one and the same.

Mid-nineteenth-century public schools were expected to teach basic literacy, strengthen students' moral character, and build citizens who would leave school prepared to discharge their civic duties. With the end of the Civil War, the conquered South presented Abraham Lincoln's successors with the monumental task of transforming four million ex-slaves into literate citizens. In ex-Confederate states, the federal government provided free public schooling for millions of black children and adults, thus forging linkages for the first time between federal action and locally controlled schools and between race and citizenship. Again, education and the common good were assumed to be closely linked. This experiment in schooling ex-slaves for social democracy, however, lasted only a decade, leaving the issues of a federal role in schooling and educating poor, minority children unaddressed for another century.

In the early 1900s, another wave of social reforms swept across the nation, making the economic purpose of public schools explicit. Preparing students for work in an industrial economy then competing with Great Britain and Germany gave impetus to the spread of vocational education. Solving the social ills afflicting the nation, such as meeting the soaring health and social needs of immigrant children, also increased taxpayers' and parents' expectations of what their locally controlled schools could do for the community and for each individual child. Yes, tax-supported public schools, even segregated ones, were still expected to make the young literate and prepare them for their moral and civic duties. But now, more than before, public schools were expected to Americanize newcomers and produce vocationally skilled graduates who could fill skilled jobs in the industrial workforce.

By the middle of the twentieth century, the individual, civic, and economic purposes of tax-supported, locally controlled public schools were firmly in place. The new expectation that a diploma from high school was essential for each son and daughter to climb the ladder of social and economic success added fervor to white, black, and foreign-born parents as they all embraced the public schools. In subsequent decades, national and local reformers framed the larger political, social, and economic problems of the Cold War, racial segregation, and international economic competition as ones that could be solved, in part, through the public schools. For Americans, faith in public schools had become gospel. The articles of faith were a jumble of beliefs that public schooling was the social glue holding the country together, an all-purpose solution to any national problem, and a personal ladder for the climb to success. That mélange of popular beliefs had become a secular religion.

As the twentieth century drew to a close, however, hard core problems of poverty, social stratification, and racial inequities remained intractable and glaring in the nation's urban and rural schools. With increased immigration from Latin America and Asia, and with fierce global scrambling for increased market share, schools again came under close scrutiny. Improvement-minded public officials and corporate critics found fault in graduates unprepared for a fast-changing automated workplace; compared to other developed nations, academic performance was low. In the early 1980s, public officials and corporate leaders feared the United States was losing its economic primacy, fueling wave after wave of unrelenting criticism of schools. The subsequent economic boom of the 1990s did little to silence these doomsayers. Gaggles of reforms calling for restructured schools, vouchers, charter schools, and making schools more business-like accumulated over two decades, reducing the zeal of middle-class parents and taxpayers for identifying public schools with the common good.

As the twenty-first century begins, the popular commitment to public schooling, albeit eroded and brittle, remains durable. Sustaining Americans' faith in tax-supported education are the many expectations for collective and individual goods that have flowed from attending public schools. Public schools are still expected to yield both civic-minded independent thinkers who care for their communities and marketable entry-level workers while remedying the grim effects of poverty and racism upon individual children.

Accommodating all of these purposes for public schools, however, might have been easier were they compatible with—rather than in tough competition for—limited resources. Constraints of money, time, and people restricted what schools could do, increasing the conflict among those championing different goals. It is no surprise, then, that school reformers often diverged in recommending what schools should do to improve.

Historically, public schools (and other social agencies) have been driven to and fro by such private and public pressures, attempting to accommodate different constituencies who criticize these institutions for falling short of their announced goals. Both democratic politics and market forces have placed impossible demands upon schools and other public agencies, already stretched between conflicting purposes. Schools, like other social institutions that serve Americans, have become contested ground over individual rights and the common good.

The founders of the nation, of course, grappled with the inherent tension between public and private, between seeking individual liberty and social order in a democratic society, between equal opportunity and the common good. Over two centuries ago, the Federalist Papers argued for and against protections from a newly formed, powerful federal government. The constitutional system of checks and balances that dispersed authority among the branches of the federal government and the states, including the Bill of Rights, were the essential compromises that resulted. The founders designed these compromises to manage the inescapable conflicts that repeatedly arise in a democracy with overlapping powers of state and federal governments and individual rights. Since then, the U.S. Supreme Court and Congress have renegotiated, time and again, the inevitable tensions between personal liberty and equality and the common good.

This dilemma still poses vexing questions about how much freedom local agents (like teachers or social workers) and clients (like students or the poor) should have in private and governmental institutions. For example, should a single mother who is dependent upon the help of a charitable organization have guarantees of individual freedom that protect her privacy from the prying questions and eyes of a visiting social worker? Should teachers indoctrinate students to be loyal to democratic principles and the nation? Benjamin Rush, writing in 1786, sought to "convert men into republican machines." Or, as he put it: "Let our pupil be taught to love his family, but let him be taught at the same time that he must forsake and even forget them when the welfare of his country requires it" (Sandel 1996, 129). An equally fervent reformer, George Counts, speaking to educators a century and a half later, entitled his book *Dare the School Build a New Social Order?* In these instances, reformers saw the schools as proper engines for indoctrination. Yet many parents and educators committed to democracy in education want schools to nurture students' skepticism and urge students to think independently, raise questions, and challenge authority.

Other deeply embedded value-conflicts about social and political equality and individual opportunity faced the founders then and have faced policy makers ever since. With increased access to public schooling in the past century, students heretofore excluded from schools or who seldom considered finishing high school have remained, expanding the teaching corps, administrative ranks, and, of course, bureaucracies. Tensions over competing definitions of equal opportunity arose when some reformers pressed for special programs for neglected families and students (e.g., ex-slaves, Mexican-American immigrants, and students who are at-risk, gifted, or disabled) while others called for programs directed to all clients, regardless of capacity or circumstance. "Common schooling for all" is the slogan of one set of reformers, while others pass out bumper stickers calling for compensatory programs for students in need of special attention. Both approaches raise fundamental questions about fairness and conflicting definitions of equal educational opportunity. The question begs for an answer: how can we renew the meaning of equity in our democracy so that individual initiative is rewarded while sustaining a commitment to *e pluribus unum*?

Social disparities permeate both school and society in our market-based economy. These inequities raise moral dilemmas. In a federal system where authority is decentralized, control over what happens in communities and classrooms is continually being contested. Some reformers argue that increasing mobility, cultural diversity, and dependence on technology in modern society requires that state, and even federal, control over schools and other public agencies should expand to better confront serious national problems. Common (but higher) academic standards and tougher accountability for educators, they argue, is necessary to provide equity to all students. Government cannot stand by and permit social inequalities to worsen.

Other reformers contend that state and federal agencies should be morally neutral mediators of private interests, negotiating with multinational corporations and individuals alike to temporarily satisfy each until a new bargain is needed. For example, if parents want to exit inadequate public schools to find better private schools, then the government, in its broker role, should permit parental choice through government-funded vouchers.

Inescapable value-laden questions arise from these opposing views: can (or should) the purposes of public schooling be harnessed to a morally neutral, tax-supported government with power dispersed among local, state, and federal agencies? Can (or should) the gap between earlier notions of civic excellence and the contemporary moral purposes of schooling be bridged by a government that actively reconciles—rather than umpires—competing interests?

Thus, the current dilemma confronting public institutions—reconciling the common good with private individual interests—becomes merely one of several equally trying moral dilemmas facing national and local policy makers, administrators, practitioners, and the larger citizenry.

As should now be evident, there are many sources for these intractable dilemmas over the past two centuries. Reformers, in their zeal to correct social ills, have designed and introduced school structures and processes that have both reconciled and exacerbated conflicts. Economic crises, wars, demographic changes, new technologies, and cultural shifts have reverberated through public schools, creating pressures for change and further tensions. The nation's founders had constructed political and constitutional compromises to manage these dilemmas but left subsequent generations the task of adapting their compromises to new circumstances.

The essays in this book address these questions and how reformers over the past century in different venues have pressed for individually driven and collective remedies to political, social, and economic inequities. The issues that we write about probe and examine these durable dilemmas that have been (and are) inherent to public schools in a democracy. We pose these issues as questions:

- How can individual liberty and the common good be better reconciled within tax-supported public schools?
- How can the tension between social integration and social stratification be eased, both in the larger society and within public schools?
- What directions should school reformers pursue in reconstructing the ideal of the common good as a goal for public schools amid unrelenting tensions over conflicting values?

We respond to these questions with no single voice. Acknowledging many disciplinary and value differences among us, we have come together to challenge the prevailing view that the common good is simply the random accumulation of individual choices that Americans make. We worry about this popular view. In the past, we have seen how this notion of the public good as a collection of individual decisions encouraged societal fragmentation and shattered joint efforts to encourage equality and social integration. We have also seen how this view of the common good has allowed elites, with more resources than ordinary individuals, to transform the public good into one that enhances their vested interests while increasing social inequities.

In challenging the prevailing view of the common good, we do not agree among ourselves about how it might be reconstructed. Our different values and experiences virtually guarantee some disagreement.

We do, however, agree on two things. First, assumptions about the common good that drive contemporary policy debates, school reform initiatives, and market-filled rhetoric about schooling need to be openly questioned. Second, the public debate over the common good is constricted, with few alternatives available for informed citizens to consider.

Our questioning derives from values we hold in common: we believe that when individual purposes trump public purposes, when private interest overcomes public interest, both children and adults in a democracy lose. In light of the historical legacy of tension between competing civic and individual values, we believe that the present reform moment requires more voices to join a policy debate that has been heavily tilted toward promoting private and individual interests over the public good.

We also recognize that what appear as dichotomies are infinitely complex and need to be worked through mindfully. For example, few question—either in theory or in practice—that maximizing ethnic, racial, and cultural diversity in public schools is a public good. What often go unacknowledged, however, are the private benefits from diversity that accrue to individuals. In a world where future politicians must seek the approval of both white and Latino voters and where corporate executives must work closely with white, African American, and Asian American managers, it is useful to have developed ties to Latino, Asian American, and African American individuals in school and elsewhere. Learning to live with future political allies, customers, employees, neighbors, and pew-mates confers both a public and a private good. Such complexities in what appear to be either/or choices will be underscored in several chapters.

Finally, the editors and authors are committed to using different disciplinary lenses to analyze the persistent dilemmas that we have identified. We have among us historians, sociologists, political scientists, and educational researchers to broaden our collective "ways of seeing" the past and present conflicts in American public schools. We believe that applying traditional and untraditional lenses to familiar policy issues can reveal uncommon insights. Drawing from different disciplines, then, these essays reframe contested policy issues inside and outside schools. All return, in one way or another, to the central tension between the public and the private, between the common good upon which public schools and democratic society are founded, and the utilitarian interests that individuals seek.

We believe that the present generation of reformers has largely ignored this tension, dismissing the persistent conflicts as if they either never existed or were trifling considerations. To the editors and authors of these essays, however, reconstructing the common good—ensuring that larger purposes for schooling involve more than serving individual needs—remains essential and unfinished work.

PART I

Ways of Seeing the Common Good in Public Education: The Past Informing the Present

Each of the five authors in this section deals historically with the public purposes of U.S. tax-supported schools by examining key moments in school reform over the past century and a half. Each assumes that some renegotiation of purposes is necessary in our time given the ever-renewing conflicts over often-incompatible goals and persistent ambiguities between public and private spheres. In drawing from past and very different contexts, each author offers a distinct historical interpretation on how previous generations of school reformers approached the dilemmas that face contemporary advocates of school improvement.

William Reese's essay examines the nineteenth-century roots of the modern conflict over the goals of American schooling. By reexamining how the early common school crusaders, Horace Mann and William T. Harris, handled similar dilemmas, Reese reminds us that current debates have deep roots. He points out that, at its inception, public education in the United States was founded on nation-building and virtue-forming purposes, with far less emphasis on improving worker productivity. Common schools were intended to instill common values across social classes, teach social cooperation, socialize immigrants, and provide the underpinnings for democracy. A concern then, as now, was that the elite did not patronize the public schools and thereby avoided the lessons of empathy, shared understanding, and social cooperation they had to offer, impoverishing the nation's future as a result.

Urban schooling was of primary interest to Mann and Harris because each saw that industrialization and urbanization had brought both vastly increased economic growth and human degradation on a new scale. These school leaders acknowledged that countering economic and social changes was at the core of the urban school's importance. Reese also clarifies that urban schools—the most likely to be abandoned en masse today—were the most innovative and the most advanced in this formative period. He underscores that neither Mann nor Harris embraced vocational education or a differentiated curriculum in response to industrialization or urbanization because these policies clashed with the essentially moral purposes of the common school.

By reminding us that these multiple goals of education are fundamentally at odds with one another, Reese highlights one dilemma that contemporary school reformers face, especially urban ones who also grapple with the implications of economic restructuring. Can public schools provide anything resembling a common socializing experience while displaying greater respect for social diversity and preparing students for a changing workplace?

Ted Mitchell examines a period of high conflict over citizenship and schooling: Reconstruction. He concludes that Reconstruction's legacy to the modern federal role in public schooling set a precedent in building a common national and social identity. During Reconstruction, he argues, white Southern opposition to federal programs on behalf of black education legitimated a more "aggressive" federal role than would otherwise have been acceptable even to Northerners. As the conquered enemy, white Southerners were briefly subject to a "colonial" military rule and an imposed "common schooling." Ex-slaves were educated at public expense just like whites, except whites were to be taught loyalty to the Northern national government. This era helped create the long-term expectation that the federal government should guarantee the educational opportunities necessary for black citizenship, voting, and other civil rights. For the first time, a federal office of education was established.

Although blacks and their Northern religious and federal government supporters did not succeed beyond the 1870s (the Southern white opposition was too strongly entrenched), their failure left a political legacy for subsequent generations. Their attempt nonetheless altered expectations about the federal role in education and realigned the national dialogue over the purposes of public schooling. Developing national citizenship was reinforced as a central purpose of schooling in the nineteenth century as a result of these expectations. At the same time, the federal government established its role in securing equal rights, one that would be called upon a century later during the Civil Rights movement.

Daniel Perlstein turns to the Great Depression and the inspiration of school reformer George Counts, who argued that public schools were doing no more than reproducing the social class inequities that existed in the larger society. Public schools, according to Counts, needed to be in the vanguard of creating a better, more socially just society.

Perlstein, in offering a detailed historical account of this Depression-era reformer's ideas, points out the tension among progressives: their narrow focus on pedagogy was in conflict with ideals for a democratic schooling that could transcend social class. He argues that the value of Counts's social critique of the role of public schools is that it spurs others to articulate their guiding values more clearly and engenders more substantive public dialogue. He seeks dialogue that goes beyond the often spurious exchanges forcing citizens to choose between artificial (or at least poorly understood) choices, such as having or not having bilingual education, school uniforms, or phonics in the curriculum.

In Rubén Donato's chapter, we turn to a story about post–World War II school districts in the Southwest, where Spanish-American parents and community leaders are sometimes in control but more frequently not. In only one of these districts did the marginalized communities have strong political representation, and it was only there that commonly accepted political levers worked on behalf of their children. From the perspective of those communities, the benefits of universal, common schooling did not automatically accrue from philosophical arguments or from policy opportunities in and of themselves. Only when these communities developed political power were they able to exploit policy opportunities and "universal" expectations to benefit their own children.

In contrast to the ex-slaves in Mitchell's chapter, the Spanish Americans in Donato's narrative did not have federal support in their bid for equal educational opportunity. Instead, they acted locally, drawing on a broad national consensus about the value of consolidated (and larger) school districts and differentiated curricula to develop a school program that addressed their own children's needs. In other districts that Donato examined, the contrasting evidence of ongoing marginalization, disrespect, and low levels of Spanish-American children's academic performance highlight the importance of acquiring political representation. Equal opportunity depends, Donato suggests, as much on power relations as on shared values about public schooling.

The final chapter in this section, by Dorothy Shipps, examines the contemporary impulse to improve urban schools by managerial reform. Drawing from historical scholarship on the development of the corporate model of schooling in the early twentieth century, Shipps concludes that modern managerial reform in schools is both more of the same and a distorted exaggeration. The corporate model of public schooling, initiated in response to broad economic and social changes, pushed the purposes of public schools toward the economically functional, in both individual and collective terms. For most of the twentieth century, public schools have been expected to provide the means to an individual's livelihood, the human capital needed for collective productivity, and the basis for national wealth.

But the range of urban school goals has been distorted and constrained by other changes. One of them is the apparent decline in the status of professional educators relative to economic leaders. Another is the internal debate among business leaders about how best to encourage worker productivity: one group advocates greater reliance on the invisible hand of markets; another would lessen market-induced tendencies to create labor-management conflict by greater worker participation. These corporate management debates transfer to schools and help marginalize more fundamental differences between conflicting purposes of urban schools. Linking the low status of educators with the low salience of equity and nation-building purposes of schooling in contemporary rhetoric and policy making, Shipps advocates that educators pay less attention to the economic purposes of schooling. Instead, they should focus on the moral and nation-building purposes of schooling that Reese found at the core of nineteenth-century educational leadership.

CHAPTER 1

Public Schools and the Elusive Search for the Common Good

William J. Reese

Looking back at our times a century from now, historians may detect one of those proverbial "turning points" in our nation's development. The "privatization" of formerly public "goods" such as public schools, to use modern jargon, has become more than an academic question, as coalitions of reformers question the nation's historic commitment to universal public education. Public schools, of course, have been controversial since their inception in the Northern states in the decades preceding the Civil War. Catholics then opposed their Protestant tone and demanded a division of the school fund, which horrified the Protestant majority and led Catholics to begin the slow process of building an alternative parochial system. Other critics in the nineteenth century opposed the idea of taxing everyone to educate the young or, while supporting the common elementary schools, called for the elimination of free high schools. Still others complained about the evils of coeducation (complaints that bore little fruit) or feared the prospect of racial integration (which proved unpopular in all regions of the nation). Yet the public schools survived these and other movements to undermine their legal right to existence, and they soon educated the vast majority of school-age children.

Even by the 1980s, a time of evident national soul-searching about the state of U.S. public schools—producing dozens of reports from philanthropic foundations and all levels of government—they continued to enroll approximately 90 percent of the relevant population. But movements had emerged from diverse parts of the political spectrum, especially from right of center, and they called for something that had long seemed unthinkable: the elimination of the so-called "public school monopoly" through a variety of means, including tuition tax credits and vouchers.

Only citizens in the coming decades will know whether the current fascination with the private sector led to a new educational order and a radically altered social landscape. What seems certain in the here-and-now often evaporates in the mists of time. But, at the onset of a new millennium, one might usefully reflect upon the nation's common school traditions as they evolved in the nineteenth century to place current debates on the schools in a broad historical context. It is important to recognize that calls for the privatization of all aspects of social life, including education, have not gone unchallenged. Although politicians on the state and federal levels debate the issue of privatization and often extol the virtues of "school choice," numerous writers have also revived interest in the idea of the "common good," of special importance in considering the place of public schools in the larger society. The "common good" is subject to various definitions, but it usually means the elevation of civic values and ideals above individual self-interest, and it has attracted the attention of a broad range of academics and public intellectuals since the mid-1980s (Raskin 1986; Novak 1989; Etzioni 1995). An age that glorified the triumph of capitalism around the globe and, according to some critics, made greed a virtue also generated its opposite, a concern with how to repair the torn fabric of community as business values and the advancement of free market ideals increasingly dominated discussions of civil society.

Without question, future scholars looking back upon our generation will note the revived interest in identifying common values in a world shaken by the vast restructuring of the world economy and consequent reassessment of familiar institutions. By the late 1980s, capitalism and free markets appeared triumphant as the Cold War ended and communist regimes collapsed. Drawing upon eclectic sources, scholars rediscovered the age-old problem of defining what constitutes the common good and its place in a pluralistic, democratic republic. They found insights in the writings of Aristotle, St. Thomas Aquinas, Alexis de Tocqueville, and other classic authors to help reformulate the moral basis for personal action and a redefinition of public life in the late twentieth century. Some theorists hail from the far left, others from the neo-conservative right, and still others eschew political labels; yet they are all concerned with how to rebuild a sense of community and social justice. Whether they fear corrosive individualism and an untrammeled market or identity politics and "alternative" families, or whether they embrace an enlightened capitalism or communitarianism, these citizens ask whether it is possible to identify and promote common ideals in a nation that so prizes both individual freedom and cultural pluralism (Raskin 1986; Novak 1989; Ford Foundation 1989; Daley and Cobb 1989; Wallach and Wallach 1990).

Similar questions were asked about school and society in the nineteenth century, when public schools were first established in the Northern states and, in the wake of Reconstruction, slowly made their appearance in the former Confederacy. An exploration of the founding ideals of public education in the nineteenth century offers some needed perspective on contemporary debates.

In the 1800s, a wide range of activist citizens assumed that the common school—publicly funded, free, and in theory open to everyone—was central to the common good and an improved society. Two leading activists—Horace Mann before the Civil War and William T. Harris afterwards—assumed that the survival of the republic, the spread of democratic values, and the stability of the social order depended upon free public schools. Only through universal public education could the children of the expanding nation learn mainstream majority values as well as core knowledge, which was deemed essential to introduce children to the best sources of wisdom from the past while preparing them for the sober responsibilities of life in a free society.

Citizens in the new century will provide their own answers to profound questions about education and the common good. To revisit the main educational ideas of Mann and Harris—the most famous school advocates of their times—provides a unique perspective on issues that continue to inspire debate concerning the best paths to the good society. Living in an age—like our own—of enormous economic and social changes, Mann and Harris offer some insights into the kinds of social tensions a common system was expected to address during its formative years. And they remind us of the various trade-offs and compromises entailed in supporting any common set of institutions in a society that simultaneously seeks individual freedom and regulated social behavior. By serving as one of the major common institutions in American society, public schools—locally controlled, tax-supported, often far removed from federal intervention, and supported by diverse coalitions of citizens—came to assume huge symbolic as well as practical importance. Above all other institutions they came to embody the nation's deepest hopes and disappointments concerning the possibilities of democracy, economic freedom, and an elevated common culture.

That schools would continue to arouse strong passions about their character and purposes would not have surprised Horace Mann. He was born in Franklin, Massachusetts, in 1796, to a farming family whose roots reached back to the colonial period. During his lifetime, America was increasingly transformed from an agrarian republic to a more urban, industrial society, one where immigrants from Ireland, Germany, and other countries changed the face of the nation. Like many other farm children, Mann knew hard work firsthand, which he said became part of his second nature, leading to fifteen-hour workdays (Tyack and Hansot 1982, 57). He received a modest education in the local district school, but, ambitious for something better, he studied with an itinerant schoolmaster, attended Brown University, and later went to Litchfield Law School. By the 1830s Mann was a rising political presence in the newly formed Whig Party. As a legislator he championed the cause of the mentally ill, antislavery, prison reform, and temperance. Alcohol consumption, he believed, was the source of much poverty in America, a common view among middle-class reformers. But it was when he decided to accept the post of secretary of the newly created Massachusetts State Board of Education in 1837—which friends and family thought would sink a rising career—that Mann unknowingly charted a dramatically new course for himself and for the cause of public education across the nation (Messerli 1972).

By the time of his death in 1859, no other figure was more associated with the public schools than Mann. He was to education what Catherine Beecher was to reforms in domestic economy, William Lloyd Garrison to abolitionism, and Ralph Waldo Emerson to American Letters. Mann was lionized by the emerging educational profession he had promoted in his countless reports, speeches at educational conventions, and published editorials and essays, which were reprinted in newspapers and school periodicals throughout the land. And his reputation only grew over time. A century after his death, the National Education Association revealed his long shadow over popular thinking about the origins of public education by sponsoring the reprinting of his twelve annual reports as secretary, the most widely read set of educational documents issued before the Civil War. To comprehend the role of common schools in attempts to promote the larger good of society in antebellum America, one necessarily turns to his writings.

Hardly a profound or philosophically impressive thinker—certainly not compared with contemporaries like Emerson, or Harris later—Mann nevertheless remains a key figure in the rise of common schools before the

Civil War. David Tyack and Elisabeth Hansot aptly refer to him as the "archetype" educational reformer of his generation. Raised in a Puritan household, Mann never dropped the moralizing side to his social thought; indeed, many scholars see this as decisive in shaping his somewhat brooding personality (Messerli 1972; Tyack and Hansot 1982, 52–58). Embracing Unitarianism, which emphasized reason and a benevolent God, he seemed typical of an array of Whig reformers who clashed with the opposition Jacksonian Democrats over numerous public policy issues in the 1830s and 1840s. He favored government subsidies for railroads and other internal improvements, actively promoting the use of government in the expansion of a free market economy. At the same time, he witnessed with horror the rise of poverty, especially in the cities, which themselves grew at their greatest rate ever in American history in the pre–Civil War decades. Into the cities flooded displaced farmers and their children who were increasingly unable to make a living on the rocky New England soil, unable to compete with the cheaper farm goods of the Midwestern states that were tied to eastern and world markets via the fabled Erie Canal, completed in 1825. In the mill towns and cities, with the first factories appeared grave social extremes: the fabulously wealthy and the abysmally poor, both given to excessive behaviors, according to many reformers (Kaestle 1983).

Moral dissipation seemed to increase alongside economic prosperity. Americans consumed more alcohol per capita in the 1820s than at any other time in the nation's history, before or since, and cities stood both as the shining example of economic growth and progress and as the worst forms of human degradation. Children hustled on the city streets, learning vice and the ways of the criminal, said many anxious citizens. As impoverished Irish immigrants arrived in New England towns and cities, especially by the 1840s, Whigs and other citizens offered dire predictions of imminent social war, pitting rich against poor, native against immigrant, and white against black, as abolitionist sentiments intensified. Like other Whigs, Mann pressed for solutions to halt the spread of social disorder, crime, race riots (already familiar in the cities), and the other evils of the day (Howe 1979). As he wrote in his *Lectures on Education* in 1845, "The mobs, the riots, the burnings, the lynchings, perpetrated by the *men* of the present day, are perpetrated, because of their vicious or defective education, when children. . . . If we permit the vulture's eggs to be incubated and hatched, it will then be too late to take care of the lambs" (Mann 1904, 2: 41). He sought a way out of potential social chaos through the widespread adoption of universal public education.

Scholars such as Carl F. Kaestle have shown that school enrollments were already rising in the North by the time Mann had risen to a position of influence and that his generation of activists was primarily concerned with shaping the system. This included attempts to centralize administrative authority, standardize the curriculum, and expand a graded system of schools (Kaestle 1983). All of this occurred at a time when politicians in stump speeches, editorialists in local newspapers, and ministers from the pulpit all lamented the presumed collapse of community, rising crime rates, incivility in the streets, and similar threats to the preservation of the republic, whose fragility seemed clear according to the moralizing reformers. As a legislator, before becoming an educational bureaucrat, Mann had actively promoted economic development and the spread of the free market system. Fearful of the darker side of social change, he and other Whigs urged citizens to champion the cause of public schools, which he called the greatest invention in history.

As he contemplated the creation of his soon-to-be-famous periodical, the *Common School Journal*, in 1838, Mann wrote that the nation's intellectual and moral development had not kept pace with its rising wealth. Convinced that individuals, especially when they were young, were capable of great improvement, he repeated the claims of Thomas Jefferson and the Founding Fathers that intelligence and virtue were the foundation of the republic, a recurrent theme in his many writings. America, he said, had a destiny to fulfill. Unlike the Old World, where learning was still cloistered and hidden from the masses, here the importance of the diffusion of knowledge was a guiding social belief. The common schools, which in theory would offer each child the same opportunities for moral and intellectual development, would help break down social animosities, teach social cooperation at a time of rising tensions, and spare the nation the horrors of European despotism, in which standing armies repeatedly crushed civilian dissent. The fruits of the common schools, however, would not appear in a season but in the next generation. There was no doubting the conclusion that "a proper education of the rising generation is the highest earthly duty" (Mann 1904, 2: 7).

Like other contemporary writers on education, Mann repeatedly argued that the education of republican citizens required something special. Countless speeches, sermons, and books during the antebellum period, at least in the North, praised the common schools as providing the foundations of good citizenship, and writers usually contrasted the American approach to the education and training of the young with the ways of corrupt, monarchical, often Catholic Europe (Mintz 1995, 108). Mann echoed these views. Like other reformers, he believed that the liberty guaranteeing respect for the laws in the political arena and the protection of private property in the economic sphere could prove dangerous when it came to public morals. The American Revolution had led to the disestablishment of religion, the traditional parent of moral behavior, in the various states, and Massachusetts, the original home of the Puritans, was the last to succumb, in 1833. Without a standing army or established churches, how would men lead moral lives? Religious revivals, powerful in rural and urban America since the turn of the century, provided one answer, as church membership soared. Sunday schools would also help. Temperance crusades, which the Whigs (often native born) championed, provided another means to guarantee right living. But lasting change seemed most likely in the education of the young, at a stage of life when individuals seemed most malleable.

Having discarded the Calvinist training of his youth, Mann absorbed the milder views of mainstream, middle-class Protestantism, which emphasized not Adam's sin and predestination but the power of the environment to shape and mold each individual (Mintz 1995, 110). He also applauded the romantic pedagogy of Johann Pestalozzi, the famed European child-centered educator, who called for innovative teaching practices and greater kindness toward children. But Mann's romanticism only went so far. What was needed, he thought, was the popularization of new forms of self-discipline, suitable for a republic. As he argued in a lecture on the history of education in 1840, unlike Europe, where despotic governments ruled, in America one could not find a "thousand-eyed police to detect transgression and crush it in the germ" (Mann 1904, 2: 242). How, then, could social order be guaranteed, given the emphasis of so many white Americans, at least, on the importance of liberty and freedom?

As Tyack argued in his influential history of urban school reform, *The One Best System*, Mann believed that "public education was mostly a kind of preventive nurture, a training in consonance with an idealized family but supplementing it in ways that prepared pupils for a more complex society" (Tyack 1974, 69). Without the usual forms of social control and restraint common in Europe, common schools took on added importance. Their special role in shaping republican values and virtues, which youth would internalize, permeated Mann's reports in Massachusetts and his many public addresses. In 1841 he emphasized that "Forts, arsenals, garrisons, armies, navies, are means of security and defense, which were invented in half-civilized times and in feudal or despotic countries; but schoolhouses are the Republican line of fortifications, and if they are dismantled and dilapidated, ignorance and vice will pour in their legions through every breach" (*Annual Report of the Board of Education* 1841, 30). Five years later, as immigration from Ireland soared, he emphasized that the newcomers in particular needed to learn to leave their "servility" to "lord or priest" on the other side of the Atlantic, for America was a republic (ibid. 1846, 95). Everyone, rich and poor, native born and immigrant, had to learn a common set of values, and these would be best taught in a universal system of public education.

Although today's educational rhetoric often regards the private sector as the savior of modern education, Mann—a firm enthusiast of private property and markets and hostile to machine-breakers and socialists of every form—offered a more critical reading of the social order. In the early nineteenth century, the lines between public and private endeavors in education were blurred as compared to later, but fears of social class division so accelerated that he and other educational leaders forcefully argued on behalf of a common, tax-supported school system. Mann realized that the children of the rich and poor still attended some rural district schools together. In addition, since the turn of the century, children of all backgrounds had sometimes attended academies, which also often taught the higher branches before the first free high schools appeared in the 1820s; these schools were often partially supported out of the public purse through land grants and other state appropriations. But the separation of rich and poor, so evident in urban environments, Mann thought, now made the need for an inclusive public system, at least for all white children, imperative. The more children lived apart, the more the social distance between them would widen, tearing civilization asunder. In the cities by the 1830s, free public education was only slowly losing its pauper stigmas as it became more inclusive of all the social classes, a dream of the reformers that was never completely fulfilled. Mann and his allies regularly complained that the rich stubbornly refused to send their children to the public schools, fearing social contamination and lowered status.

Throughout his corpus of writings, Mann bemoaned the continued reliance of the rich upon private schools. Without the full support of the wealthier residents, he said, teachers and children in the common schools would remain demoralized and the republican goal of equal access unfulfilled. In his first annual report to the Massachusetts legislature, he admitted that the bad habits of some poor children in the common schools drove the rich out of the system, thus hurting its popularity. The rich claimed that "some of the children in the public school are so addicted to profanity or obscenity, so prone to trickishness or to vulgar and mischievous habits, as to render a removal of their own children from such contaminating influences an obligatory precaution" (*Annual Report of the Board of Education* 1838, 54). This removal of "the intelligent portion of society" (that is, the richest families) from actively supporting the common system haunted Mann throughout his life (ibid., 55). How could reformers make something "common" appealing to everyone, rich and poor, native born and immigrant? How could something be made common but uplifting, available to all, like "the common blessings of heaven?" (ibid. 1841, 32). The key challenge of public education, he affirmed in 1849, was to make something "common" excellent, "good enough for the richest, open to the poorest" (ibid. 1849, 18).

Despite all their worries about the state of society and especially the social problems of the cities, Mann and his generation were cautiously optimistic about the future. Theirs was a generation still close enough to the Revolution to revel in the triumph of the forces of republicanism over monarchy. While rejecting the French side of the Enlightenment, which in its extreme forms leaned toward atheism, reformers shared some of the key assumptions of Enlightenment thinking, especially the idea of progress, the perfectibility or at least improvement of humanity, and the notion that institutions could be arranged in a rational fashion to avoid the anarchism and destruction that had been unleashed on the Continent after 1789 (Cremin 1957, 8, 13–14). Middle-class Protestantism, clearly Christian but without the Calvinist trappings of the past, offered a softer, gentler view of the child, who while often born into questionable families and difficult circumstances might still be rescued from the immorality of parents and dangers of the streets. The moral purposes of the schools and the nondenominational Protestant values taught there held out the prospect that the younger generation would weather the serious social and economic changes that so altered the character of American society during Mann's lifetime.

The contradictions of poverty and progress were never fully reconciled in the thinking of Mann and his contemporary reformers. As Michael B. Katz and other scholars have noted, they often had an ambivalent attitude toward economic growth and change, which they embraced though simultaneously feared because of its degrading effects on many citizens (Katz 1968).

But the schools of the city—where the greatest social evils allegedly existed—ironically were the sites of innovative school practices that tangibly demonstrated ways to popularize the system. The concentration of student populations enabled city systems to establish the first age-graded classrooms, which allowed a more standardized curriculum. Because of their presumed superiority as teachers of young children and their low salaries, women were increasingly hired in the primary grades. Whatever the reality, they were seen as gentler and more effective than the proverbial Ichabod Cranes of the day (Kaestle 1983). In addition, high schools, which were open to all academically qualified students but in reality mostly enrolled a small number of middle-class adolescents, were first established in the towns and cities. Many hundreds of academies and private schools closed their doors, unable to compete with these secondary schools, which had a well-paid teaching staff with a low class size that worked in often magnificent buildings (Reese 1995). And through a series of compromises that angered critics on every side, Mann and other school reformers built a strong political following for free schools in the North, promising equal opportunity, moral training, recognition for the most talented students, and the values needed to ensure the survival of republican virtue.

To build a common system in a pluralistic nation, antebellum school reformers worked diligently to appease critics in an effort to build a political consensus in favor of free, tax-supported education throughout the North. As Maris A. Vinovskis and other scholars have demonstrated, Mann used a wide variety of arguments to promote public education, depending upon the audience, the changing political climate, and pressure from outside critics. The famous Massachusetts reformer never doubted that the main aim of education, in addition to providing access to basic academic subjects to ensure literacy, was moral training. He did not shy from claiming in a famous report in the 1840s that education led to higher rates of productivity in future workers, anticipating the human capital theories that would grow popular in the middle of the twentieth century (Vinovskis 1995, chap. 5; Tyack and Hansot 1982, 62). But, overall, he wanted the common schools to teach a nondenominational form of Christianity, including morning prayers (such as the "Our Father") and the reading of passages, usually without comment, from the King James version of the Bible. This satisfied the Protestant majority, though some Protestant sects and especially the rising Catholic population opposed this separation of sectarian religion from education and called his approach to schooling "Godless."

Like most nineteenth-century educators, Mann assumed an intimate connection between morality and economics and that moral education was the main purpose of the public schools. "Arithmetic, grammar, and the other rudiments, as they are called, comprise but a small part of the teachings in a school," he affirmed in 1838. "The rudiments of feeling are taught not less than the rudiments of thinking. The sentiments and passions get more lessons than the intellect. Though their open recitations may be less, their secret rehearsals are more" (*Annual Report of the Board of Education* 1838, 58). As any college graduate knew after taking the usual courses in political economy and moral science, certain moral values helped promote the making of worthy individuals. As the homilies of Poor Richard and the maxims of political economy showed, laziness was primarily the root of poverty. The lack of self-restraint, will, and attention to right behavior produced most personal and social distress. While practicing the cardinal principles of the school—punctuality, application, delayed gratification, obedience to just authority, and so forth—children could imbibe the kinds of values that led to lives of respectability, if not necessarily great material success. Without a "thousand-eyed police" to watch over the citizenry, the republic needed common institutions not only to train the mind but also to instill an ethos of responsibility and self-control. Railing against the popularity of "trashy" novels, the evil effects of street corner society, and the visits of too many parents to the grog shop, Mann sounded much like a Puritan in Babylon (ibid. 1840, 60).

Very few educators before the Civil War wanted the schools to teach what would later be called vocational education. They nevertheless generally believed that the hard work of the classroom, the attention to moral propriety, and the lessons learned outside of textbooks and recitations at school held real importance in the shaping of responsible individuals. Mann and other school reformers were terribly fearful of the prospect of class war; they watched the rich separate from the poor in ever-exclusive urban neighborhoods and patronize expensive private schools. Although they fretted over excessive competition for school honors in some classrooms, educators generally concluded that the common schools should reward and advance the most talented pupils. As Mann wrote in the early 1840s, the genius of the American political system was its destruction of primogeniture and entail and other feudal practices. The Founding Fathers had championed the political equality of all free men, and schools needed to guarantee "that celebrity or obscurity, wealth or poverty, should depend on individual merit" (ibid. 1842, 70).

Mann realized that schools were not equally funded. Some school districts, he said, spent seven times more per capita annually in educating their children than their poorer neighbors. Nor were all children able to attend for the same number of years, since most poor children had to withdraw from school prematurely to work to help support their families. But the great dream remained: widespread access to free education, where at least all white children would compete for school honors and receive a basic education in the rudiments and in moral values useful for the rest of their lives.

To labor was an inevitability, not exactly a curse from Adam and Eve's wayward acts in the Garden of Eden, but a necessity nonetheless. Investment in education, Mann continually argued, meant that the rocky soils of New England could be turned to good uses, as well-educated, industrious men, women, and children enjoyed a high standard of living overall compared to areas with richer soils but poorer educational advantages (ibid. 1842, 101–9). Becoming educated was not only inherently and morally good, it was also a wise investment. "An educated people is a more industrious and productive people. Knowledge and abundance sustain to each other the relation of cause and effect." And, in a nod to Adam Smith, the father of modern political economy, Mann wrote that "Intelligence is a primary ingredient in the Wealth of Nations" (ibid. 1847, 40). Believing in the overall beneficence of the economic system while fearful of the rising gap between rich and poor, the famous Massachusetts Whig urged each individual to defend the idea and reality of a fluid social system, where success and failure were based on merit rather than family background or inheritance.

The social thought of Horace Mann illuminates well the kinds of compromises that were required to gain the support of the majority of Northern citizens for the common schools. Protestant teachings were watered down to a nondenominational core, offending some sectarian Protestants and many Catholics. While fervently antislavery, Mann was mostly critical of abolitionists and refused to lend his prestigious name to the cause of school integration in a celebrated court case in Boston, fearful of offending those who otherwise supported the public system (Kaestle 1983, 214–15).

Recognizing the real inequalities in school funding from district to district, he nevertheless helped to reinforce the idea that individuals could overcome disadvantage through hard work and application. He did not seriously ask whether structural problems in the economic system rather than individual failings per se led to the widening gap between rich and poor.

Nevertheless, the famous educational leader was a man of his age and social position, predisposed to believe that compromise and consensus were essential to the survival and expansion of the common schools (Tyack 1974, 109). Like most Whigs, he advocated more financial and community support for local schools, and he shared the wider views of middle-class, forward-thinking people of his times that education was a positive force, indeed a panacea for larger economic, political, and social ills.

At the time of Mann's death, public schools still faced innumerable critics, from Southern slaveholders to sectarian opponents to those citizens who were apathetic or opposed to higher taxes and probably dismissive of much reform rhetoric as humbug. Yet the public schools had endured, and Mann was destined to wear the crown as the leading educational leader of his day.

After the Civil War, that mantle was worn by William T. Harris, a towering figure in education until his death in 1909. Like most educators of the late nineteenth century, Harris regarded Mann as the greatest schoolman of the age. Harris was probably the best-known educator of the postbellum years (Tyack 1974, 43, 66). Like Mann a New Englander, he was born in East Killingly, Connecticut, in 1835, and he attended an assortment of district and other schools. Withdrawing in good standing from Yale College in his junior year, Harris headed West, to the boom city of St. Louis. After trying his hand at a number of jobs, he became a teacher and then rose rapidly up the expanding bureaucracy of the city system, becoming superintendent in 1868. During the next twelve years he wrote annual reports to the school board that, like Mann's, became among the most read educational documents of his generation. An exceptionally bookish individual, he founded the nation's leading Hegelian journal, became an early president of the National Education Association, and was to many contemporaries an odd combination of philosopher and administrator. At a time when the idea of the common school—that all children should in theory have access to the same standard curriculum—was increasingly under assault from a range of critics, he became his era's most eloquent defender of humanistic study in public education and its role in shaping the good society (Curti 1935, chap. 9; Leidecker 1946).[1]

Harris's reports and countless writings have all the earmarks of the nineteenth-century educator's faith in the power of formal schooling to advance personal mobility, social stability, and the progress of the nation. Cities and an expanding industrial workforce were transforming America away from its rural and agrarian roots, and Harris thought that the schools would only grow in their influence and salutary effects upon society. Like Mann, he believed that the schools taught moral as well as intellectual values, many of them rooted in the past but highly serviceable in a world of vast social change. The translator of Hegel's *Logic* into English, Harris believed in the inevitability of change, witnessed daily as newcomers displaced from the countryside or from Europe poured into America's cities and swelled the industrial workforce. Schools, he often said, were only one among the many institutions that educated the young, but they had a special role to play in the preservation of republican values in a world undergoing rapid change.

Fully aware that the majority of America's children lived in the countryside or small villages, Harris hitched his star to the cities, which remained for most career educators the epitome of educational progress. With the Confederacy vanquished, the Republican Harris, who like Mann officially downplayed the importance of politics in educational decision making, believed that the common school would spread across the nation, including the reconstructed South. Cities would remain the guiding lights of educational reform, for here one found the sophisticated innovations of the age, from graded classrooms to the standard curriculum to the free high school. His reports as superintendent understandably dealt with these matters and others affecting the urban schools, including the question of coeducation, foreign-language training, and the place of public education in an industrial society (Leidecker 1946). Like Mann he sought community consensus to build the widest possible support for the public sphere.

By the 1870s, vocal reformers of various stripes were convinced that the public schools needed to abandon the common curriculum. Although the Northern economy boomed immediately following the Civil War, the late nineteenth century was plagued with horrific panics and depressions; a severe depression occurred in the 1870s, further downturns appeared in the 1880s, and a terrible depression—the century's worst—hit the nation between 1893 and 1897. By the 1870s, industrial strikes, lockouts, and labor-capital violence were pronounced, leading some reformers to conclude that the schools needed to prepare youth for specific jobs to help quell labor disturbances and to weaken the appeal of socialist agitators and trade union leaders.

Harris endorsed the ends but not the means. He had no doubt that the schools taught the knowledge and values that would lead to productive lives of labor, but he steadfastly opposed turning schools into centers of job training despite his praise for the expansion of an industrial economy. As his tenure as superintendent in St. Louis came to a close, he noted that "There has been for some time a popular clamor in favor of the introduction of the arts and trades into public schools. It has been supposed by self-styled 'practical' writers upon education that the school should fit the youth for the practice of some vocation or calling." But, he asked, "Who can tell, on seeing the child, what special vocation he will best follow when he grows up?" (*Annual Report of the St. Louis Schools* 1880, 126–27). In the years to come, manual training would ultimately enter the schools, despite his early objections, and by the turn of the century it would help pave the way for the adoption of actual vocational programs and a differentiated curriculum.

Harris, however, steadfastly defended an older common school tradition. Although it was increasingly seen by many reform-minded critics as a bastion of reaction and tradition, the common school seemed to him the best general preparation for adulthood. Like educators of the antebellum period and many in his own time, he applauded the efforts of schools to identify and reward individual merit, to enroll children of all social classes, and thus to help keep the social order fluid, not fixed as in aristocratic Europe. In an age where jobs disappeared and new ones were created almost overnight through technological innovation, narrow trade training seemed dysfunctional, not practical at all. Harris thus defended the common curriculum with uncommon fervor.

Because so many children dropped out of school to work by the age of twelve, it seemed imperative to Harris that they receive the best moral training and academic education possible. Without question, new habits, already emphasized by school leaders decades before, remained vitally important to survival and success in the new urban-industrial world. The rhythms of work were no longer guided by the rising and setting of the sun or the seasons but increasingly, for many Americans, by the factory whistle and the whirl of machinery. And so Harris, sounding much like an earlier generation, spoke of the universal "moral virtues" taught at school, such as punctuality, delayed gratification, industry, self-reliance, and obedience to authority. These helped "civilize" the young by teaching them the values essential for survival in an increasingly interdependent workaday world (ibid. 1870, 18). He applauded the rise of large-scale corporate enterprises, which reshaped the world of business, government, and schools, and he believed that labor-saving devices would ultimately liberate laborers from considerable drudgery, freeing them to enjoy a better standard of living and time for leisure and self improvement (Tyack 1974, 73).

Intellectually, the heart of the common school was the course of study. Not surprisingly for a well-educated person with special strengths in European (especially German) philosophy, Harris was well versed in the history of pedagogy and what would later be called the curriculum. Fairly cosmopolitan in academic tastes, he called the five main areas of study in the common schools the "windows of the soul." They all opened the unlettered child to a world that transcended time and space, family, community, and nation, allowing the young to drink from the wellsprings of humanity while moving forward to make their own unique contributions to society. He believed that there was a "common stock of ideas" that the schools should make available to everyone (*Annual Report of the St. Louis Schools* 1870, 110).

During the middle of the depression of the 1870s—as labor strife worsened and calls for a more practical education intensified—he steadfastly refused to bow to critics. "It must never be forgotten that the school has its chief work in initiating the pupil into the inherited wisdom of the race as a preliminary to his original additions to the same," he wrote. "Unless he knows what has been thought, observed, and done, he runs the risk of traveling round in a narrow circle of his own, and wasting his life in repeating discoveries long since made" (ibid. 1877, 186).

As Herbert M. Kliebard has written, no educator of the Victorian era so consistently defended humanistic education and an academic course of study in the schools as Harris (Kliebard 1995, 31). The "windows of the soul" could unfailingly widen the perspectives of school children. Whether rich or poor, white or black, immigrant or native born, all children had rights as citizens to academic instruction, no matter what their likely destination in life. Arithmetic and mathematics, Harris said, were eminently practical for all the usual reasons, whether counting change or measuring angles to repair a roof; they also introduced the child to an abstract world of relationships unique to these subjects (*Annual Report of the St. Louis Schools* 1870, 112; 1874, 76). English and grammar allowed children and young people to learn how to speak, write, and communicate with others, permitting them to escape from the narrow confines of home and neighborhood. These subjects opened up the world of books, with all their new ideas that exposed everyone to worlds beyond what was familiar to them. Life otherwise remained fairly "circumscribed" (ibid. 1870, 111).

History and geography, too, had the potential to transport children imaginatively outside of their own small space on earth. History taught all the things humankind had accomplished, those that embarrassed as well as those that inspired (ibid. 1871, 169; 1872, 177; 1874, 77; Reese 1995, 117–18). Geography, closely related, revealed the worlds literally beyond one's doors. For example, it taught how food was grown, how climate shaped human industry, and how humans and nature acted upon each other. "Shut up the geographical window of the soul and what darkness ensues!" Harris wrote in the 1870s (*Annual Report of the St. Louis Schools* 1870, 112; 1871, 168; 1872, 177; 1874, 76). Art and literature, in turn, offered exposure to the aesthetic realms, including some appreciation for painting, music, and fine literature (ibid. 1870, 112; 1874, 77–78).

These subjects seemed to offer the young equal access, in theory, to an elevated culture that Harris thought was their birthright. As immigration swelled and fears for social order mounted, nativist movements had waxed and waned since the 1840s, but Harris pressed for ways to make the public schools more inclusive of the newcomers. Unlike Mann, who in response to sectarian critics had advocated Bible reading in the school without comment from teachers, the St. Louis superintendent endorsed the local policy he inherited when he took that post. For decades neither prayers nor Bible reading were allowed in the schools, helping to draw more Catholics into the St. Louis system (McCluskey 1958, chap. 7; *Annual Report of the St. Louis Schools* 1873, 16–17). As German immigration swelled, Harris worked with their (usually Republican) representatives on the school committee, adding the first (and German-inspired) kindergartens found in a large public system, open to African Americans as well as to whites (Troen 1975, chap. 5). He believed firmly in the addition of German-language instruction in the schools; this led to the closing of several private schools in the city in which German was the language of instruction (ibid., 55–56, 65–73). Throughout his tenure as superintendent, Harris also wrote long defenses of coeducation, the high school, and other aspects of the system to counter various school critics.

Harris resigned from his post in St. Louis in 1880, though his career as an educator was far from over. He served an unprecedented tenure as the U.S. commissioner of education (1889–1906). He remained a controversial figure for his defense of the common school in an age that soon endorsed vocational education, a differentiated curriculum, more racially segregated education, and wholesale assaults on foreign-language training, first Latin and then German and others during World War I.

Standing on the shoulders of Mann, Harris was a giant in his own right, defending the common school as part of a grand republican experiment. If practice followed theory, the schools would break down the chauvinism of various groups, teach a common core of moral values and academic subjects, reward individual talent, and prevent the hardening of social classes in the larger society. Some children might find the core academic subjects difficult, boring, and unpleasant, but Harris was convinced that in early efforts to replace academic with vocational education lurked the specter of "caste education," which should be resisted at all costs. "The public school is the instrumentality designed for the conservation of true democratic principles," he proudly asserted in 1876. "It protects one class against another by giving an opportunity to the children of all classes for free competition in the struggle to become intelligent and virtuous. An aristocracy built on the accident of birth, wealth, or position can not resist the counter-influence of a system of free schools wherein all are given the same chances" (*Annual Report of the St. Louis Schools* 1876, 111–12). Here was a voice of the nineteenth century whose words would have caused even the sometimes dour Horace Mann to smile.

Harris was perhaps the last prominent educator to endorse the idea of the common school as the key to the survival and perpetuation of the republic. His ideas were outdated by the time of his death in 1909, and schools, as he predicted, continued to grow ever more important, but not in ways he would have approved of. Vocationalism became the single most important change in the schools of the twentieth century, built upon a diversified curriculum oriented toward various streams, tracks, and other divisions of pedagogical labor. Harris was fond of sprinkling his prose with metaphors that revealed his biases in favor of the common school: he liked to talk about the "common stock of ideas" or "common ground" on which children stood in the American educational system. Such views also disappeared for the most part in the twentieth century, as various philosophies on the "differences," not similarities, of children rose in importance as a matter of theory as well as practice.

At the dawn of the twenty-first century, educators no longer speak of public schools as part of some grand republican experiment. Such language is anachronistic in a world where the material goals of formal schooling tend to dominate debates about schools and their effectiveness, and where criticisms of state institutions have accelerated. As late as the 1920s, Catholics had to fight against efforts to close down their alternative to the public system, something inconceivable today. Since the 1980s, support for privatization of many sectors of the economy and of state welfare has only accelerated. Former mortal enemies—Catholics and fundamentalist Protestants—occasionally even lobby together for public monies for private schools, the vast majority of which remain church-based. Activists, especially in the Republican Party, press the claim that the common good would be strengthened by market competition, providing the public schools with more incentives to innovate. Moreover, various proposals—such as tuition tax credits, savings plans for private school tuition, and vouchers—have the potential to weaken the financial basis of what is often called the public school monopoly. The U.S. Supreme Court will undoubtedly face challenges to recent court decisions, such as in Wisconsin, that have upheld the use of public funds for private religious schools in Milwaukee, but the outcome remains uncertain.

History provides some valuable perspective, but not answers, to grave matters of public policy in the contemporary world. Whether the great experiment to promote the common good through public schools continues to find favor is an open question. To Horace Mann and William T. Harris, public schools helped promote moral training, intellectual development, and a deep regard for academic and civic values that transcended the perspectives of family, group, and community. They assumed that education taught the sturdy virtues of hard work, application, and achievement that in a general way promoted personal success and overall economic growth. But they would have been horrified by the largely materialistic purposes of modern education, summed up in a pithy way by the television ad a few decades ago: "To get a good job, get a good education." Like Emerson and other moral philosophers of the day, Mann and Harris were more concerned with teaching the young how to live a good life, not simply how to make a good living. How to promote the common good and build a better society will undoubtedly guide citizens and policy makers in the coming years, who will have to ask anew what particular role public schools should play in that process.

CHAPTER 2

Turning Points: Reconstruction and the Growth of National Influence in Education

Ted Mitchell

Freedom. . . . It is necessary to define that word, for it is most apt to be misunderstood.
— *O. O. Howard, commissioner of the U.S. Bureau of Refugees, Freedmen, and Abandoned Lands, 1864*

Almost as soon as our armies came here, school teachers followed.
— *Major W. L. Van Derlip, U.S. Bureau of Refugees, Freedmen, and Abandoned Lands, 1870*

Confederate New Orleans fell to Union forces during April of 1862. On April 25, a victorious David Farragut and his fleet steamed into the harbor and the period of Federal occupation began; so too did the general government's first experiment with a new task and a new term: reconstruction.

Three issues set the Reconstruction era apart and make it a critical turning point in both the history of the American state and in the history of American education. First, Reconstruction marked America's first large-scale experience as a conquering force, and the strategy and tactics of occupation, combined with what many saw as a moral imperative to rebuild republican sentiment in the South, encouraged the expansion of the role of the central state in a wide range of policy domains, but especially in education.[1] At the same time, emancipation set free nearly four million slaves into an economic structure and a social system that not only could not absorb them as free labor but did not want to, except upon terms that mirrored, as closely as possible, the slave system that had until so recently regulated the lives and labor of African Americans. For Northern legislators, and even more for members of the vocal and powerful abolitionist movement, the vulnerability of the Freedmen created a moral problem of enormous proportions. Together, these two demands created support for an unprecedented level of federal intervention and regulation in the economy and social system of the South.

The second compelling feature of Reconstruction is the signal clarity with which contests over access and control and ideals of liberty and order were played out in the educational arena. Ideological clashes between planters and reformers, between Freedmen and their self-appointed benefactors, and between individual states and the general government raised to the level of practical policy the debates that had simmered since the founding of the republic. The traditional need to balance the rights of states, for example, with the needs of the nation took on significant meaning in education during the period. What lay at the center of this debate was not only an abstract matter of constitutional principle, nor the more immediate issue of race relations, but an equally fundamental set of tensions over the nature of civic life and citizenship. The resolution of these issues, the re-balancing of state and national interests in favor of notions of *national* citizenship, and the transmission of limited and limiting ideas of citizenship for Freedmen, in particular, became paradigmatic in the future understanding of political education, North as well as South, whites as well as blacks (Mitchell and Lowe 1983).

Finally, the critical feature of Reconstruction is and always has been the issue of race. In Reconstruction, as at no time since the drafting and ratification of the Constitution, the connection between race and citizenship became a pressing matter of public policy. None knew the stakes involved better than the ex-slaves themselves. One of the marked advances in Reconstruction historiography has been the greater understanding of the actions of Freedmen in securing and defining freedom on their own terms (Anderson 1988; Foner 1988; Berlin 1992). The determination and the clarity with which ex-slaves sought to live their freedom surprised many whites of both sections. Moreover, the activities of Freedmen did much to influence policy during the Reconstruction era. Particularly in education, as W. E. B. Du Bois put it, "with perplexed and laggard steps, the United

States government followed in the footsteps of the black slave" (1975, 81). The debates over black citizenship, enfranchisement, and education were complicated and often internally conflicted. The struggles put American attitudes about race on public display, exposing divisions and contradictions that are with us still. It is no wonder that historian Eric Foner called Reconstruction "America's Unfinished Revolution" (Foner 1988).

The interplay of these three elements, the rise of federal power, the question of the locus of citizenship, and the central issue of race make the Reconstruction era an important "turning point" in the history of American education. As David Tyack and his colleagues have shown, occupation and reconstruction in the South created the "Constitutional Moment" during which public schooling was established in law in the Southern states. Similarly, occupation and reconstruction also reformed the idea of education in the Northern states, establishing and creating cultural norms and political mechanisms for the expression of federal interest in education (Tyack, James, and Benavot 1987). Today's policy debates over national tests and national curriculum standards, to name just two issues, reflect the unfinished nature of the Reconstruction arguments over the federal role. Yet the very fact of these debates and the substantial federal presence in education owe much to the changes in policy and philosophy wrought during Reconstruction.

EDUCATION FOR LOYALTY

New Orleans had always prided itself on its schools. Indeed, New Orleans was nearly alone among Southern cities when, in 1841, it created free public schools for white children. Throughout the 1850s schools of all sorts, public and private (many of the latter were Catholic schools taught in French), prospered. Even during the war years, schools remained open and embraced a commitment to the cause of Confederate nationalism (Mitchell forthcoming; Faust 1988). Occupation created new challenges for the schools and their patrons. By the end of 1863, the second year of occupation, it became clear that many in New Orleans subscribed to the point of view that the public schools had become "federalized" and thus not suitable places for the children of the city. In 1863, a mandate from the headquarters of Nathaniel Banks, commander of the Department of the Gulf, required "the singing of National airs in our schools and the inculcation of Union sentiments by the teachers"; this became the object of civil disobedience as half of the enrolled students were kept away from school for several days by their parents in protest. Some stayed away longer. By 1864, only 12,511 of the city's 37,664 school-age children attended public schools, a drop of over one-third from prewar estimates. Meanwhile, private schools, always important in New Orleans, grew in both size and number (Doyle 1960; MacNair 1864). Rebel "flight" and the political character of the city's private schools soon became an issue of concern for the occupation force and its appointed educational officials.

Shortly after the promulgation of an order in 1862 requiring citizens to take a loyalty oath, Union loyalists began calling for teachers in both public and private schools to be "required, not only to take the oath of allegiance to the United States, but to give bonds—and heavy ones, neither to encourage nor permit the expression of sentiments unfriendly to the United States government in the schools under their charge" (Daily Delta 1862). The following year, the occupation forces under Banks went even farther, enlisting a force of special agents to ferret out seditious activity in private schools. Using extraordinary powers granted them by Banks under martial law, these agents appeared without warning at several of the city's most prestigious girls' schools on the morning of May 8, 1863. Demanding to see all curricular materials as well as the copybooks of students, the agents left no stone unturned. Throughout the month of May, the scene was repeated in school after school, and at least half a dozen schoolmistresses were brought before the Provost Court to answer charges of treason. Yet despite the vigorous efforts of the special agents, the most damning pieces of evidence brought before the court were copy books in which students had drawn the Confederate flag. Several teachers were fined and all were humiliated, to the delight of the unionist press, which commended Banks's agents for "bringing to light the evils prevailing in these treasonable nurseries" (Doyle 1960).

In July 1864, Banks went a step further, creating a commission to "visit, examine, and report upon the organization, studies, and general tendencies, and the character of the teachers of all the private schools." Like the special agents the previous year, the commissioners enjoyed broad military powers and were "authorized to visit any premises for this purpose," with instructions to "call upon the Provost Marshal for assistance, if required" (Doyle 1960).

Not surprisingly, the commission found several kinds of treasonous activity in the schools. Some of this took the form of Confederate teaching or the singing of "Dixie." But more complex was the stance of neutrality that most teachers took, neutrality that the commission regarded as a kind of sin of omission. As the army-appointed superintendent of education put it, "with American born citizens, adults or children, there is no such thing as neutrality at this crisis. . . . [I]t is an absurdity in principle and an impossibility in fact." The fundamental error, from the commission's point of view, was the idea advanced by some (posing as neutrals) that "it is wrong to teach . . . children any idea of patriotism towards their country, because they would be teaching them *politics*." The commission's response was absolute. "We scarcely," it wrote to Banks, "know how to find words sufficiently strong for the expression of our detestation of such casuistry." Banks's commissioners were "of the opinion that the teaching of patriotism or love and respect for the constitution and laws of one's country . . . can never, without a direct perversion of the plainest meaning of words, be denominated as *politics*" (MacNair 1864). Yet as we will see, what was plain in one setting would become bedeviling in another. Just this issue, the meaning and limits of "political" education, was to have a long life in the region, taking on renewed and confounding significance when Southerners and Northerners together considered what it meant to educate the millions of newly emancipated and newly enfranchised Freedmen.

It is telling that the occupation developed such a hard-edged educational program to deal with the perceived disloyalty of white Southerners. Washed aside in these "times of great political trouble" was the careful balancing of liberty and order that had so captured the mind of the republic's founding generation and that so informed the establishment of limits to state authority in the debates over the Constitution. Abandoned, too, in the heat of national crisis, was the Jeffersonian idea of "the general diffusion of knowledge" as a means of checking incursions by the government on the rights and liberties of citizens (Kaestle 1983; Wood 1991; Rakove 1996). Banks sought to create a citizenship of loyalty to the country, to its government, and to its institutions. "We take it upon ourselves," the commission concluded without irony, "to say that the instruction of the youth of this country (particularly of this section of it) in a proper regard for the constitution and laws of the country, as well as a love and respect for the magistracy created by law for the government and protection of the country and the execution of its laws, is . . . a moral obligation." For the commissioners, the matter was a simple one. "Let the youth of the country be properly instructed in their obligations to the country of their birth, and the institutions of the country are safe. . . . [N]eglect that and all hope is gone" (MacNair 1864).

John MacNair, superintendent of education for Louisiana under the occupation, was outraged by the New Orleans revelations and made a point of driving home the commission's conclusions. "Can the gentlemen of the General Assembly," he asked rhetorically, "realize that in many of the private schools in this city, persons are instructing our youth who avow themselves 'rebels,' or 'rebel sympathizers?'" The war, he feared, could go on "interminably" or "to extermination" if "a part of our children be allowed to be taught treason." Arguing against the pretense of neutrality and pointing to the "evasive manner of answering" exhibited by some teachers, MacNair warned the legislature that "[I]t is high time that the question of loyalty or disloyalty should be well settled in all the schools of the city and State . . . time that such shallow pretenses and subterfuges be put down and that the arm of our government make itself felt, if necessary, for its own quiet and safety, even in the schoolroom." In Mac-Nair's view, "[O]ur state government owes it to itself, to our general government, and to the blood of our dead heroes . . . to see that the poison of sectionalism and disloyalty be allowed to spread no further. . . . [T]he children of the State, so long as they are on American soil and beneath the American flag, *must be taught loyalty to that flag, and to none other*" (MacNair 1864). For unionists engaged in the occupation, the need for the general government, as well as the state government, to defend itself *in* and *by* education took on paramount importance. In their search for educational means to eradicate Southern disloyalty, the occupying forces could rely on two distinguishing features of the time.

First, as suggested above, an emphasis on unflagging and unquestioning loyalty to the government replaced the more contingent rhetoric of loyalty that marked earlier expressions of the relationship between the government and its citizens (Kaestle 1983). In that more contingent understanding, loyalty was something that governments earned by protecting the liberties of the people and by providing for the common good, as defined and pursued by virtuous citizens (Wood 1991). In the republican view, states could easily *not* be worthy of loyalty and should, in such instances, be recalled to their true mission and purpose. The Civil War showed dramatically that the "general government" could develop an identity and interests that were more concrete than abstract and more open to contention and actual civil strife than the framers of the Constitution might have imagined. Through the debates over slavery and over sectional and states' rights, the vocabulary of citizenship changed over the period in both the North and the occupied South. Those views became polarized. As David Potter has shown, the "sectional crisis" over slavery drove Southerners to ever more extreme defenses of the independent sovereign rights of states and drove Northerners to extreme defenses of the idea of union and of the sovereignty of the Union. The war decided the issue of slavery. It also decided, at least temporarily, the issue of sovereignty in favor of the central state. Under the urgent demands of occupation, this translated quickly into an educational program that focused in a single-minded way on inculcating loyalty to the general government (Potter 1968). The longer the war dragged on and the clearer it became that Southerners would continue to oppose the emancipation of enslaved African Americans, the more possible it became to see the national government, not the people, as the ultimate protector of liberty. This perception was to have telling consequences (Bensel 1990).

Second, for the first time the general government had placed the civil affairs of an entire region under control of the military. This willingness to use the coercive power of the state to direct civic affairs originated during the war and occurred in both the North and the South, largely as a means of quelling dissent and of mobilizing economic resources (Bensel 1990). What was new in the occupation of Southern cities like New Orleans was the speed with which the schoolmaster followed the army and, indeed, how quickly the army made the school its formal ally. That alliance spoke clearly of the perceived instrumental utility of schools in creating the kind of loyalty that the occupation forces believed lay at the foundation of a stable social order. Schooling, during occupation and reconstruction, became a direct instrument of central state policy. For a time, initially in the unmaking of Confederate loyalty and then in development of schooling for the Freedmen, the creation of citizens became a province of the federal government with schools as its tool of choice (Foner 1988).

In occupied New Orleans, the replacement of civil authority by military authority in educational affairs was barely masked by the appointment of a civilian Bureau of Education. That board proceeded rapidly to develop loyalty tests for teachers, to replace the Confederate texts currently in use with "sound" Northern ones, and, as we have seen, to require patriotic performances in schools. The military investigation of private schools showed the intent of the general government to extend its reach into civil society and to eliminate Confederate loyalty by rooting out disloyal and "neutral" teachers. But in Louisiana, as elsewhere in the South, emancipation altered the terms of the debate. Important as the unmaking of Confederate citizens might be, far more significant, in the long run, was the work of the federal government in making citizens of the region's four million freed men, women, and children. Here, too, the military arm of the general government, in concert with private philanthropic and missionary groups, took on the job of schoolmaster.

EDUCATION FOR FREEDOM

"My friends," Illinois congressman S. W. Moulton asked a crowd of former slaves at a Washington, D.C., celebration in 1867, "do you understand fully the import of freedom, liberty, and citizenship?" He, like nearly every white leader, felt duty bound to make sure. "By being free," he intoned, "you are not thereby discharged from the obligations of citizens— from responsibilities and from labor to support yourselves and your families." Indeed, he reminded his audience, the opposite was the case; "with citizenship your responsibilities begin; you stand erect before the world as men and women." This, for Moulton and so many other white leaders, was the theory. But Moulton was more honest than most in expressing aloud their fears when he asked "have you the mantle and moral qualities to enable you to take care of yourselves in the race of life?" That, he concluded, "is one of the questions that you alone can solve" (Moulton 1867). Neither Moulton's paternalism nor his racism was unusual, even among white abolitionists. They reflected the struggle among even the highest-minded whites in coming to terms with black citizenship and in moving beyond the abstractions of egalitarian rhetoric. It was somehow easier to talk about equality when blacks were not free.

The Freedmen hardly needed to be reminded of such matters; for them, the issues of freedom, liberty, and citizenship were neither abstract nor long-term. Freedmen were never simply the objects of Reconstruction policies, despite the efforts of Northern reformers to treat them that way (Du Bois 1975; Berlin 1992; Anderson 1988; Litwack 1979). Just as recent historiography has embraced a more complex view of white Reconstruction as an interplay between abstractions and realities, so too have historians come to understand the importance of the interplay between white and black during Reconstruction and after. Ex-slaves were not simply "witness to Reconstruction," they were active agents on their own behalf. In the matter of education, Du Bois was even stronger in characterizing the contribution of freed slaves when he remarked that "Public education for all at public expense was, in the South, a Negro idea."[2]

Du Bois was right. But this tells only a part of the story. Policy and practice did not often follow the desires or the expectations of the

Freedmen. Reconstruction education policy can be seen as an ongoing set of interlocking conflicts, between blacks and whites, between Northerners and Southerners, and between different factions within the party of Reconstruction. At stake, simply, was the question of what kind of citizens blacks would be and how best to prepare them for that role. Significantly, what was not at stake was the issue that had dominated discussion of public education since the beginning of the republic: whether the federal government should have standing in the establishment and operation of public schools. That question was swept aside by the tide of war.

The massive expansion of schooling for former slaves both established a federal role and rooted firmly in the mind of the North and the South an association between public education and freedom for the ex-slaves. First as an element of occupation, particularly in the Gulf under Banks and in Tennessee under Ulysses Grant, the education of "contraband" slaves in camp evolved into full-fledged schools and school systems. Banks's General Order in 1864 created a Commission of Enrollment in the Gulf, and six months later another general order created the first Board of Education for Freedmen in the occupied South (MacNair 1864; Banks 1864). In the Department of the Tennessee, John Eaton, a Vermonter and Dartmouth graduate, was put in charge of providing for the safety and well-being of more than 100,000 fugitive and confiscated slaves.

A central task for Eaton was directing the increased traffic from the North of "benevolent persons . . . whether offered by independent workers or societies." As Eaton observed, "almost as soon as the desperate condition of the Negroes became known in the loyal states, representatives of various organizations found their way to the settlements and cities, aiding in the educational as well as the relief work among the suffering refugees." The military partnered in this work from the first, providing "transportation, rations, quarters, and places in which to teach" for teachers who were accredited by Eaton and his staff. While highly desirable—"saving," as Eaton's orders reminded him, "the Government the cost of labor" in providing for the Freedmen's education—the presence of the aid societies caused increasing complications (Eaton 1907).

By means of providing support for the aid societies' teachers, Eaton's department "was thus put into direct relations with the agents of the aid associations. Yet," Eaton recalled, "the connection of the Department with such teachers was, after all, somewhat informal":

I could do little more than advise with regard to the distribution of teachers and the location of schools. I had no authority either to superintend their schools, enforce the needed discipline, secure uniformity of schoolbooks or regulate in any manner the conduct of teachers and agents. Under these circumstances, the work of the Department could be efficient only in part. (ibid., 194)

Particularly vexing for Eaton were the "frictions and jealousies bound to come when so many independent agencies are working side by side." Among these, the most problematic was "the not unnatural loyalty of each agent to what he conceived to be the interest of his particular organization." This led "occasionally to forms of self-seeking" that were "strangely at variance with the heroic self-sacrifices which the same individuals were constantly making." The net result was "a lack of systematic co-operation" that, to Eaton's mind, called for "some central authority." In orders sent to Eaton on September 26, 1864, just such authority was given. By this order, Eaton was given the responsibility to "arrange all . . . details pertaining to the education of Freedmen," including the appointment of "Superintendents of Colored Schools," to which all teachers would report. The Federal Government, in the Department of the Tennessee, had created its first school system with John Eaton as its superintendent.

Education became, for Eaton and the army, one of the many services to be provided to the Freedmen, and Eaton set about organizing schools in the same way he had done for the distribution of rations, the allocation of jobs, and the organization of a post office for the refugees. In time "the school hours, the question of classification, the text books, and matters of school organization and discipline were put entirely in the hands of the superintendents appointed by me" (ibid.). Education of the Freedmen had become a military problem, and as such it was handled within the frame of military policy and military organization. This carried three major consequences.

First, the general government had, for the first time, created an organized school system of its own. In keeping with the pattern of all organizations, this system rapidly developed clients and constituents for whom a continued federal interest and presence became a priority. These included the Freedmen themselves, the benevolent societies, and sympathetic Southern whites who came under the protection of the federal armies. Second, in a more complex way, the appropriation by the national military and the national government of the education of Freedmen established a specific rather than a general national interest in schools. It also established a precedent for the assertion of national interest over those of states and localities. Third and finally, for Northern and Southern observers alike, the education of Freedmen became inextricably linked with federal initiative and with the exercise of military power. For Southerners, the very fact of Freedmen education became associated with defeat; for Northerners, it was associated with victory. For casual observers from both regions, the education of African Americans became, regardless of its form or content, something that was imposed upon the South by the federal government. How people felt about that imposition depended largely upon one's sympathies and sectional loyalties. It is certainly the case, as Louis Harlan and others have shown, that the fact and the symbolic meaning of federal imposition galled many Southerners and fueled the vehemence of the eventual Southern white reaction to the Reconstruction program of black education (Harlan 1958). In the shorter run, though, aid societies quickly became indistinguishable from their federal hosts and, together with the Freedmen themselves, captured and directed what educational momentum there was in the region sheltered and defined by the power of the military. As the Freedmen's Bureau was to find out, a system of schools that was forced on the South could only be sustained by force. The bureau superintendent in Louisiana put it clearly in 1867: "it would be impossible" to sustain schools in "several parishes"; they would simply "not be tolerated" and could only be carried on "as guarded by United States troops" (Alvord 1867a). It was largely to meet this need that the Reconstruction Congress created the Freedmen's Bureau at the end of the war.

EDUCATION FOR CITIZENSHIP

Leroy Pope Walker, Jefferson Davis's first secretary of war in the Confederacy, argued that the war's "great question," namely, "shall Negroes govern white men, or white men govern Negroes," would be answered in the years following peace. "Remember now," he urged a correspondent, "universal emancipation and universal suffrage go together." He foresaw with horror a time in the near future when "the ballot is free alike to black and white—My God!" he exclaimed, "the infamy of such a possibility!" (Harris 1962). One did not need to be a Confederate like Walker to wonder how the Freedmen would respond in their new roles as citizens. The attempts by Northern teachers and the Freedmen's Bureau to frame civic virtue and to articulate a vision of citizenship in which blacks actually participated were wildly antithetical to anything in the experience of the

South and were opposed as such by Southerners and many in the North. Yet even within this radical context, in political education as in so much else about Freedmen's education, lessons on citizenship carried both an expression of freedom and exhortations to duty and responsibility, attempting the familiar task of balancing liberty and order in a context framed by both abolitionist rhetoric and deep-rooted racial prejudices.

"When parents come to me and ask for the establishment of schools," wrote one superintendent in 1868, "their plea is 'you know, sir, we are citizens now and we want to learn our duty.'" And much of the material in Freedmen's texts did indeed focus on duty. "The abolition of slavery has made an alteration in the condition of the freedmen," read one lesson in the *Freedman's Second Reader,* and it "laid upon them corresponding duties." Some "are bewildered by liberty," continued another lesson; "such should learn to appreciate the duties of liberty." Meeting these duties required individual and collective virtue, as "liberty . . . cannot be enjoyed for a long period without the virtue of a whole people," and the virtue of a whole people depended upon each winning a "victory over ourselves, producing purity and rectitude of character" (Alvord 1868).

Following Noah Webster's example, Freedmen's texts made an explicit connection between the development of individual virtue and civic virtue. They also created an image of the state as an independent moral authority, reversing the idea that the state is responsible to the people. In answering the question "What is Government?" the *Freedman's Third Reader* (1865) makes a telling analogy. "Suppose a man says to his son, you must not tell a lie. . . . [I]n such a case, the father makes a law." If the father hears that the son has told a lie, the father gathers evidence from "brothers or schoolmates," and if "proved that the lie was told . . . concludes that his son is guilty. This is to judge the case." Finally, the father "punishes the liar; that is, he executes the law." In this way, the text defines the legislative, judicial, and executive branches of government, but, far more important, it places the state in the allegorical role of parent, setting and monitoring laws from an incontestable position. When Eric Foner argues that "even the most paternalistic educators viewed their efforts to reshape the character of blacks as a way of equipping them to make decisions for themselves," he takes care to differentiate between decisions that are inside a boundary of acceptable behavior and those that are decisions about the boundaries themselves (Foner 1988). Ideas of appropriate civic action as promoted in school texts encouraged broad participation and the robust exercise of citizenship. Yet as black political participation became a reality, the acceptable range of black political activity narrowed, resulting in a clear and unmistakable contrast between the rhetoric of citizenship and the reality of participation.

Limited experiments had given the franchise to free blacks in Louisiana during 1865, but the passage of the Reconstruction Act of 1867 finally gave the vote to all Freedmen of the ex-Confederacy. Former Confederate congressman and educational reformer J. L. M. Curry called this action "the blunder of the centuries," and it filled conservatives of both sections with dread (Curry 1885). Even several of the Freedmen Bureau's superintendents worried that, without proper political education, the Freedmen would quickly become the "prey of vice and the pliant material of base politicians." The commissioner of the bureau himself, John Alvord, reported the plight of the black voters who "at the place of voting . . . look at the ballot box and then at the printed ticket in their hands, wishing they could read it." At each elbow is "the party politician with professions and assertions," causing the Freedmen to "feel their ignorance." By "the vigilance of friends" Freedmen might be kept from influence or intimidation, "but they now possess, and are therefore conscious of individuality—that they must judge and act for themselves. 'We must have learning' is the common remark," heard from the new citizens. As a result, the Freedmen's Bureau redoubled its efforts early in 1867 toward adult education. "As immediately as practicable," Alvord instructed, "we urge that adults . . . be brought into evening and Sabbath schools." For adults and children alike, the bureau set out to answer the call from the National Teachers' Association for "the speedy preparation of all those who need it for the exercise of the rights of citizenship" (Rickoff 1864, 303). Threats to independent decision making came not only from designing politicians but also from the threatened hegemony of the old order. Bureau officials shared the common understanding that "many planters wish to keep [Freedmen] in greater ignorance, that their votes may be the more easily controlled. Hostility to the schools increases," the same superintendent observed, "as the colored people are 'getting too smart' and cannot be entirely controlled, especially in their political relations."

Citizenship education for ex-slaves touched deeply held beliefs on every side. John Greenleaf Whittier's poem "The Free Children," included in the *Freedman's Second Reader* (1865), built one kind of enthusiasm, reinforcing the joy freedom brought to the millions of former slaves, as did the reading exercise "Freedom should give freedmen freedom from fretting." But the spirit of freedom in the context of citizenship and politics required the same kind of personalization Webster had sought in his paeans to Washington. In a remarkable set of stories, the *Freedman's Third Reader* created a pantheon of black heroes around whom swirled the energy and the self-confidence of freedom and through whom educators hoped children would learn the uses of political liberty. On one level, biographies of Toussaint L'Ouverture, Phillis Wheatley, Frederick Douglass, and Paul Cuffee demonstrated the ability of blacks to rise above hardship through hard work and diligence, the traditional themes of the rewards of virtue. On another level, they made a virtue of opposing tyranny and fighting oppression. Cuffee, who had been "dragged from his home in Africa" by slave traders, purchased his freedom and used his wealth to help escaped slaves flee to Africa. L'Ouverture led the Santo Domingo slaves in revolt but was noble enough to spare his former master and help his family to safety. These tales were designed to quicken the spirit and stoke the fires of liberty among adults and children alike. Of central significance is that the story of L'Ouverture, not of Washington or even Lincoln, carries the iconographic message of the ideal Republic:

Thus, through the genius, wisdom, and efforts of Toussaint L'Ouverture, a nation of freedmen had been created out of Negro slaves; and their leader had succeeded in teaching them that virtue, order, industry, and necessary self-restraint were, under God, the only sufficient guarantee of civil and social liberty. (*Third Reader* 1865)

The message of these stories, individually and collectively, is clear. First, Freedmen were encouraged through the telling of history to act politically on their own behalf. Black freedom required opposition to oppression in the past, and vigilance, if not action, would be required in the future. Second, at every occasion the stories work to discredit slavery and those who defended it. In pointed ways, the stories paint slavery as the antithesis of virtue and slaveholders, even if kind, as lacking moral integrity. Finally, as an act of historical restoration, the stories begin the development of an iconography and a collective memory regarding liberty and freedom that celebrated agency and effort even through the slave period.

Southern whites who read these books, or heard of them, expressed outrage or else counted them up as examples of the wrongs committed by the Federals and their agents. Critics complained about the inclusion of "politics" in the schools. In answer, Alvord argued that sectional interests in the Confederacy had so perverted the region's understanding of the nation that "in the present state of society in the South any tuition which does not include some information upon the character and condition of our whole country will fail of producing what is most needed, an intelligent and loyal population." In so saying, Alvord identified an important rationale for "nationalizing" the idea of citizenship and reinforced the importance of loyalty in the construction of an educational regime in the South. He also drew a distinction between national political aims and "politics in a partisan sense." Any accusation that the latter "are taught in the schools is without foundation in fact" (Alvord 1867b). This was precisely the point at issue. For Alvord, for the Freedmen's Bureau, and for a vocal segment of the Northern population, the interest of the nation and that of the general government had become joined during the war and so also became nonpartisan and thus somehow nondebatable. For the South, the counterpoint continued to be important, namely that the states, or a region, might have interests different from and perhaps opposed to the interest of the general government or even to a majority of states. In such a situation, despite having fought and lost a war over the issue, Southerners continued to feel that state sovereignty reigned. As Reconstruction persisted, schooling became a battlefield on which was fought not only the war for Freedmen's education but, increasingly, the war between states rights and the interest of the general government.

SOUTHERN OPPOSITION AND THE NATIONAL INTEREST

Locally, whenever the chance arose, Southern whites reclaimed their governments and reestablished their educational ideologies. In New Orleans, where Banks had done so much to root out disloyalty from the schools, the return of Confederate sympathizers to power in 1866 brought about the near elimination of Freedmen's Bureau influence and the near destruction of the city's school system. Testimony taken by congressional investigators following the New Orleans Riots in 1866 recorded that 110 teachers had been dismissed for pro-federal sentiments. Asked how many "who were really for the Union" remained in their posts, one witness answered that he "did not know of one." Such incidents became more and more frequent across the South under presidential reconstruction, as Andrew Johnson's policy of appeasement allowed what General Joseph Holt called "the barbarism of the rebellion . . . a renaissance" (Alvord 1867a). Radical reconstruction was a response to the perceived failures of Johnson's policies and to the obdurate Southern sympathy for the Confederate cause.

In the North, abolitionists and reformers did not spare their invective.

"The hands from which the President's proclamation has released" the Freedmen, William Garnett wrote in the *North American Review* (1865, 540), "are still clutching after them." The South, like a wild beast, "deprived of its prey, has been subdued into cajolery and deceit," and yet "it still keeps its eye on its victim." Andrew Rickoff, in a speech to the National Teachers' Association, remarked about Confederates that "the fell spirit that animated them is not destroyed . . . and must be exterminated" (1864, 304). Lyman Abbott used different terms, which would have been easily understood by Benjamin Rush or Noah Webster to express a similar sentiment: "We have not only to conquer the South—we have also to convert it. We have not only to occupy it by bayonets and bullets—but also by ideas and institutions. We have not only to destroy slavery—we must also organize freedom" (Abbott 1864, 250). For Rickoff, this change would come "not in the light of gleaming sabers and the conflagration of cities and towns, but in the radiance that shall beam from the thousand primary schools" (1864, 304).

In an irony of epochal proportions, Southern opposition to the education of Freedmen and to the spread of common schooling in the region fueled demands for an increased federal role in the education of the nation's children. In the charged atmosphere of the war, Southern intransigence to a form of social reform that had gained wide acceptance in the North galvanized an aggressive kind of educational policy making that would not have been possible in other circumstances. Arguing in favor of the establishment of a federal department of education, Rickoff told his audience that events have demonstrated that the government "in Washington . . . must recognize the cause of general education as a part of its care" (ibid., 304). He was not alone. The president of the National Teachers' Association, J. P. Wickersham, told the audience at his presidential address in 1865 that the "great lesson we have learned in the last four years is that the United States of America is a *nation* and not a co-partnership of States; and as a nation, our Government ought not to release itself from all responsibility regarding education." Wickersham went on, reminding his listeners that during the war "it was found that a government like ours could not always depend upon the several state governments for its soldiers or its money." In ways similar to the nationalization of defense, "the necessity now exists for the establishment of a department of public instruction in Washington." To Wickersham's mind, "a start in this direction has been made by the establishment of the Freedmen's bureau." Only, he concluded, "when our youth all learn to read similar books, study similar lessons, submit to similar regulations in the schools, we shall become one people, possessing an organic nationality, and the Republic will be safe for all time" (Wickersham 1865, 297). Although no national system of texts emerged, the federal presence in education was institutionalized by the creation of the Office of Education in 1867.

RECONSTRUCTION AS TURNING POINT

Reconstruction marks a decided turning point in the history of education, for it was the Reconstruction, and in particular the work of the Freedmen's Bureau, that brought the nation-state into active agency in creating and maintaining educational programs. It was the victorious Yankee *state*—as army, as president, as legislature, and as treasury—that determined, directly and indirectly, the course of educational development in the states of the ex-Confederacy. This direct agency by the national state on its own behalf is a striking contrast to the diffuse nature of the relationship between the state and the schools that had preceded it. Yet during Reconstruction, the Yankee state confiscated lands and buildings for educational use, protected schools for former slaves by force of arms, appointed an inspectorate for Southern schools, determined access and content in these schools, provided funds directly for the support of teachers, and, perhaps most telling of all, made readmission to the Union contingent upon Southern states adopting constitutional provisions establishing Northern-style common schools (Tyack and Lowe 1987). In these critical ways, Reconstruction marked a new era in the relationship between the general government and the schools, one in which schools became more directly than ever before instruments of state policy and state power.[3] But when Reconstruction ended, much of this ended, too. The general government retreated, literally and figuratively, closing the Freedmen's Bureau in 1870 amidst protests from its officers and supporters in Congress, leaving the direction of Southern policy to Southerners and leaving the scores of teachers, black and white, worried that "much that has been gained will be lost" (Alvord 1870).

Nellie Morton, a missionary teacher, reported that one of her students had told her "We've no chance—the white people's arms are longer than ours." "What we want to do is lengthen the colored people's arms till they can reach as far as their old masters," Morton explained (quoted in Foner 1988). And for a period, the ex-slaves, the federal government, and the aid societies, although often at odds, did just that. But by 1877, the old masters' arms had proved again to be longer than the arms of the Freed-men. Black Codes disenfranchised former slaves; school laws were man-aged in a way that eliminated or reduced funding for black schools; and the sharecropping system stripped many Freedmen of what little economic independence they had. As Du Bois put it, "The river has its bend . . . the slave went free, stood a brief moment in the sun; then moved back again towards slavery" (1975, 30). But despite these reverses, the Reconstruc-tion era has influenced profoundly the future of American education.

In the first place, those efforts changed fundamentally the terms of the national debate about citizenship, about education, and about the role of the central government regarding both. By the end of Reconstruction, many who argued hardest for the emancipation of the slaves and the establishment of civil rights for Freedmen had come to see the federal government as the single most powerful protector and guarantor of "the complete civil and political equality of the colored race" (Chamberlain 1864). This idea—that the general government was the protector of civil liberties rather than the entity against whom one's rights needed to be pro-tected—compromised a century of political talk about the relationship between citizens and the nation-state. Driving the point home further, the states were widely seen to be the villain. There were the depredations of the individual states that needed guarding against, and the Fourteenth Amendment set up protections and at the same time reified the moral superiority of the general government. It is in this light and in the glare of the war itself that loyalty to the government made sense in ways it had not before. Similarly, as a result of the extraordinary moral authority created around the state by the war, the federal government enjoyed a legitimacy and an imperative for action that it had never had before. The govern-ment's colonial attitude toward the South and the expansion of its power in general relied on this imperative. Together, these elements of the Civil War and Reconstruction altered the terms of citizenship, making it much less contingent and much more focused on loyalty, and making the gov-ernment, through schools, an active force in making citizens.

In the second place, the numbers of individuals and constituencies who became stakeholders in publicly supported education grew. The magnitude of the emancipation made compromises possible that had not been possible and made for odd partnerships. The alliance between the government's Freedmen's Bureau and agents of a host of religious organi-zations in providing teachers, books, and money for Freedmen is but one such example. Just as significant was the recognition among the liberal press and in the radical Congress that if education was a solution to a national problem, then it required public attention at the highest level, or it would be compromised by local prejudice. New Orleans stands as the clearest example of the need for the protection of the national interest against incursion from local forces, and it was a telling one at the time. By 1870, when the Freedmen's Bureau closed its operation, the Northern public did not need convincing that education was a matter of national importance, too important to be left solely to the states. Thus, Congress created the first federal Office of Education in 1867, at the high tide of sentiment in favor of national responsibility for the education of the Freedmen. After Reconstruction, it was impossible to return to the voluntarism of the 1820s or the localism of the 1840s. The disparate voices calling for a national influence on public education were annealed in the heat of the war and its aftermath.

In the third place, Reconstruction policies did alter the actual educational terrain, the landscape against which all future educational policy making would take place. As David Tyack and Robert Lowe have shown (1987), congressional pressure on Reconstruction legislatures and conventions resulted in provisions in each of the constitutions of the former Confederate states providing for free public education. On the ground in the South, Reconstruction helped lay the foundation for Southern public education by providing support and protection for ex-slaves engaged in their own education and by establishing thousands of schools of their own throughout the region (Anderson 1988). The Freedmen's Bureau also developed a capacity within the general government to carry out educational programs. This capacity and the logic behind it became institutionalized by the establishment of the federal Office of Education. Most significant of all, passage of the Thirteenth, Fourteenth, and Fifteenth Amendments to the Constitution during Reconstruction extended ideas of citizenship and created a new and broader template for the discussion of civil rights, altering the locus of debate regarding access to education. Within the logic forged in the fires of Reconstruction, the federal government has remained the locus of debate in the twentieth century. The national government has served in our own time the role it served in Reconstruction, combating by force of arms persistent patterns of local resistance to ideas of equality and acting as the ultimate guarantor of civil rights. Although Reconstruction-era policies may have been generated by the most atypical of circumstances, those policies have had a history that has lived on, making it one of the critical turning points in the history of American education.

CHAPTER 3

"There is No Escape . . . from the Ogre of Indoctrination": George Counts and the Civic Dilemmas of Democratic Educators

Daniel Perlstein

On February 18, 1932, George Counts challenged the annual meeting of the Progressive Education Association (PEA) with a speech that electrified listeners. A well-known Teachers College sociologist, Counts praised the achievements of the child-centered educators gathered before him. Nevertheless, Counts charged, progressive teachers' refusal to articulate a critique of the social order prevented students from confronting the misery and injustice of Depression-era America. In small groups, the educators weighed Counts's speech, "Dare Progressive Education Be Progressive?" deep into the night. The next day, other talks were canceled so that the convened educators could further discuss his charge (*Progressive Education* 1932b, 288). Published as an article and then enlarged into a pamphlet, Counts's speech reshaped and revitalized American debates about the schools' role in the quest to realize the democratic ideal.

Counts argued that, despite the constraints on Americans' lives, new ideas can transform students and citizens. He forcefully reminded educators that teachers committed to the protection and expansion of democratic schooling faced the paradoxical task of simultaneously promoting the critical thinking of individual students and indoctrinating shared democratic commitments. Teachers' work, moreover, transcended classroom method. Educators, Counts stressed, were uniquely able to mobilize Americans to join together in challenging social injustice.

Despite its rhetorical force, Counts's speech and its intense reception are in some ways puzzling. Counts offered little sense of what he meant by indoctrination or how it could be reconciled with the child-centered practices he praised, and his critics had far better arguments against the use of indoctrination than Counts could muster in its support. Moreover, no educational researcher had done more than Counts himself to expose elite domination of public schooling and thus to suggest that calls for schools to lead in the progressive transformation of American society were hopelessly quixotic. Still, educators did not dismiss Counts's challenge as empty rhetoric, and the manifesto long outlived critiques of it. To this day, Counts's short speech continues to generate far more interest among scholars than the rest of his lengthy, pioneering career as a sociologist of education (Lagemann 1992).

Ironically, Counts's very inability to detail what he meant by indoctrination or to reconcile it with child-centered pedagogy hints at his work's lasting appeal. As David Tyack has noted, tension between aspirations for individual freedom and the maintenance of a democratic order—tension at the core of a liberal democracy—have shaped educational thought in the United States since the American Revolution (Tyack 1966a). This tension persisted, William Reese suggests in this volume, when nineteenth-century school reformers worked to create a system of common schooling amid the social divisions that were coming to mark American life. Counts, in turn, attempted to reconcile and extend the dual aspirations of liberal democratic schooling amid the new social and economic conflicts of twentieth-century American life.

Counts's effort did much to revitalize Depression-era debates about the democratic potential of schooling. These debates brought together liberal and radical educators in fruitful dialogue and common action. The final irony of Counts's call for indoctrination is that its main beneficiaries were liberal progressives, who were pushed by Counts to more militantly work for open-ended classroom inquiries into controversial social problems.

Neither liberal progressives nor social democrats like Counts have achieved the prominence in public school affairs enjoyed by the corporate influences that Dorothy Shipps analyzes in this volume. In recent years, efforts to discipline students and teachers by means of standardized tests, together with market-inspired proposals for charter schools, vouchers, and other forms of privatization, have dominated discussions of school reform. Attacks on public schooling by the right have led scholars such as Harvey Kantor and Robert Lowe in this volume to reconsider the revisionist critique of bureaucracy. If the role of bureaucracy in education merits reassessment, so too does the work of reformers like Counts, who sought to promote social justice through the system of public schooling. His call for indoctrination and the response it generated suggest the enduring power of democratic appeals in American education as well as the barriers that continue to prevent their realization. Counts's vision of teaching in and for a democracy epitomizes the challenges that continue to face educators struggling to reconcile the demands of social justice and individual freedom amid the social divisions of American schools and life. After outlining the evolution of Counts's argument from a critique of progressive education to a fuller indictment of American schooling, I will trace its origins and educators' response to it.

THE CALL

Counts opened his 1932 talk on a celebratory note. Progressive education, he extolled, "has focused attention squarely upon the child; it has recognized the fundamental importance of the interest of the learner; it has defended the thesis that activity lies at the root of all true education; it has conceived learning in terms of life situations and growth of character; and it has championed the rights of the child as a free personality" (1932, 257). Nevertheless, Counts charged, the failure of progressive education to articulate a social analysis limited its usefulness in solving the real problems of American life and restricted its benefits to a narrow, privileged stratum of students.

In "elaborat[ing] no theory of social welfare, unless it be that of anarchy or extreme individualism," Counts argued, progressivism reflected

the viewpoint of the liberal-minded upper middle class who provide most of the children for Progressive schools—persons who are fairly well off, who have abandoned the faiths of their fathers . . . who pride themselves on their open mindedness and tolerance . . . who are genuinely distressed at the sight of unwonted forms of cruelty, misery, and suffering . . . but who, in spite of all their good qualities, have no deep and abiding loyalties . . . who are rather insensitive to the accepted forms of social injustice, who are content to play the role of interested spectator in the drama of human history, who refuse to see reality in its harsher and more disagreeable forms, and who, in the day of severe trial, will follow the lead of the most powerful and respectable forces in society, and, at the same time, find good reasons for so doing. (ibid., 258)

In Counts's view, the individualism and freethinking promoted by child-centered educators had been well suited to the pioneer era of free land and a self-sustaining family economy. By the 1930s, however, this individualist pedagogy inevitably "deal[t] with life . . . in a highly diluted form," neglecting the grimmer aspects of industrial production, and thus serving "to justify a system, which exploits pitilessly and without thought of the morrow, the natural and human resources of the nation and the world" (ibid., 258–60).

The "bitter . . . struggle" provoked by the Depression, Counts argued, was no passing phenomenon. Although humanity had achieved "mastery over the forces of nature," the creation of a society of plenty also required a reorganization of social structures and values. Counts's analysis suggested that students needed to understand certain social laws as well as to master processes of thinking. In order to "come to grips with life in all its stark reality," progressive educators needed to "develop a realistic and comprehensive theory of social welfare, fashion a compelling and challenging vision of human destiny, and become somewhat less frightened than . . . today at the bogeys of *imposition* and *indoctrination*" (ibid.).

Within a week of his February PEA speech, Counts addressed the winter meetings of the National Education Association's National Council of Education and Department of Superintendence on similar themes. By April, he had combined the three talks into *Dare the School Build a New Social Order?* In this work, Counts broadened his critique.

Counts took no comfort in the fact that most American students did not attend child-centered progressive schools. Like elite progressive schools, public schooling, he charged, was "perpetuating ideas and institutions suited to an age that is gone." The traditional public school, no less than the progressive private one, based its curriculum on an anachronistic vision of democracy that "made security an individual rather than a social goal." Much like the progressive school student's self-centered diet of individual growth, the public school student's "spare ration" of "intellectualistic" study discouraged commitment to democracy and to one's fellows (1978, 3, 19, 23, 35).

In both progressive and public schools, Counts charged, this hidden curriculum of individual security and advancement constituted "imposition with a vengeance, but not the imposition of the teacher or of the school. . . . [It is] the imposition of chaos and cruelty and ugliness produced by the brutish struggle for existence and advantage." This "prospect of our becoming completely victimized and molded by the mechanics of industrialism" was, for Counts, "far more terrifying than any indoctrination in which the school might indulge" (ibid., 23–24).

Counts did, however, find cause for optimism. America's "economy of plenty," together with the enduring strengths of its democratic traditions, meant that for the first time in history the ruling classes might surrender privilege without a violent fight. A transformed curriculum, Counts envisioned, could reshape national ideals and democratize America's inevitably collective future" (ibid., 41, 46, 49).

The conclusion that schools inevitably indoctrinate and that neither child development nor academic study offered a basis by which to determine the curriculum left Counts with a dilemma. Although individual critical thinking discouraged democratic solidarity, it was nevertheless an essential element of democratic citizenship. Recognizing that partisans ranging from Soviet Communists to the Methodists of his Kansas boyhood indoctrinated what they held to be the Truth, Counts denied that his indoctrination entailed "the establishment of a state church, the formulation of a body of sacred doctrine, and the teaching of this doctrine as fixed and final." Eschewing the advocacy of specific reforms, he would "promote the fullest and most thorough understanding of the world," without "deliberate distortion or suppression of the facts" (ibid., 8–9).

At the same time as he called for "the fullest and most thorough understanding of the world," however, Counts maintained that any people needs "great faiths" or "great passions" and that "every great venture of mankind" requires "a supreme act of faith." The "most genuine expression" of American democracy, he claimed, had "little to do with our political institutions: it is a sentiment with respect to the moral equality of men." By "revitalizing and reconstituting" for industrial times the American Dream of a "society in which the lot of the common man will be easier and his life enriched and ennobled," indoctrination, he proposed, would make possible the massive social planning needed in the modern economic world and "combat all forces tending to produce social distinctions and classes" (ibid., 9, 19, 35, 37–38; Morlan 1932, 341). Schools, Counts imagined, could simultaneously promote understanding and faith.

Counts worked tirelessly to win educational organizations and the public to his vision of education in the service of social change or reconstruction. At a contentious three-day meeting, the PEA's Board of Directors conceded two months after Counts's speech that the development of individuality alone did not guarantee the development of social consciousness. Schools, the PEA acknowledged, "cannot build for social idealism and a living faith without coming to grips somewhere with the controversial issues perplexing our changing social order." In order to clarify how the schools could fulfill their expanded role, the board appointed Counts to head its newly created Committee on Social and Economic Problems. As principal author of the committee's report, *A Call to the Teachers of the Nation* (1933), Counts sought both to justify a curriculum that critiqued existing American life and to convince teachers that they were obliged and able to make such a critique (*Progressive Education* 1932a, 329-30; 1932b, 289; Bovard 1941, 45).

The Depression, Counts warned, was "symptomatic of a profound conflict . . . between the social forms of production and the private system of distribution." Expressing outrage that there were Americans who "starve today in the presence of plenty," Counts argued on behalf of the PEA that Americans needed to decide in whose interests the economy was "to be managed. It might be made to serve either the few or the many; it cannot be made to serve both" (Counts et al. 1933, 12–13, 15–17).

Appeals to a pioneer past free of economic (and racial) divisions offered Counts a means both to explain Depression-era difficulties and to justify claims that social harmony was at the core of American values and experience. In the day of the pioneer, democracy and individualism had been "intimately linked together." The crisis of the 1930s, in Counts's analysis, reflected Americans' reliance on this "tradition of individualism . . . to operate a social structure that is marked by the closest interdependence." Although "the ideals of democracy" are securely "rooted in American culture, . . . the democratic tradition, in its historic form, is in conflict with the basic trends of the epoch." Democracy's commitment to individual freedom for "cultural and spiritual growth," he concluded, could be guaranteed "only by the abandonment of economic individualism" (1938, 12, 13, 15–17; on the neglect of race and class conflict in progressive educators' historical analysis, see Perlstein 1996).

The task of reconciling America's democratic ethos with the requirements of the age was a preeminently educational one. "Our basic need is for clarification of purposes and the dissipation of moral confusion. . . . The most urgent and crucial task of our generation, both for education and for society in general, is the development of this community of purpose." The repudiation of "a social system that fails to make full use, for the benefit of all, of the productive resources of the nation," Counts urged, "should be bred in [students] from earliest infancy" (1933, 10).

Already in *Dare the School Build a New Social Order?* Counts claimed that teachers, "representing as they do, not the interests of the moment or any special class, but rather the common and abiding interests of the people," were uniquely positioned to articulate the public good. Still, he urged, "a spring never rises higher than its source. So the power that teachers exercise in the schools can be no greater than the power they wield in society." In order to achieve their vocation, teachers needed to "throw off [their] slave mentality" and organize (1978, 25–27). *A Call* elaborated both Counts's claim that teachers embodied the general interest and his claim that they could not represent that interest unless they organized.

According to Counts, the inevitably political nature of the curriculum, the needs of most students, and the evolving nature of American life all compelled teachers to represent democratic interests. The guise of neutrality not only preserved individual success, social conformity, and mechanical efficiency as the controlling ideals of the schools, but it also created a "completely formalized" and irrelevant curriculum. Since the great majority of students sprang from the producing classes, teachers owed allegiance to them rather than to the ruling classes or the state. Mixing his own ideals with claims about the beliefs of American educators, Counts argued that teachers could "never be reconciled to a social order that . . . needlessly violates the deepest loyalties of their calling." Happily for teachers, in America's emerging "collectivist society," the school could realize its mission to promote the general welfare and to serve as "an agency for the abolition of all artificial social distinctions," rather than continuing to promote the social mobility of a few exceptional individuals (Counts et al. 1933, 18, 20–21).

In order "to play a positive and creative role in building a better social order," teachers needed to "emancipate themselves completely from the domination of the business interests, reorganize the procedures of the school, and redefine their own position in society" (1933, 20). Counts took his campaign to justify teacher organizing beyond the PEA. With Counts serving as its research director, the American Historical Association's Commission on Social Studies observed that "the age of individualism and *laissez faire* is closing and a new age of collectivism is emerging." Echoing Counts, the commission worried that because of "the timidity and weakness of the profession . . . the teacher seldom dares to introduce his pupils to the truth about American society and the forces that drive it onward" (American Historical Association 1934, 16, 75–76).

Counts recognized that schools alone could not transform the social order and that progressive indoctrination was possible only in the context of "some profound social movement or trend" (1929, 68). The simultaneous inability of the schools to engage in radical work in a society where "private gain-seeking is the dominant motif" and need for schools to take the lead in social reconstruction brought Counts "face to face with the paradox: the school must participate in the task of social reconstruction, yet until society is already transformed the school can scarcely hope to function effectively." Counts's answer for democratic teachers was to work at "building a new society . . . simultaneously both within and outside the school" (Counts et al. 1933, 23–24).

Increasingly in the 1930s, Counts took his own advice, becoming a leading activist in the American Federation of Teachers. As a unionist, he continued to argue that teachers' "derivation from the ranks of the people, their relatively disinterested position in society, their freedom from the ties of large property, their traditional loyalty to the popular welfare, and their whole outlook on life tend to identify them overwhelmingly with the fortunes of the democratic process" (1938, 292). Yet if Counts's analysis led him to a leading role in the development of teacher unionism, it also led him to consistently demand that teacher unions not limit themselves to questions of working conditions but rather be active agents in the democratization of American education.

Counts's entire life prepared him to articulate a social reconstructionist progressivism consistent with the American Creed. Born in 1889, his childhood on a Kansas farm was the stuff that sentimental progressive dreams were made of. Late in life he would fondly recall the chores of farm life: "carrying in wood and corncobs for the fire . . . milking the cows, feeding the animals, removing manure from the stable, cutting down trees, sawing logs . . . plowing the land, planting grain, cultivating the fields, and harvesting crops of many kinds." When he witnessed his first automobile at age thirteen, he was driving a team of horses. Through farm work and a strict Methodist upbringing, Counts acquired not only "practical skills and knowledges" but also "moral character and discipline" (1971a, 151, 153).

After leaving the family farm, Counts attended a Methodist college, found work as a high school teacher, and then studied sociology and education at the University of Chicago. His 1922 study, *The Selective Character of American Secondary Education*, demonstrated that the high schools perpetuated social inequalities. His 1927 *The Social Composition of Boards of Education* documented class bias in school board membership. Always a reformer guided by moral concerns, Counts argued that if schools were not above politics then they should respond to it.

Born in one age of seemingly unparalleled social change and then, in the 1930s, confronting another, Counts found in indoctrination a means to reconcile faith and reason, independence and civic solidarity, order and justice. "Like my people," he would reflect late in life, "I regard myself as a cross between a Jeffersonian Democrat and a Lincolnian Republican, struggling with the old problem of human freedom and equality in the age of science and technology" (1971a, 164).

THE RESPONSE

However much it stunned his listeners, Counts's call for indoctrination was not unprecedented. The attempt to justify social justice with appeals to purportedly original American pioneer values drew on Frederick Jackson Turner's claims about the pivotal role of the frontier in American history. The image of social harmony in pioneer society reinforced Counts's view that Depression-era America could transcend the social divisions of the industrial economy. Although Counts often regretted the racial oppression of black Americans (1932, 258–59; 1951; 1962, 51–52), he and other social democrats believed that, if America could evolve gradually and abolish class conflict without a fundamental reordering of its political structure, then the more epiphenomenal division of races would disappear even more easily. Like appeals to the frontier, the social democratic vision of race-blind social justice, soon to find its definitive statement in Gunnar Myrdal's *An American Dilemma* (1944), offered Counts and other progressives a means of reconciling notions of the common good with recognition of the reality of social conflicts (Urban 1978, vi; Goodenow and Urban 1977, 172).

Since 1927, a group of Teachers College faculty under the leadership of William Kilpatrick had been discussing the role of education in the development of new forms of social cooperation and welfare state liberalism. Counts's 1932 speech built on the work of these colleagues and such scholars as Charles Beard, together with the efforts of a broad range of Americans who were seeking social and political alternatives through education during the Depression years. Still, Counts's efforts crystallized what was at stake in broader discussions of social reconstruction. His call for indoctrination became the focal point of discussions among socially minded progressive educators and intensified his colleagues' activity (Merriam 1934; Washburne 1940, 424–46; Tyler 1991, 35; Hook 1991, 38; Cremin 1961, 234–35; Krug 1972, 235).

Counts's reasoning appealed to many progressive educators. Although Harold Rugg denied fomenting "social control indoctrination," his practice seems close to Counts's ideal. "In my books," Rugg claimed to

present "the problem"—giving the facts concerning the health of our people, their financial resources, the inequalities of financial support throughout the country, the needs of the people, the new governmental services available, the description of experiments being made to attempt to solve the problem. This is not teaching or preaching the socialization of medicine. It's merely posing a pressing problem and supplying historical data which may be helpful in leading to a solution. (1941, 272–73)

Some radical educators advocated indoctrination without the caveats that Counts and Rugg added. Economist Broadus Mitchell urged American teachers to show students the need for a more systematic and far-reaching national revitalization program than was offered by the New Deal. "The truth is not something to be searched for and, when found, put in one's pocket," Mitchell wrote. "It should be handed about generously and with a will" (1934, 16). Theodore Brameld's support for indoctrination in the schools reflected his view that the class struggle to establish socialism required extra-constitutional means to overcome bourgeois domination, including the dictatorship of the proletariat. If one believed in the necessity of a revolutionary avant-garde to lead the proletariat, then a similar ideological avant-garde in the classroom made sense (Brameld 1935). Zalmen Slesinger questioned Counts's assumption that public schooling, a state institution, could be steered to democratic purposes, but in demanding that critiques of the class structure determine teachers' lessons, Slesinger advocated more indoctrination, not less (1937, 273).

From the moment Counts's speech was discussed at the PEA's 1932 meeting, however, indoctrination had far more critics than supporters. Not all progressive educators embraced social reconstruction. Whereas for Counts the Depression epitomized the need to institute planning, philosopher Horace Kallen was committed to limiting the role of government in Americans' lives. "The alterations of good fortune and bad" that mark the American economy every 30 years, Kallen complacently argued, "are no more than the natural weather of existence." Claiming that industrial capitalism had benefited the common man more than any society in history, Kallen condemned Counts and his supporters as Stalinist "apostles of the schemes of salvation" (Kallen 1934b, 2, 3, 14; see also 1934a, 55–62).

Kallen embraced the very individualism that Counts repudiated. Social reconstructionism, he charged, "expresses its judgments in statistical composites; it substitutes numbers, averages, and graphs for people; it talks of masses instead of men, of classes instead of individuals." Like lived experience, "intelligence is born in doubt, it grows by inquiry, discrimination, selection, testing. [It] cannot be alienated from the individual." To present doctrines as anything other than theories to be tested in examining and confronting the world, in Kallen's view, was "to abort actuality, it is to make the end into a means, the means into an end. It is to affirm that man is made for Sabbath or for the church, for the state, for whatever institution. It is to affirm the conventional lie that individuals exist for 'society,' not for themselves and each other." Progressives, Kallen concluded, faced a choice between "indoctrination of the 'American dream' transformed by Marxism or fascism or indoctrination of the religion of freedom as the sciences practice freedom" (1934b, 7–8, 12, 19–20, 22). Like Kallen, Walter Lippmann dismissed the possibility that schools could articulate the common good as Counts envisioned. "The ideal of a conscious pursuit of the common good," Lippmann responded to Counts, "is at war at a thousand points with the vested interests and special desires of sections of the community" (1933, 20; see also Kohl 1980).

Echoing Chicago teacher organizer Margaret Haley, Counts's proposal synthesized appeals for popular control and teacher professionalism (Haley 1981 [1904]; Weiner 1996; Cremin 1961, 226). Still, the call for indoctrination, with its suggestion that teachers possessed the expert knowledge, hints at social efficiency (Goodenow and Urban 1977, 170). Indeed, philosopher Sidney Hook saw in Counts's radicalism the same middle-class sensibility that Counts had exposed in child-centered schools. Indoctrination, Hook charged, "substituted a paternalistic conception of welfare for the vision of democratic mutualism and political liberty central to progressive education" (1963, 104–5).

Even progressives who embraced social reconstruction tended to reject indoctrination. Elsie Clapp was one of those asked to respond to Counts's PEA speech. A protégée of John Dewey, who had gained a national reputation as the director of a Kentucky community-centered school, Clapp seconded Counts's view that child-centered education had neglected social problems and the social life of the child. She rejected, however, Counts's promotion of "indoctrination." Rather than pretending that they are omniscient and dictating ideological critiques of the social order, democratic teachers, Clapp believed, should engage in learning activities with their students. "The process of living and learning and doing," she replied to Counts, was itself "revolutionizing" (1932, 270). As if remembering her debate with Counts, Clapp would elaborate years later that "changes in living and learning are not produced by imparting information about different conditions or by gathering statistical data about what exists, but by creating by people, with people, for people" (Perlstein 1996, 634).

Progressivism's leading lights also rejected indoctrination. William Kilpatrick argued that "Simply to indoctrinate [children] with what has been taught is to indoctrinate them against thinking" (1935). And again, "Democracy, to be itself, cannot indoctrinate even itself" (1939). Echoing Kilpatrick, Alan Griffin argued that there is no "way of 'indoctrinating' [the student] in the democratic ideal. . . . We could indoctrinate *against* the values of any particular authoritarianism, but that would leave our victim at the mercy of the next plausible fixed system that came along" (1942, 83).

Like Counts, John Dewey dismissed the invocations of absolute freedom made by many child-centered educators. "There is no such thing as liberty in general," he argued. "One has to examine what persons *can* do and what they *cannot* do" (1935, 41; Counts 1962, 76). Freedom, for Dewey, is the power to affect one's environment, not some natural state. It is inevitably social. Like Counts, Dewey rejected the notion that some neutral science could define educational objectives. Rather, Dewey argued, social neutrality is an impossible and unworthy goal for teachers. "Social conditions," he observed, "are running in different, often opposed directions. . . . The schools will surely, as a matter of fact and not of ideal, *share* in the building of the social order of the future according as they ally themselves with this or that movement of the existing social forces. . . . Because of this fact the educator . . . is constantly compelled to make a choice. With what phase and direction of social forces will he throw in his energies?" (1934a, 12). Still, Dewey rejected indoctrination. Advocating a planning rather than a planned economy, he saw "an important difference between education with respect to a new social order and indoctrination into settled convictions about that order" (1934b, 10). As an alternative to either apolitical notions of critical thinking or indoctrination, Dewey called for teachers to set up democratic situations for students.

Also among those taking a dim view of indoctrination was progressive philosopher Boyd Bode. Like Counts, Bode applauded progressives' democratic faith in the individual and in the power of intelligence "to create new standards and ideals." He also dismissed "the pathetic hope" that one could decide what to teach "by relying on such notions as interests, needs, growth, and freedom. . . . 'Maximum development' of the individual," Bode argued, "is in itself an empty phrase. . . . Shall we say, for example, that a pupil with a pronounced talent for business needs a commercial course . . . or a comprehension of the evils inherent in a system of free competition. . . ? The answer will not be revealed by any educational microscope." In Bode's view, teachers' refusal to become exponents of democracy as a way of life left "progressive education with no guiding principle except random interests and hypothetical needs." Without a guiding principle, teachers in turn had no basis on which to guide students. Like Counts, Bode reasoned that the absence of a guiding principle, no less the presence, "means that in our attempts to 'socialize' the school population we are really practicing 'imposition' on the sly" (1938, 10, 12–13, 40, 43, 68, 84; see also Childs 1956, 136).

Bode, however, rejected calls for indoctrination:

We take too much upon ourselves if we announce that our purpose is to win "believers in the democratic vista." The teacher's work is done when he has made the issue clear as best he can. Education becomes propaganda when we set out deliberately to make converts; and, moreover, we get hopelessly messed up if the doctrine for which we seek converts is a doctrine that it is wrong to seek converts. (1938, 81)

Moreover, when the teacher is required "to set down beforehand in his lesson plan the answers that are to be elicited from the class, then spontaneous and effective teaching gives way to dreary, soul-destroying pedagogy" (Bode 1940, 156–57, 159). Bode's response to Counts, even more than Counts's call for indoctrination, articulated the case for synthesizing child-centered pedagogy and democratic commitments in American schools.

Counts's call generated wide discussion not only among educational theorists but also in journals that targeted teachers and administrators. Educators closer than Counts or Bode to the classroom raised practical objections to indoctrination. "Those of us who have not taken leave of our senses," wrote Allentown, Pennsylvania, superintendent William Connor, "know that the schools and schoolmasters are not generally going to be permitted *to take the lead* in changing the social order" (Krug 1972, 239). Most teachers, Paul Hanna noted, had little background in philosophy and the social sciences. They "would find themselves quite incapable of understanding and dealing with contemporary social problems" (Hanna

1932, 273). One Arkansas educator found the reconstructionists no help in his insistent inquiries as to whether European history should or should not be taught in seventh grade (Krug 1972, 247).

Still, the lively discussion that Counts's call provoked among New York City high school teachers focused on philosophical and social rather than practical issues. According to Tilden High School's Louis Schuker, opinions about contentious social issues reflect interest as much as logic. Consensus would inevitably reflect the ideology and interests of dominant groups. Democratic teachers, on the other hand, rightly rejected indoctrination because it "recalls rigid orthodoxy, unimpeachable dogmas, ruthless liquidation of contrary-minded minorities and opposition to all change" (Schuker 1934, 6–7, 16–17). Finding the logic of New Deal programs self-evident, Walton High School teacher Jefferson Purcell encouraged students "to develop their own conclusions logically and in terms of social benefit." The liberal teacher, according to Purcell, "must under no condition, try to force the students into accepting his own philosophy except insofar as the truth is its own indoctrinator" (1936, 47, 50). Abraham Lincoln High School principal Gabriel Mason instructed teachers to "permit students ranging from the ultra-conservative to the ultra-radical to express themselves freely, frankly, and fully" in class. Even when dealing with universally recognized evils like lynching and unemployment, "the teacher has no right to say, 'This is the truth, because I think it is the truth.' . . . In considering these topics in a liberal and pedagogical fashion . . . their inherent and intrinsic fallacies will themselves lead to ethical points of view" (Mason 1935: 38–39, 41).

The conviction that open debate would allow students to discover the self-evident logic of New Deal policies suggests that there may have been more indoctrination occurring in the classrooms of opponents of indoctrination than they realized. Whether or not they embraced indoctrination, New York's teachers accepted Counts's premise that their professionalism required them to infuse the curriculum with contemporary concerns and to define their work in terms of democratic values (Guinness 1934, 69; Tauber 1935, 31).

Charging social reconstructionists with disinterest in teachers' daily work, scholars have argued that Counts and other progressives had little impact on the nation's classrooms (Cremin 1961, 233; Moreo 1996, 30–31). In fact, the schools did not lead the struggle to build a new social order. And yet, if one judged Counts by a more modest standard, then his efforts appear more impressive.

Under Counts's editorship, *The Social Frontier*, the flagship journal of social reconstruction, devoted considerable space to the indoctrination question. By its second year, the journal had achieved a circulation of 6,000 (Moreo 1996, 32), a substantial number for an academic journal in Counts's day or our own. Even "the volume of criticism of reconstructionism," as Edward Krug remarks, "was in itself a kind of tribute to its pervasive appeal" (1972, 238).

Whether educators embraced or rejected indoctrination, Counts's manifesto encouraged them to inject contemporary social problems and social justice into the curriculum (Threlkeld et al. 1932, 191; Katz 1966). By raising the question of the goals of the curriculum, the call for indoctrination challenged the notion of a neutral science of education (Counts 1930, 169–71). No doubt debates about the democratic purposes of education, and with them social and historical analyses, occurred with more frequency among teacher educators, hundreds of whom studied at Teachers College, than in elementary and secondary schools (Cremin 1961, 231). Still, through *Scholastic* magazine and the textbooks of Harold Rugg, social reconstructionists reached several million American students and provided them with the opportunity to reflect upon pressing social controversies (Rugg 1941). If George Counts did not transform the social order, he did nevertheless demonstrate the power of social critique in education.

CONCLUSION

In 1935, Counts joined with Reinhold Niebuhr to investigate factionalism in New York's Teachers Union. They argued against excluding Communists from the union. "If liberal and labor forces cannot form a united front," the two maintained, "there is no hope" of countering the ascendancy of reaction in America (Wattenberg 1936, 147). Counts was never a Communist, but social democrats like Counts, in David Hollinger's apt phrase, shared with Communists a "community of discourse . . . within the terms of the cosmopolitan ideal" (1975, 144–45). In 1935, Counts remained convinced that, despite sectarian differences and social conflicts, American teachers, students, and citizens shared fundamental principles. This belief that shared values, if properly applied by educators, could overcome social differences united Counts with Dewey and other progressive critics of indoctrination.

By the late 1930s, however, the reconstructionist moment had passed, and Counts had moved away from the optimistic tolerance of 1935. The rise of Nazism and second thoughts on the Soviet Union combined with conflicts closer to home. In February 1939, Counts published a long article attacking the activities of Communists at Teachers College. Counts now saw in United Front activities a malicious effort to control or destroy liberal voices. Spearheading a campaign to purge Communists from the American Federation of Teachers, Counts worked secretly with New York State's Rapp-Coudert Committee and the House Un-American Activities Committee (Counts 1939; Eaton 1975; Iversen 1959; Murphy 1990; Goodenow and Urban 1977).

Just as the alliance of liberals and radicals had suffused reconstructionism with simultaneous attention to liberty and justice, the rupture of the left-liberal alliance divested reconstructionism of its militancy and élan. Still, Counts's change of heart did not shake his conviction that education took its direction from social analysis rather than from the laws of learning, and he continued to advocate indoctrination even after he abandoned social reconstruction. By the time he wrote the NEA Educational Policies Commission's *The Education of Free Men in American Democracy* in 1941, Counts had become more sympathetic to the liberal tradition, to old-fashioned patriotism, and to the claims of individual conscience and freedom. Still, he condemned curricula that gave students only questions but no answers. He saw "the cultivation of democratic loyalties" as a core function of the school (1941, 34, 53–54). And the development of these loyalties required a conscious and explicit program. Throughout his life, Counts continued to hold that it is "quite impossible to launch and operate a school . . . without making a thousand choices positively involving values, from the architecture of a building, to the materials in a textbook, to the personality of a teacher. . . . There is no escape . . . from the ogre of indoctrination" (1962, 74–75).

The dilemmas that Counts confronted as he sought to reconcile critical thinking and democratic solidarity have been with American educators, in various forms, since the American Revolution. "The quest for a balance between order and liberty, for the proper transaction between the individual and society," David Tyack observed, creates a conflict "inherent in the education of the citizen" (1966a, 31). In addition to the conflicts within the democratic ideal, schools wrestle with conflicts between the democratic purposes of education and the sorting and training functions of the school. It is no wonder that Counts was unable to articulate a viable program of indoctrination with which to reconcile the enduring aims of democratic education as they were manifest in mid-century American life.

Today, industrial battles are no longer the locus of Americans' ideological and social conflicts. Yet faith in shared values and in the political efficacy of citizens has also declined and, with it, the belief that reason and loyalty can be combined. The specific concerns facing democratic educators are therefore different from those Counts addressed. Still, today as in Counts's day, educators committed to fighting for social justice must define the democratic values that would shape their curricula and reconcile imposition with student-directed inquiry. Teacher professionalism must balance self-interest and the common good, and teachers must respond to the crises of democracy outside as well as inside their classrooms if they are to fulfill their democratic obligations (Niece and Viechnicki 1987, 150).

Today, as in Counts's day, social concerns shape educational affairs. "Schooling," as Counts himself put it,

does not simply reflect a culture or civilization. Nor is it derived automatically through a process of assembling and analyzing data. Always at the point where an educational program comes into being, definite choices are made among many possibilities. And these choices are made, not by the gods or the laws of nature, but by men and women working both individually and collectively—by men and women who are moved by all of those forces and considerations which move them in other realms of conduct, by their knowledge and understanding, their hopes and fears, their purposes and loyalties, their views of the world and human destiny, and their position of power in the social structure. (1971b: 1–2)

In Counts's day, the call to indoctrinate strengthened not only those who embraced his appeal but also those liberals who challenged it. In responding to Counts, liberals were led to more fully and militantly articulate their own vision of democratic education. As they did so, they joined Counts in demonstrating the poverty of educational visions grounded only in notions of growth, freedom, academic skills, or social efficiency. Today, as in the 1930s, curricular reformers—whether advocating multiculturalism or shared civic literacy, direct instruction or whole language—risk failing to address the fundamental questions facing Americans and their schools. Unable to provide a road map for democratic educators of his day, Counts offers no sure guide for our own. His efforts, however, make at least this much clear: without a crusading commitment to social justice, child-centered pedagogies are incoherent and sterile. Only by reconstructing society can we educate the whole child.

CHAPTER 4

"No One Here to Put Us Down": Hispano Education in a Southern Colorado Community, 1920–1963

Rubén Donato

Throughout this volume, scholars have been raising provocative questions about the persisting dilemmas in American public schools. Notwithstanding the profound tension between cultivating the common good and serving individual interests, reformers have always believed that free public education for all children would somehow improve society. Early in their history, public schools were given the dual tasks of preparing children for future employment and promoting common democratic values. But what school reformers envisioned and how public schools actually functioned became a serious topic of discussion for educational historians only after the 1960s.

Discussions focused on how public schools reproduced the social and economic structure, the hypocrisy in the promise of democracy, and the illusion of educational reform. Scholars began to generate difficult questions about how race, class, ethnicity, and gender played out in American public schools (Katz 1971; Greer 1972; Spring 1972; Tyack 1974). Important in these discussions was the fact that public education differed over time and location for various groups of people. The educational experiences of southern and eastern European immigrants, for example, was different from those of their northern European peers. Similarly, schooling for African Americans in the South was different from that in the North (Tyack 1974; Anderson 1988; Olneck and Lazerson 1988).

Over the past three decades, we have become more acquainted with the schooling experiences of Mexican Americans in the Southwest (Carter 1970). Although some scholars did write about Mexican Americans in schools during the first half of the twentieth century (Manuel 1930; Reynolds 1933; Tireman 1948; Sanchez 1951), it was the work of Guadalupe San Miguel (1987) and Gilbert Gonzalez (1990) that provided a more critical understanding of what it was like to be Mexican American in public schools. The focus of their work was geographically different (San Miguel concentrated on Texas, Gonzalez on California), but they arrived at similar conclusions regarding the educational experiences of Mexican Americans.

Among other things, they found that large percentages of Mexican American children attended segregated classes or separate schools, they were viewed as inferior by most educators, they were channeled into low, average, or vocational tracks, few graduated from high school, and even fewer went on to college. Moreover, throughout these two seminal works a dominant theme recurs: the possession of political and educational power by Anglos and the subsequent disenfranchisement and marginalization of Mexican Americans. In other words, Anglos were primarily responsible for defining the common good for their own children as well as for Mexican Americans. Missing from this literature are examples where "Latinos" were in positions of authority; that is, local conditions where Latinos were able to determine the educational fates of their children.

Uncommon as it was, there were some communities where Latinos were autonomous. In this chapter I will focus on one such community and examine the schooling experiences of Hispanos—a segment of the Mexican American population—in San Luis, Colorado, between 1920 and 1963. Located in southern Colorado, Hispanos in San Luis have always had political and educational control. What difference did their control make to Hispano students? How did schooling for Hispanos in San Luis differ from that of their Hispano counterparts in nearby school systems and communities where Anglos were in control?

HISPANO LEGACY AND DEMOGRAPHY

Historians have been documenting the unique history of "Hispanos" in southern Colorado (and northern New Mexico) for decades. By the early twentieth century, Hispanos had been living in northern New Mexico for centuries and in southern Colorado for several generations. In 1598, Spanish settlers arrived in New Mexico via Mexico. The colonists, led by

Don Juan de Oñate, built permanent settlements, dug for precious metals, and converted Native Americans to Christianity. Isolated for many years, this northern outpost of the Spanish empire was used primarily as a mission field and a military buffer. Communication between Spanish Mexico and this colony was rare; the colonists were left to fend for themselves (Stoddard 1973). As a result, they developed a culture that bore little resemblance to a true "Mexican" identity. In fact, this region was part of Mexico for only 27 years, and therefore these Hispanos were officially "Mexican" for only one generation.[1]

After the U.S.-Mexican War in 1848, the American Southwest began to change dramatically. By this time, "Spanish Americans" were well established economically and socially. Indeed, they were the original settlers and pioneers of this section of the Southwest (McLean and Thomson 1924). In the middle of the nineteenth century, Anglos started to arrive in large numbers. They came into this territory and shattered the "cultural isolation" of the Spanish American. Anglo cattlemen from California and Arizona invaded Hispano grasslands, Mormon colonists moved into southern Colorado from the Utah area, and eventually the Colorado territory was established in 1861, thereby cutting off the San Luis region from Santa Fe control. The resulting loss of land shifted the economic base and "changed the Hispano-dominated system into an Anglo-dominated system in which Spanish Americans were sole occupants of the lower strata of society" (Stoddard 1973, 10). Hispano communities that had previously enjoyed unquestioned autonomy became politically disenfranchised, socially marginalized, and economically displaced. However, some Hispano communities remained autonomous and were able to maintain social, political, and economic control.

These resilient communities were primarily located in northern New Mexico. Still, there was at least one such community in southern Colorado, the town of San Luis. Situated in the southern section of Costilla County, San Luis and its surrounding villages stand out as a counter example of the ways in which Anglos came to dominate the political and social spheres of Colorado in the latter half of the nineteenth century. Although both whites and Hispanos moved into the southern part of the state after the 1850s, it was the white population that established social, political, economic, and educational control in most communities (Simmons 1979). This occurred in the southern Colorado communities of Monte Vista, Del Norte, and Trinidad, but not in San Luis. The juxtaposition of the Hispano experience in these three communities against that in

San Luis can shed much light on the relationships between autonomy, educational success, and the local definitions of the common purposes of schooling.

It was difficult to generate an accurate count of Hispanos in the towns of Monte Vista, Del Norte, and Trinidad because no such records were available at the time. School districts in Colorado, however, were required to produce census reports that accounted for every person between six and twenty-one years of age. These reports included the child's age as well as his or her place of birth, national origin, and parents' national origin. In all of these reports, Hispanos were referred to as "Spanish Americans" or simply "Spanish." With this information it was possible to produce a general picture of the Hispano population in each of these communities. For example, in the years between 1935 and 1950, Hispano children constituted half or more of the school-aged population in each of these communities (Del Norte School District 1924, 1950; Monte Vista School District 1925, 1950; Trinidad School District 1925, 1950).

However, this did not necessarily mean that all these youth were attending school. One way to find out how Hispanos were faring in school is to compare the overall school-age population to those who were graduating from high school. Hispano graduation rates were low in each of the three communities where Anglos controlled the system. For example, although 17.4 percent of Trinidad's school-age population was Hispano in 1925, they constituted only 2.5 percent of the high school's graduating class that year (Trinidad High School 1925). By 1950, the Hispano school-age population increased to 49.5 percent; however, only 18 percent of the graduating class were Hispano (Morning Light 1950).

Del Norte always had a large Hispano population; it made up 52.2 percent of the school-age population as early as 1924. Yet, in 1925, less than 1 percent of high school graduates were Hispano (San Juan Prospector 1925). By 1950, when the Hispano school-age population had risen to 59.3 percent, less than 40 percent of the graduating class was Hispano (Del Norte High School 1951).

Monte Vista had a similar pattern. In 1920 there were no Hispano graduates in the high school (Monte Vista High School 1920), and even when Hispanos made up more than half of the school-age population in 1950, they accounted for less than 15 percent of the graduating class (ibid. 1950).

These three communities shared certain social, political, demographic, and educational traits. Prominent among these were large Hispano school-age populations, lowered expectations for Hispano students, and few Hispanos (compared to whites) graduating from high school. There was a paucity of Hispanos in leadership roles (in the schools and communities), a perception (in the larger community) of Hispano inferiority, and a lack of Hispano voice in educational affairs. Very few Hispanos were elected to county positions, city councils, or school boards of education. In Monte Vista and Del Norte, Hispanos were generally seen as outsiders and lived on the margins of civic life (Aherns 1968; Borrego 1946).

Trinidad was a little different. The community was not dichotomized as Hispano versus Anglo. It had an unusual multiethnic European population, with a large number of Italians. Given this multiethnic blend, Trinidad seemed more tolerant toward Hispanos. For example, Hispanos were employed there as police officers and fire fighters during the 1940s and 1950s, a period when most Anglo-controlled communities in the region refused to consider them for such positions.

Notwithstanding Trinidad's more tolerant environment, Hispanos lacked a voice in school affairs. Very few Hispanos were elected to the school board, there were almost no Hispano teachers hired in the district before 1950, and Hispano students were heavily tracked into general and commercial classes. This began to change by the mid-1950s as more Hispanos were hired in the schools, more were completing high school, and more were placed in college prep tracks (Donato 1999).

SAN LUIS

The schooling experiences of Hispanos in Monte Vista, Del Norte, and, to a lesser extent, Trinidad were typical of the time. This kind of marginalization and concomitant lack of autonomy was commonplace in most communities in the Southwest and was especially true for Spanish-speaking people in Texas and California (San Miguel 1987; Gonzalez 1990). Schooling for Hispanos in San Luis, however, was different. San Luis, the Costilla County seat, is the oldest town in Colorado. Settled by Hispanos in 1851, it is one of the few places in the state where Hispanos both established and maintained control of the county, the town, and the schools (Borrego 1946). Hispano mayors, assessors and clerks, sheriffs, commissioners, treasurers, justices of the peace, and constables have historically been the norm in Costilla County (*El Democrata* 1928; Bean 1927; Snyder 1948). As Thomas Borrego noted, "In Costilla County where the 'Spanish' element has remained in the majority, they are still actively in control of the county. County official personnel, teacher, and school board positions are filled mostly by 'Spanish' people. This fact, although resented by some 'Anglo' residents of the county, cannot be altered" (1947, 7).

San Luis and its surrounding villages were among the first to organize schools in the state; some, in fact, were organized before Colorado achieved statehood in 1876 (Jaramillo 1955, 11).[2] Given the low tax base and socioeconomic status of the population of Costilla County, public schools had always struggled. Many school buildings were inadequate, books were outdated, and some schools found it difficult to hire teachers with proper credentials (Nash 1949; Bean 1927). Despite these economic hardships, Hispanos—except for three small villages—controlled, managed, and taught in the schools (*El Democrata* 1927; Snyder 1948; Silver Jaramillo, personal interview, July 1997). In an era when many school districts in the region refused to employ Hispanos, San Luis was the exception, especially during the 1920s and 1930s.[3] In Costilla County in 1949, 33 of 42 public school teachers were Hispanos and 9 were Anglos (*Costilla County Free Press* 1949).

Costilla County was remote, isolated, and sparsely populated. In 1946 there were 2,604 school-age children in the county, and the largest number of them were in San Luis (Peccolo 1949, 64). The San Luis educational system, however, was not ideal. There was no public high school; access to a high school education in San Luis was available only through a private Catholic school. The problem was that large families could not afford even the small tuition for all their children (Zack Bernal, personal interview, October 1998). As a result, many students in the San Luis area did not attend high school. Thus, only a small number of high school graduates went on to college from this community. During World War II, however, Hispanos in San Luis began actively to seek remedies to the educational needs in their community.

The San Luis Institute

Many San Luis Hispanos joined the armed services and then, following the war, they returned to the community. In the early 1940s, a group of Hispano veterans got together for the purpose of finding ways to enhance the educational opportunities within San Luis. *The Southern Coloradan* noted that several Hispano veterans—Richard Maes, Gilbert Maes, Larry La Combe, and Joe Barela—became adamant about establishing an institution of higher education in the town (Adams State College n.d.).

Specifically, they wanted to establish a two-year academic program and vocational training (Adams State College 1945, 1951–52). Hispanos in San Luis were insistent; they sought to transform the town's Works Progress Administration building to house the program.

The initiative and building were available, but there was no one to teach post-secondary education. Hispanos sought help from nearby Adams State College in Alamosa. College officials were receptive to the idea. The institute was discussed and approved, and classes began in 1943. As the school newspaper noted:

[T]he new San Luis division called the San Luis Institute of Arts and Crafts sort of grew up like Topsy. Few Coloradans probably know of its existence. Dr. [Ira] Richardson [Adams State College president] had an old community WPA building given to the state and around this structure he built a college serving a population that is 90 per cent Spanish-American. . . . The amazing thing about this unique college is that the building was acquired without cost to the state, built or improved upon partly by the faculty, students and volunteer help. (Adams State College n.d.)

President Richardson was aware that Hispanos in the San Luis area had few opportunities to pursue higher education. In fact, the newspaper for the college noted that "Dr. Richardson's small, hard-working faculty is giving some ambitious young men and women, who have felt that they've been discriminated against, at least a smattering of higher learning" (ibid.). The institute began as a small program, serving seven to twelve full-time and part-time students. As more Hispanos were discharged from the military, enrollments began to soar. "I remember that almost all of us who got discharged from the military went to college," said Alfirio Sanchez, a former teacher in San Luis (personal interview, September 1998). Opportunities to further one's education, said Salomon Chavez, a former teacher and school administrator, became available with the San Luis Institute (personal interview, October 1998). Relatively large numbers of Hispanos were enrolled in the institute's vocational program, where they received training in agriculture and in industrial and mechanical arts. Most of those in the academic program became teachers. Preservice teachers took course work during their freshman and sophomore years in the institute and went to the main campus in Alamosa for their junior and senior years.

The establishment of the San Luis Institute was a turning point in the community. It "not only made it possible to earn college degrees," explained Salomon Chavez, "but it also allowed us to train teachers for our community." The San Luis Institute, however, was more than a place where students attended classes; it was also the center for many social, cultural, religious, and athletic activities and events. Hispanos formed the Newman Club, a Catholic organization; the Outing Club, a camping, nature, and conservation group; the *Centennial*, a newspaper; and the Chorus group, which specialized in Spanish songs and dances. There were also athletics and other extracurricular activities (Adams State College 1945–50). Hispano students remember the institute as an extremely safe place to attend college.

The institute also housed its faculty members in San Luis, and a number of the professors were Hispanos and Hispanas. Julian Samora, who later became a prominent scholar, started his career at Adams State College and the San Luis Institute. Eva Borrego, Cornelio Gallegos, and Bridget Olguin also taught there for a number of years. In addition to the Hispano faculty, students recalled that the Anglo faculty—Winfred Mott, Ascha Nash, Alice Wright, and Luther Bean, among others—were well received. The presence of Samora and Borrego, however, seemed to be crucial to the institute. "Eva Borrego and Julian Samora were great professors," said Alfirio Sanchez. "They always pushed us and wanted us to better ourselves. They made a lasting impression on my life. I will never forget them" (personal interview, September 1998).

It was difficult for many students to leave the institute and continue at Adams State in Alamosa to complete their bachelor's degrees. Concerns about distance, money, and being in the minority were prominent in the minds of those attending the institute. However, James Mascarenas, a former student and teacher in San Luis, remembers that attending college in Alamosa was not that bad because there were a significant number of Hispanos from San Luis and its surrounding villages in attendance (personal interview, September 1998). In addition, a significant number of Hispanos from other communities in the San Luis Valley were also present at Adams State.

The Struggle for a Public High School in San Luis

Some Hispano students from Costilla County who earned their college degrees at Adams State College during the 1940s and early 1950s returned to be employed as teachers and administrators in the San Luis public schools. Many began to realize that Mercy High School was unable to serve the majority of students from southern Costilla County. Although the private high school had done a commendable job for a number of decades, there were too many Hispanos who were unable to attend. Yet, establishing a public high school in San Luis was not a simple matter. The school-age population in San Luis was not large enough or wealthy enough to establish a public high school, so consolidation was inevitable. That is, successful creation of a high school would entail the cooperation of several villages in the county—Chama, Los Fuertes, La Valley, San Pablo, Garcia, Jaroso, Mesita, New Acacio, and San Acacio. In addition, a few village school systems in southern Costilla County were controlled by Anglos but needed to be involved in the process. These districts had historically avoided institutional relationships with Hispano communities.

However, during the late 1940s and early 1950s, a movement toward school district consolidation was gaining momentum in Colorado and, indeed, throughout the nation. Voters in southern Costilla County realized that their children would have access to a free public high school only if they consolidated. In 1949, a bill to consolidate public schools was passed by the 57th Colorado General Assembly. "The purpose of this Bill," wrote Charles Peccolo, was to "enlarge the areas of the school districts so that better and more equal educational opportunities will be offered to the children; to provide a larger tax base; and to provide better facilities, teachers and equipment" (1949, 4-5). State officials sought "a complete reorganization of school districts in Colorado by 1952" (ibid.). Silver Jaramillo, a former teacher, principal, and school superintendent in San Luis, remembered that small Anglo communities in southern Costilla County were nervous about unifying with school systems controlled by Hispanos. Although some Anglos were supportive, many Anglos feared they would be "beaten up" in the political process (personal interview, July 1997).

Almost everyone in Costilla County understood that cultural and economic differences "needed to be considered in the reorganization plan" (Borrego 1947, 9). Residents had begun to realize that the reform could offer the "best opportunity for educational attainment" for everyone. Anglo and Hispano community members understood that the only way to make free secondary education available to their children was to join together. What was needed to accomplish this, according to Thomas Borrego, was the "pooling of all resources, whether 'Spanish' or 'Anglo' in nature, to provide the best schools possible" (ibid., 8).

Jaramillo began the crusade to establish a public high school in San Luis in the early 1950s. With support from Adams State College, the Colorado State Department of Education, and some interested school board members in southern Costilla County, he persuaded residents from ten school districts in the area to vote in favor of a "union high school district." Jaramillo and several state officials "visited nearly all of the board members of the various districts, discussed plans and set a date for the meeting to evaluate the feasibility of this consolidation." On August 17, 1953, "ten school districts voted to become a Union High School District" (Jaramillo 1955, 22). To ensure equal representation, the county superintendent appointed ten members—six Hispanos and four Anglos—to the "Centennial High School District board" (San Luis School District 1953).

As soon as the community had voted in favor of the new high school, Jaramillo was asked to assume the role of superintendent. In less than a month, he had hired several teachers, the San Luis Institute building was transformed into the new high school, used appliances were donated to the school, and three used buses were purchased. "People knew we meant business," Jaramillo said, "when we drove in town with these buses. The community was finally convinced that we were going to have a free public high school in San Luis" (personal interview, September 1998).

On the first day of school in the 1953 fall semester, 95 students showed up at Centennial High; the following year 178 students were attending classes regularly (Jaramillo 1955, 22, 34). By 1960, high school enrollment had increased to 242. In 1961, the high school was staffed with ten teachers, a principal, and a superintendent; the superintendent, the principal, and five teachers were Hispano (Centennial High School 1960–62).

Education and the Common Good at Work in San Luis

People who were involved in founding Centennial High School seemed to have a specific vision: school board members, administrators, and teachers fostered an environment that allowed Hispano students to thrive. Unlike those in Monte Vista, Del Norte, and, to a lesser extent, Trinidad, teachers and administrators at Centennial High (many of whom were themselves Hispano)[4] expected a great deal from their Hispano students, and they sought to provide them with the skills, confidence, and opportunities needed to excel academically. From the beginning, Hispano students were encouraged to take algebra, chemistry, and geometry. In the mid-1950s, the Rocky Mountain Area Project—a grant from the Ford Foundation to small rural schools in Colorado—gave Hispanos at Centennial High the opportunity to take algebra II, trigonometry, physics, and other advanced courses (Jaramillo 1955, 30).

In 1961, 17.3 percent of students at the school made the honor roll, with a grade point average of 3.0 or better. That percentage was probably typical of any U.S. high school at the time, which in and of itself was a sign of the school's success, given that most of the students at Centennial High were Hispanos (*Costilla County Free Press* 1961), a population that had not previously shown such academic achievement. Although data were unavailable to determine how many Hispano students dropped out from Centennial High, oral interviews suggest that the dropout rate was extremely low. Charlie Jaquez, a seventh-generation San Luis Hispano, recalled that the graduation rate was always high at the school: "It was very unusual for students to drop out from Centennial High," said Jaquez. "I guess you can say that the dropout rate was low because students felt comfortable in the system" (personal interview, September 1998).

Chris Martinez, who taught biology at the school during the early 1960s, said that students at Centennial High succeeded "because parents valued education, the school was staffed with dedicated teachers, Hispanos controlled the schools, and kids did not have to deal with discrimination" (personal interview, September 1998). There was another reason why Hispano students at the high school performed relatively well. Abie Duarte, a former teacher and the principal at Centennial High, maintained that Hispano youth performed well because "there was no one here to put us down." It made a difference, he said, that "Hispanos were teachers, principals, superintendents, and school board members." Unlike many other schools systems where Hispanos attended, continued Duarte, San Luis "did not have a structure that was oppressive" (personal interview, June 1997).

Duarte explained that he did not understand the nature of oppression and the implications of autonomy until he moved to the Denver metro area. He remembered some Hispano families who had left San Luis for economic reasons, and he was disturbed to see how life had changed for these families in the city. In San Luis, he said, families were respected and had status in the community. In the metro area, their lives changed. Families experienced a total loss of dignity and self-respect: "In San Luis [Hispanos] may have been needy, but they knew who they were, they had pride, and most of all, they had self-respect" (personal interview, June 1997).

Arnold Chavez, a student from San Pablo who attended Centennial High during the late 1950s and early 1960s, remembered the mutual respect between teachers and students: "Teachers were part of the community, they were extended family, and they cared about us." Many teachers had been raised in the community and were related to some of the students. "My cousin," Chavez said, "lived across the street from us, and he was a teacher. His wife was also a teacher. I used to see how they lived. They were not wealthy, but they had a better life than we did. . . . So I always thought I needed to further my education." Hispano parents, he said, "expected their children to respect their teachers," and in return "teachers respected us" (personal interview, November 1997).

There was no doubt that Hispano educators and parents from San Luis and its surrounding villages saw schooling as a means to a better life. Education, however, was seen not only as a vehicle for social mobility but also as a means to achieve self-respect and give back to their community. This was evident in the decisions people made as to who would run their schools. Although Hispano school board members ultimately controlled the district, Superintendent Jaramillo was a major player in the decision-making process. He hired school administrators, teachers, and counselors, helped shape the curriculum, and dealt with the politics of education within and outside of the community. Arnold Chavez remembered that, when he was a student at Centennial High, Silver Jaramillo was the superintendent. "He was articulate," said Chavez, "he was respected in the community, and he represented us well. He not only communicated well with people in the San Luis area, but he also had the skills, presence, and ability to command respect from educational professionals in Denver. . . . He was an excellent role model" (personal interview, November 1997).

Duarte, the principal, also played an important role. Unlike the administrative indifference many students felt in Monte Vista, Del Norte, and Trinidad, students at Centennial High School described how Duarte listened to their concerns, attended to their academic needs, and inspired them to succeed in everyday life (Centennial High School 1960–62). The school was unusual: it was a place where Hispanos were in charge, where students felt comfortable and encouraged to excel academically, where racial discrimination was not an issue, and where mutual respect was found. And, as we shall see, the unique educative experience offered at Centennial High had a profound effect on Hispano students in terms of the pursuit of post-secondary education.

Hispanos at Adams State College

Adams State College was established in Alamosa in 1925, when few Hispanos in the region were attending high school, when still fewer were graduating from high school, and when college was a remote possibility for most of them. Despite these realities, Hispanos from the San Luis Valley did begin to attend Adams State College when it opened its doors. College enrollments were relatively small, increasing from 103 in 1925 to almost 500 in 1960. Hispanos had always had a presence in the college: in 1925 there were 17 Hispanos out of a total enrollment of 102; in 1935, 42 out of 204; in 1946, 38 out of 169; in 1955, 70 out of 257; and, in 1964, 122 out of 1,013 (Adams State College 1935, 1946, 1955, 1964).

Adams State yearbooks reveal that the majority of the Hispano enrollment came from many southern Colorado communities. A significant number of Hispanos who attended, however, were from Costilla County. Many came from San Luis and the small villages in the southern part of county—Garcia, San Pablo, San Acacio, Chama, La Valley, Jaroso, San Acacio, New San Acacio, Mesita, and Los Fuertes. Between 1955 and 1962, 86 Hispano students from San Luis and the southern part of the county attended Adams State College. In contrast, there were only 88 Hispano students from Monte Vista, Del Norte, and Trinidad combined (Adams State College 1955–62). What is particularly noteworthy about this comparison is that the Hispano population in San Luis and the southern part of the county was less than half the size of the combined Hispano populations of Monte Vista, Del Norte, and Trinidad.

The number of Hispanos from the San Luis area enrolled at Adams State College was not surprising. Early on, graduates from Our Lady of Mercy High School established a tradition of attendance, alumni from the San Luis Institute continued this trend, and the establishment of Centennial High School made post-secondary education both accessible and possible for many Hispano students in the San Luis area.

CONCLUSION

One of the paradoxes about the legacy of American public schools was that, though reformers struggled with many complex issues, they did not question who defined the common good. In the belief that free public education for all children would promote the common good, improve society, and cure the nation's social ills, Hispanos, like their Mexican American counterparts, were excluded from these discussions. Consistent with the evolution of public education, Anglos in Del Norte, Monte Vista, and Trinidad defined the common good and operated schools in ways that benefited their children. Hispanos lived on the margins in these school systems and, for the most part, were left to fend for themselves. Moreover, Hispano parents were excluded from educational decision-making processes. In these school systems, the outcomes were clear and negative. Hispano students were generally looked down upon by educators, held to low expectations, tracked into average/low classes, and rarely told about the benefits of a high school diploma or going on to college. It is not surprising that high school completion rates for Hispanos were much lower than for their Anglo counterparts.

In contrast, Hispanos in San Luis defined the common good. They were the majority on the school boards and in school administration, and many of them were teachers. They created an educational environment in which Hispano youth felt comfortable, free from racial discrimination, and held to high expectations. Hence, the majority of Hispano students graduated from Centennial High, they were encouraged to take academically challenging courses, and many of them went on to college. Within the context of this community, unique sociocultural circumstances evolved: Hispanos in the San Luis area never knew what it was like to be marginalized, to be looked upon as inferior, to be ignored by educational professionals, or for their children to be treated unequally in their schools.

What San Luis and its surrounding villages can teach us is the importance of autonomy. Contrary to conventional wisdom that Latinos were unable to determine their educational fates, this study shows what can happen when Hispanos had the power to control their schools, the authority to run them, and the freedom to define the common good. Hispanos in the San Luis area were able to achieve this in no small way because, as Centennial High School principal Duarte suggested, there was no one there to put them down.

CHAPTER 5

Echoes of Corporate Influence: Managing Away Urban School Troubles

Dorothy Shipps

Many modern-day school reformers acknowledge an inheritance from the Progressive era (1880–1920), when our current public system was formed. Often, they spotlight its organizational structures or governance as the core of that legacy. Reformers typically blame the limitations of those structures for the problems they encounter in changing schools, especially urban schools. As a result, the "factory-like," "industrial," "bureaucratic," "monopolistic," or "democratically controlled" school system we inherited from that earlier era have all become accepted arguments for change (see, for instance, Sizer 1984; Kearns and Doyle 1989; Hill, Pierce, and Guthrie 1997; Lee, Bryk, and Smith 1993; Chubb and Moe 1990).

In this chapter I examine another striking resemblance between the two eras: a preoccupation with economic justifications for urban school reform, and the privileged status of business critiques and management solutions. A century ago, reformers adopted and rationalized many favored reforms based on their reputed economic benefits to individuals and the newly industrializing urban society. The current era has at its core a resurrected and strengthened version of this notion. In both eras, reformers have agreed that whatever public schools do to improve individual students' job opportunities has direct economic consequences for the nation as a whole, and for cities in particular.

In the Progressive era, different proponents had their own economic justifications for reform. Corporate leaders criticized urban schools for failing to respond to a newly industrialized, centralized, and increasingly integrated world economy. They joined forces with other elite progressives who envisioned the need for a rationalized, less politicized school system, and who eventually accepted the benefits of adopting corporate models of governance. Still other progressives sought greater social justice and democratic participation in school governance but welcomed powerful allies from the corporate community when their interests and values seemed to overlap.

Today, corporate critiques of urban schools are again a source of economic justification for change. Business organizations and leaders seek to refashion urban schooling in response to the new technology-driven global economy. Their allies are again elites: local and national political executives, faculty at select universities, foundation heads, and union leaders. Their plans to improve urban school systems mimic corporate restructuring—a more recent model of corporate governance—while embracing competition as a means of improving quality within schools and among them. Again, management solutions for the problems of urban schools are among the dominant themes in reform proposals; and, again, community-based reformers with social action agendas welcome powerful corporate allies.

These similarities raise several questions: How are economic justifications and management reforms linked? How does our current concept of urban schooling reinforce business values and economic justifications? And, ultimately, who has the moral authority to elevate some educational goals over others and propose acceptable accommodations when values clash? These questions were initially raised and debated in the 1960s and 1970s by a group of historians writing about business influence during the Progressive era. Their insights provide a starting point for thinking about corresponding issues today. Below I describe their contributions to our understanding of that era, then compare their insights to the present day.

Drawing on historical literature to explain current reform rhetoric invites an examination of differences. After exploring those differences, I conclude that a decline in the status of educational leaders relative to business leaders and the accelerated transfer of management debates into universities and schools help to explain the urgency economic justifications have today. Our modern preoccupation with the "victory" of capitalism over other forms of economic organization is another difference that adds to the modern sense of urgency, although the accompanying millennial fervor certainly echoes that of the turn of the nineteenth century. Mid-century changes in expectations about equality and citizenship also argue against superficial comparison: they left their own residue of governance structures in urban schooling that involved courts, teachers' unions, and federal funding streams upon which current reform arguments also rest. Taken together, I contend that these changes have intensified the patterns of corporate and economic influence on urban schools that were begun over a hundred years ago.

Public ideas, the rhetoric by which problems are defined and solutions conveyed, have a singular place in reform (Reich 1988; Kingdon 1995). This rhetoric, rather than the practice of urban school reform in particular contexts, draws my attention. Economically justified and management-focused reform rhetoric frames much of the current political debate about how to improve urban schools because it is voiced by powerful corporate interests with a largely unrivaled moral claim: the educators who presented a competing vision in the past have been largely discredited. These corporate interests are supported by political allies who share their renewed millennial vision about global free markets and the role of education in fostering them.

This chapter is also a call for a contemporary countermovement, one that echoes another aspect of the Progressive era in its emphasis on social learning, group deliberation, and the development of citizens in a democracy. When the current era fades, our urban schools will be changed. My hope is that they will not have been excessively distorted by an economic rationale: their equity mission dismantled by market competition or their civic education purpose diffused by managerial fixes.

THE CORPORATE LEGACY

I use the term corporate leaders in reference to a relatively small, elite group of businessmen (and, recently, women) who run the nation's corporate enterprises, including those who manage the business associations to which these enterprises belong. Currently referred to as executive officers and chairpersons, these individuals function as salaried representatives of powerful institutions today, whereas their counterparts in the Progressive era were corporate owners and presidents (Mizruchi 1992). All have had uncommon access to high-level elected political officials and government agency heads, the wealth of large corporations to draw upon, and the ability to affect local and regional economies simply by making narrow "business" decisions. Moreover, they are highly organized. Although they have not always spoken with one voice, they typically speak in a common language and have been unified on many issues.[1]

A body of work written about four decades ago first clarified for us how the earliest corporate leaders and their economic conceptions of public life helped shape—some said dominate—Progressive-era debates over the structure, governance, and control of urban public schools. These historians had a crucial impact: they taught us how our current urban school systems are a legacy of structures built during that era. As the only public institution supported by a mandate of mass attendance, it remains significant that the shape of public schooling was so heavily influenced by the corporate elite of the time.

Transfer of Business Values to the Schools

Writing in the early 1960s, Raymond Callahan was among the first to explore corporate influence on urban public schools during the Progressive era. For him, this meant explaining the impressive influence of Frederick W. Taylor's ideas about "scientific management" on school leaders in the early decades of the century. Although scientific management assumed a hierarchy of workers and managers as well as apolitical corporate governance, Taylor advocated that both workers and owners acknowledge a shared interest in maximizing income and output. That done, management became a "technical matter of discovering the 'one best way.'" It also rationalized the centralization and specialization already occurring in the workplace and gave managers an "agenda" for continual reform (Waring 1991, 11–12; see also Kanigel 1997).

Callahan focused on the expectations and self-image of the generation of public school superintendents trained in the era. They became primary conduits for the "cultural diffusion" of high-status corporate practices and values to low-status schools. Schools succumbed to business influence because, as a group, urban superintendents were "vulnerable" to the criticism and pressure built into a "pattern of local support and control" that had made their jobs highly insecure (Callahan 1962, viii). The preponderance of businessmen and sympathetic professionals on local boards of education further encouraged superintendents to adopt business-like conceptions of schooling (Counts 1927; Cronin 1973).

Callahan added a second force to the momentum: the nearly complete capitulation of those men who taught the first courses of educational administration at the universities. They introduced business and industrial procedures and terminology to educational administrators in courses that focused on efficiency, financial, legal, and organizational issues.

Callahan coupled his vulnerability and indoctrination theses with "the great strength of the business community and the business philosophy in an age of efficiency" (1962, 179). Business tycoons were highly visible and widely admired. It seemed to him "inevitable" that business values would influence public schools, and he described almost irresistible forces driving superintendents to see themselves by the end of the Progressive era as "general managers" rather than as pedagogues or scholars (ibid., 199).

His theses drew both applause and criticism for many years, joining an important debate about the underlying question: who are the transmitters of business management models into schools, and how does it happen?[2]

Economic Conceptions of Public Life

Joel Spring, writing a decade after Callahan, focused his analysis on the era's economic construction of public life, emphasizing its corporatist aspects. He was commenting on the progressivism of Samuel Gompers, Jacob Riis, Theodore Roosevelt, Herbert Croly, and John Dewey more than the efficiency of Frederick Taylor.[3] Concerned with the effects of corporate influence on the structure and purpose of modern mass schooling rather than on superintendents or other intermediaries, Spring argued that progressive reformers' ideas buttressed corporate influence. As Christopher Lasch put it, "[Spring] both complements and corrects Raymond Callahan's earlier study . . . which identified the efficiency movement too narrowly with Taylorism and thereby missed the congruence between 'efficiency' and progressivism" (1973, 23).

Spring tied the Progressive era to an economic construction of society through the notion of the "corporate state." In explaining the source of these ideas, he frequently quotes Herbert Croly's *The Promise of American Life*. Croly had argued that America's promise was to be achieved by emulating the organization of the newest and most modern economic institutions: the huge, often multinational, corporations and unions. In these large institutions, entrepreneurship and individual competitiveness were subsumed under a larger corporate will, a sublimation encouraged by business paternalism. Croly's argument was formed, Spring tells us, in reaction to congested urban life and the disintegration of small-town relationships. The social disruption that resulted from the new urban/industrial environment drew corporate, labor, and political leaders together into a reform coalition that sought to head off social unrest, perhaps even avert socialist revolution. Cheap meals, health care and inoculations, playgrounds and showers, social clubs and adult education programs made urban workers' lives more pleasant, even as these amenities were rationalized by business, labor, and political leaders as a means to foster more productivity and maintain social peace.

If progressives provided the ideology, "America's capitalists constructed its foundation" (Lazerson 1973, 278). Paternalistic corporate leaders were expected to provide guidance for improvements in public services much as they provided the organizational models for linking individual enterprises into combines and schools into districts. In public schooling they did so by demanding that schools prepare students for their roles as cooperative, efficient industrial workers and by encouraging school systems to add social services that corporations were themselves modeling.

Spring's reviewers commented on the pessimism (sometimes referred to as romanticism) in his argument; he was writing as much about the nightmares of the era as about its ideas.[4] He left little room for the possibility of a public system designed to further goals other than social control for economic efficiency, but he unearthed a second enduring question: how does our conception of the role of schooling in society reinforce business values?

Balancing Extremes

David Tyack complicates themes raised by Callahan and Spring in a series of writings beginning with *The One Best System* in 1974. Like Callahan, Tyack underscores the role of superintendents and other educators in legitimating and transmitting scientific management, efficiency, and corporate bureaucracy to schools. Like Spring, he recognizes that the desire to smooth over social disruption was also strong.

In Tyack's account, superintendents are both initiators and translators of centralization and standardization in the schools. They seek security in their own professional status even as they remain susceptible to influence from a host of social forces. He also draws a more complete picture of allies and advocates who bring a corporate vision to the management of urban public schools. In addition to the "interlocking directorate" of educators and politicians that Callahan and Spring describe are "the business and professional elites of the cities" (Tyack 1981, 58).

Tyack clarifies how informal processes of centralization, standardization, and specialization that were influencing public schooling in the nineteenth century laid the groundwork for Taylorism after 1890, as urban elites gained control over schools. In the process, Tyack began an "analysis of the organizational and functional similarities between the public school system and the (urban) political machine" (Schultz 1975, 379; see also Cutler 1976).

Tyack explicitly links scientific management to the growth of complex corporate governance structures designed to enhance technological expertise and "take schools out of politics" (1974, 107). From the beginning, he tells us, scientific management applied to schooling created its own problems of anomie, rigidity, complacency, and irresponsibility for which the application of more efficiency and expertise was no solution. Taylorism was "notably successful" when applied to school management issues, but it also left a residue of organizational consequences that would bedevil school leaders and reformers for the remainder of the century. For these reasons, among others, he does not see the interests of corporate management and progressive reformers on the same side.

In *Managers of Virtue*, Tyack and his co-author, Elisabeth Hansot, clarify how centralization, bureaucracy, and efficiency also encouraged a practical countermovement that sought democratic participation for teachers, students, and parents. The countermovement had its own philosophical basis in social learning through group deliberation, and it followed the evolutionary and social philosophy of John Dewey. These progressive "social reconstructionists" emphasized that schools were instrumental to the development of citizenship in a democracy, whereas "administrative progressives" highlighted their role in preparing workers for the economy (1982, 119, 202). Thus, Tyack and Hansot reinterpreted the hegemony of Spring's "corporate state" as a conflict of worldviews.[5]

Tyack neither dismisses nor fully embraces the concerns raised about corporate influence by Callahan and Spring; instead, he elevates another aspect. He explores the millennial expectations of school leaders in the Progressive era, presenting it as an effective, if infrequently used, counterweight to corporate influence. Callahan described the prestige of corporate leaders in the Progressive era, arguing that they were admired because they embodied the age of efficiency. Spring hinted that corporate leaders saw themselves as moral agents.[6] David Tyack highlights the importance of the moral authority of those who would lead in education.

Initially in *The One Best System*, and with greater force in *Managers of Virtue*, he clarifies that Progressive-era school leaders had the moral authority to resist, as well as elevate, the business values pressed on them by corporate leaders and an economically defined society. The nineteenth-century image of the superintendent as "exemplar of approved virtues" did not die in the twentieth century (Tyack and Hansot 1982, 68). In part, this reflected the remarkably consistent background, gender, religious affiliation, ethnicity, and race of those who became superintendents. Tyack compared superintendents' careers to those of religious leaders in their self-selected conservatism and long socialization. Progressive-era superintendents saw themselves and were seen as "guardians of decorum and morality" (ibid., 177). Thus, Tyack raises a third question: who has the moral authority to elevate some educational goals over others and to propose acceptable accommodations when values clash?

Borrowing from the Corporate Closet

Today the public schools continue to adapt new business efficiency techniques in what seems to be a constant recycling process. Scientific management, it turns out, was only the precursor to a host of ever newer management theories aimed at encouraging greater worker productivity and, hence, greater national wealth. Over the years these theories have included the "Scanlon" plan, management by objectives, job enrichment and rotation, participatory decision making, sensitivity training, quality control circles, total quality management, and "intrepreneurship," a reference to corporate managers who adopt the creative stance of entrepreneurs. These theories have developed into applied techniques like downsizing, benchmarking, outsourcing, and the like.

The developers of these new management theories are a group whom Stephen Waring refers to as the "management mandarinate" (1991, 7), a term apparently borrowed from Peter Drucker. Management mandarins codify and market management theory to corporate leaders and beyond. They have been preoccupied since World War II with a series of attempts to overcome problems that the adoption of scientific management helped to create. The new management theories have been influenced by the attempt either to perfect Taylorism or to ameliorate its tendency to create labor/management conflict by adopting more corporatist forms of governance within the firm. Although "essentially fungible" in that both accept the primacy of management solutions to market problems, according to Waring, the two schools have traded blows for years, and they often have different views on whether centralization or decentralization, command-and-control accountability or worker participation should be preferred in firms (ibid., 187).

These trends in management theory have echoes in the management reforms prescribed for and adopted by schools. Just as corporations respond to the management problems created by Taylorism with new management techniques, so schools respond to similar problems engendered by their Progressive-era management legacy. They do so by borrowing the latest technique from business, whether from the corporatist school (e.g., decentralization, worker participation) or the neo-Taylorist school (e.g., centralization, command-and-control accountability).

Many of these business management trends have been transferred to the public schools from outside. Corporate leaders, business authors, and other entrepreneurs have written panegyric texts on how to transfer management techniques—management by objectives, total quality management (TQM), or benchmarking—into public school settings (see, for instance, Morrisey 1976; Sallis 1992; Murgatroyd and Morgen 1993; Kearns and Doyle 1989). The transfer is also initiated by educators and other insiders who seek cultural support from local elites by adopting a language of business management when they want to justify changes they believe are needed (Walberg et al. 1988; Lieberman 1989).

As Callahan and Tyack taught us about the Progressive era, the translators and transmitters of management techniques and efficiency measures into urban schools are often school leaders themselves. Urban superintendents remain vulnerable to elite boards of education as well as to corporate- and foundation-sponsored research debates. They continue to be indoctrinated by their training in graduate schools of education. Education school professors repackage business techniques for the public schools, marketing them as the latest in school reform. When they do so, they earn added cachet in an academic environment that diminishes their disciplinary expertise and highlights their ability to borrow from more prestigious applied disciplines like economics, business, and management sciences.

As has been true in the past, the transfer of management methods from businesses to schools begins with a critique about school failure. Business has contributed mightily to the current critique, much of it orchestrated through a tight network of chief executive officers that make up each state's Business Roundtable. In 1989, the National Business Roundtable began a nationwide campaign encouraging its state and local affiliates to reform the local public schools. Locals were expected to work with the state governors and mayors, devoting no less than ten years of sustained effort to restructure local school systems (NBR 1990, 1996; Fosler 1990). Other national business groups, like the National Alliance of Business and the Conference Board, have responded by writing and disseminating "how to" pamphlets for CEOs and business groups seeking to push school policy in the direction of corporate restructuring (NAB 1989, 1990; Ashwell and Caropreso 1989; Brothers 1992). These reports persistently draw parallels between good business practice and good schools. In cities, local business associations—among them the Cincinnati Business Committee, the Commercial Club of Chicago, "the Vault" in Boston, the Seattle Alliance for Education, and the Los Angeles Educational Partnership—have been strong advocates of business management transfer to the local public schools.

Speaking on behalf of corporate business groups and their own institutions, CEOs like Norman Augustine of Lockheed Martin Corporation, Jerry Hume of Basic American Foods, Louis V. Gerstner of IBM, David T. Kearns of Xerox Corporation, Richard M. Morrow of Amoco, Ronald Gidwitz of Helene Curtis, Owen B. Butler of Procter and Gamble Company, and hundreds of others have criticized schools, calling them unresponsive and unaccountable to consumers, complacent monopolies in desperate need of restructuring. Although their criticisms may seem uniquely linked to public schools, they are drawn from the most recent management theories in business.

David Kearns clarifies the link when he describes school restructuring as a process that parallels Xerox Corporation's response to Japanese competition threatening its hegemony in the copier business. He laments that schools do not have the same market incentives: in order for corporate management theories to improve education, schools must have the same competitive forces working on them as do corporations. Since market incentives are lacking, part of management reform for the schools is to create them, through charter, magnet, or voucher schools, benchmarking, and various forms of privatization. In addition, he is clear that educators cannot be trusted to do this: "business will have to set the reform agenda" (Doyle, Cooper, and Trachtman 1991, 5).

Corporate leaders in cities act locally, but they are predisposed to engage in educational policy making because of the way that business groups across the country have adopted views about schooling that are similar to Kearns's. The Cincinnati Business Committee director put it this way: "The business community took the subjectivity out of educational judgments. It was 'Let's find out what it costs, how many people are served and the results.' When you put information on that grid, the answer leaps out" (Bradley 1993). In a June 1997 personal interview, the education spokesperson for the Illinois Business Roundtable described the link between management in business and accountability in Chicago's schools:

> I suppose it sounds negative to say this, but (senior management) holds it over the heads of (teachers and principals) if they don't do their job. Just like in the sense in which getting fired is held over the heads of people in private industry if they don't perform. Nothing wrong with that. (If) people are willing to pay you to do a job, they ought to have something to say about how you do it.

If this business critique and educator complicity were the only mechanisms of cultural diffusion today, then little would be different from the Progressive era. However, modern-day diffusers of corporate management reform no longer profess to eschew politics in the schools; many are themselves politicians seeking control. School reform in the contemporary era has also responded to global changes that enhance the impact of powerful politicians and corporate leaders.

The Politician's Role in Cultural Transmission

As a series of recent studies have shown, governors and big city mayors are reversing the Progressive-era taboo against mixing electoral and party politics with public school governance (see, for instance, Bryk, Hill, and Shipps 1998; Shipps, Kahne, and Smylie 1999; Yee 1998; Portz 1997; Rich 1996). They use catchwords like "accountability" and their recent experience in "reinventing" local and state governments to assert new authority over the school systems in their jurisdiction.

These political leaders bring to school governance their access to political party resources and fund-raising connections as well as their authority to demand cooperation from other government agencies like parks, police, and health departments. As elected leaders with broad constituencies and strong party affiliation, they have a hearing in the halls of Congress (and with federal agencies) to which few school superintendents are privy. As chief executives, politicians are familiar with the latest management improvement strategy and are eager to enlist business allies to help them fix the public schools. The salience of management reforms in the schools is heightened by their own efforts to "reinvent" the operations of other departments in local government through strategies like outsourcing, privatizing, and downsizing (Osborne and Gaebler 1992).

State and local politicians work closely with corporate business leaders on many levels. The local corporate elite are taxpayers and constituents, potential contributors to political campaigns, official or kitchen-cabinet members in city and state government, and captains of industry and commerce who provide jobs and local economic development (Stone 1989). Their privileged status in city hall (and the governor's mansion) gives them special clout over schools when local politicians take control. At the 1989 national conference entitled "Can Business Save Education?"—a question to which the answer was a foregone conclusion—Delaware governor Pierre S. DuPont IV clarified for the assembled corporate executives that his conditional "yes" hinged on applying "tried and true principles that have helped each of your businesses prosper over the years" (Allen 1989, 1).

Frequently, the local business elite initiates a politician's interest in urban schools. In Chicago, for instance, a consortium of city and statewide business associations crafted and then lobbied for the law empowering Mayor Richard M. Daley in 1995 (Shipps 1997). In Charlotte, North Carolina, corporate leaders influenced the city's political leaders by selecting and funding school board candidates compatible with their new agenda to restructure (and de-bus) the schools for the purpose of enhancing the local business climate. The city's superintendent then became the spokesperson for the chamber of commerce in recruiting new businesses to the area (Mickelson 1999). Similar patterns have been seen in recent school reform efforts in Baltimore, Boston, Pittsburgh, Seattle, Cincinnati, and Los Angeles (Bryk, Hill, and Shipps 1998; Portz 1997; Rich 1996; Stone 1998).

Urban political leaders have strong pressures to take up school problems (Beinart 1997; U.S. Conference of Mayors 1996). Their efforts to increase the tax base and attract (and hold) the middle class in cities make them especially vulnerable to the recommendations of economic elites. A financial crisis and/or teachers' strike further raises the salience of the corporate critic's arguments about management failure, and simultaneously highlights business leaders' putative financial expertise (Shipps and Menefee-Libey 1997; Jones, Portz, and Stein 1997).

Not only have local politicians added their resources and support to the corporate critique, but the critique has also been buttressed by a renewed emphasis on markets at a time when alternatives to markets have been discredited. The corporate critique claims that a fundamental flaw underlies school problems: a lack of competition that would spur new management solutions. It seems elegant and simple, promising to manage away labor and financial problems while rebuilding accountability.

Reviving the Economic Conception of Public Life

Although the modern economic conception of society is not the same as that which so strongly influenced Progressive-era reformers, it dominates once again, this time with renewed millennial urgency and the added importance of recent economic theory and research. Pollsters agree that "economics and economic news is what moves the country now," and this consensus applies to education (Beatty 1998, 32). Recently, *The New York Times* pronounced that "the economic rationale for schooling has triumphed" (Bronner 1998a, 1).

This ratcheting up of economic rhetoric can be explained by the modern (and peculiarly American) sense that we are living in unprecedented times, in which capitalism has triumphed over all other forms of economic organization for nation states (Gray 1998). The victory marks simultaneously the "end of history" as a driving force for disputes among nations and a discomfiting dependence on economic competition and consumerism that takes its place (Fukuyama 1989).

Many progressives also saw something akin to the "end of history" in their sights as they marveled at the wealth-producing capabilities of international industrial combines and financial markets. All that was needed was their perfection and systematic expansion around the globe. Today's millennialists believe that the dominance of capitalism is an "unabashed victory" of Western economic liberalism over communism and other forms of planned economies, marking the end of humankind's "ideological evolution" (ibid., 3). All that remains is to extend systematically the ideological victory of the mind to the material world. This creates "a world dominated by economic concerns in which there are no ideological grounds for major conflict among nations" (ibid., 17).[7]

Conceptually, this American economic worldview pits government against market, as did its predecessor in the Progressive era.[8] In *The Commanding Heights* (1998), Daniel Yergin and Joseph Stanislaw describe a battle between governments and markets that has altered the policy direction of institutions as globally powerful as the World Bank, as local as the city of Philadelphia, and as far-flung as Africa. Most of the world, they argue, has already entered the "post reform" stage of a century-long battle of ideas between socialists and capitalists: a battle of ideas between the mixed economy consensus that emerged after World War II and a loose band of free-marketeers. Anti-Keynesian freemarket economists and antisocialist political leaders were the intellectual winners. The antidote to government control that hardened bureaucracies, stifled incentive, and discouraged fiscal discipline, they argued, is market control through privatization of national industries, deregulation of business, outsourcing of unionized work, and decreased government services. By this reasoning, nations not yet benefiting from the renewed global economy have only their own governments to blame.

The current era mimics the Progressive era to the extent that international flows of capital and transnational production processes influence both corporations and governments. As economist Alan Taylor claims, "These days it's just getting back to where it was a hundred years ago" (Kristof 1999). In *Globalization and Its Discontents* (1998), Saskia Sassen reminds us that global markets were powerful mechanisms through which those few with capital influenced government policy in the Progressive era. Today, technologically induced speed, growth among investors, concentration of wealth, and interconnectedness have increased the effects of this global speculation and decreased the capacity of governments to regulate businesses and markets. Sassen describes the power over governments held by transnational firms and global markets as a kind of economic citizenship that is unavailable to any individual (1996; see also Reich 1991). Not surprisingly, this global market ideology has been broadly recognized as a force in national education policy (Borman, Costenell, and Gallagher 1993; Fowler 1995; Lawton 1996; Martin 2000).

There is no denying that economic globalization creates political tensions by pitting governments against one another in competition for transnational corporate jobs and global capital. Cities are especially affected. Cities are economic and cultural centers that generate and disseminate global beliefs, innovations, and information, establish coalitions, and monitor implicit contracts (Knox and Taylor 1995). Many of the nonfinancial resources needed for global production are mutually dependent and place-bound, and they are concentrated in cities (Sassen 1991). Such arguments encourage corporate executives to view cities as specialized centers of economic functions (e.g., finance, labor, communications). For their part, urban politicians sanction incentives to corporations unimagined since the Progressive era.

Thus, not only states but also city governments compete to provide production resources to corporations. Reforming the local schools becomes one of the ways that cities engage in this global competition. When formal schooling is seen as a key element of productive capacity—a view reinforced by the decline of manufacturing and the rise of information-based industries in the United States—the quality of the local public school system takes on renewed importance for business leaders and local politicians alike. On the one hand, school policy becomes labor policy; on the other, schools reflect the information resources of the community. Urban school systems are seen as engines of economic development when corporate and local political leaders cooperate in their governance and redesign.

Some who protest the results of this economic conception of urban public life wind up reinforcing it. They point to growing inequalities—widening income gaps between the rich and the poor, rising rates of childhood poverty, extreme concentration of wealth in the hands of a tiny few, and falling real wages for the bottom quarter of the population—all of which are most apparent in cities (Hacker 1997; Gray 1998). These inequalities are defined in monetary terms. They overlook the inequities of re-segregation in urban schools, growing gaps in access to higher education between blacks and Hispanics and others, and worsening disparities in curriculum resources and expectations that accompany children of color and poor children under school restructuring. They also discourage awareness of schools as micro-communities where abilities to communicate with others and basic ideas about citizenship are formed. As Robert Reich observed "it has lately become unfashionable, indeed in poor taste, to notice such things" (1998, 33).

Corporate Leaders as Moral Guides

As the generals of the victory of capitalism over communism and as the leaders of the latest boom economy, corporate executives again have lofty status. Wealth has returned as a mark of competence and worth. Again, it seems our nation is turning to corporate leaders to provide us with models and morality lessons for the public schools.

Raymond Callahan argued that corporate leaders in the Progressive era had a higher social standing than other elites, and Joel Spring suggested that they saw their work in ethical terms. David Tyack and Elisabeth Hansot place superintendents in the role of moral exemplars, guardians of virtue, at least by their own lights.

Today, corporate leaders take on the social ills of the day as unelected leaders whose mettle has been proven by the conspicuous success they have had in making money for shareholders. A few even run for office assuming that their high status and self-confidence will transfer into political success. As one put it, "companies realize that with their elevated status as the dominant social institution, comes elevated responsibility" (Alberthal 1999, abstract).

In contrast, educators in the role of superintendents have seldom had lower status. Their moral authority as leaders has been eroded to the status of functionaries, bureaucrats. At times their advice is seen as quaint and befuddled, at other times opportunistic and pernicious. For instance, in the months preceding Chicago's famous reform of 1988, the superintendent and his staff were relegated to the status of "bureaucratic blob," desperately clinging to their prerogatives in the face of a completely failed school system (Chicago Tribune 1988). Presumably, their irresponsible selfishness tainted whatever they sought for the schools. Seven years later, amid a new round of management reforms, the moral authority of Chicago's school administrators had fallen so low that anyone formally trained in education was considered disqualified to lead the school system (Shipps, Kahne, and Smylie 1999). Significantly, the new leader's title is now the CEO, and his experience is that of a city bureaucrat and lobbyist. In 1997, one Chicago business leader explained, "I like the idea of a more business oriented (school leader), not necessarily the professional education type. Maybe that's just because I'm kind of down on professional educators now because I don't think they've done the job to manage their own profession" (personal interview, June 1997). Professional educators in Seattle, San Diego, and Washington, D.C., have also recently been dropped as district heads in favor of military, corporate, or political men who are expected to better manage urban schooling.

Corporate leaders' appeal as models for school leaders is partly based on their putative success as leaders of ideological victory. It is also based on their professed concern for the poor and the weak. Perhaps if the business critique of urban schools were always couched in the drier, more abstract language of economists, it would have less popular appeal. Instead, corporate leaders and business mandarins alike invoke the rhetoric of moralists grieving over the waste of young minds and lost opportunities. In doing so, they challenge educators on their own ground.

If corporate leaders have the moral status to successfully promote their own solutions to public school problems, then what is the ethical context of their decision making? According to business ethicists, three theories characterize the ethical aspirations and behavior of corporate leaders: "Friedmanite" nonethics; "stakeholder" ethics; and the less prevalent belief that corporations have an ethical duty to ameliorate social problems. The Friedmanite position denies that business has any ethical responsibility; the only responsibility of business is to increase its profits, avoiding the infliction of harm in the process, if possible (Friedman 1970). The stakeholder view asserts that corporations have an additional responsibility to customers, employees, suppliers, and occasionally to society at large (e.g., avoiding environmental degradation). The father of modern management, Peter Drucker, espouses something close to this view (Schwartz 1998).

Drucker is manifestly moral in his advice as well as intellectually omnivorous. An international figure whose first of 29 books professed to expose the spiritual and social origins of fascism, Drucker has been described as a mandarin who worked to "make capitalism corporative and corporatism capitalist" to correct the dysfunctions of Taylorism (Waring 1991, 78–103). At a time when Daniel Bell pictured the corporate organization as impersonal and spiritually deadening, Drucker saw it as a liberating community with "intrinsic morality" (Beatty 1998, 121). His early writings admit that management's power in the firm is theoretically "irresponsible" and illegitimate when it lacks a moral justification (ibid., 46). As befits a moralist, Drucker provides the missing justification in the form of contracts between workers, customers, and suppliers on the one hand, and managers on the other. For instance, post-industrial knowledge workers should subordinate their workplace demands to the corporate goals set by senior managers and become "corporate citizens with corporate virtue" (Waring 1991, 87–91). If the bargain is properly struck and workers engage in self-control, then corporate management has the potential to eliminate poverty, continue the expansion of mass education, and create social mobility.

Although Drucker eventually became less confident about the possibility that such corporate social contracts would provide the benefits of the "self-governing planned community" in cities, he remained hopeful about management in the nonprofit sector (Drucker 1998). Management, he asserts, is indispensable to successful nonprofits—and presumably to successful schools—as well as to smoothly functioning corporations. "It masters the economic circumstances and alters them by conscious directed action," and its function always remains the same, "to get more results out of the same resources" (Beatty 1998, 104, 174).

Despite the potential for contractual side-effects that benefit the public, both the Friedmanite and stakeholder views agree "it is *not* the purpose of business to do good" (Bowie 1995, 598); as independent values, fairness and equity do not trump corporate survival and profitability (Jones 1995; Clarkson 1995; Lippke 1995).

A small minority of corporate leaders (and academics) holds a third view. For them, corporate ethics require involvement in social policy making. First, corporations have a duty to repay the benefits of government-provided infrastructure (e.g., roads, schools). Second, as citizens under the law they have the political responsibilities of citizenship. Third, they have the moral responsibility to use their enormous economic power as stewards (Bowie 1995). Typically this view is expected to result in corporate philanthropy.

Only rarely do corporate leaders claim their interests in school reform are altruistic and dutiful. When they do, however, they prescribe the same management reforms that their more profit-oriented counterparts envision: clear goals set by managers; accountability sanctions for teachers, students, and schools; and market-like competition to motivate everyone. Franklin Bobbitt's "civic duty" of business to provide the standards against which education will be judged is but one example of an application of corporate social responsibility loudly echoed by the most dutiful of corporate leaders today (Callahan 1962, 83).

MID-CENTURY INTENSIFIERS

New twists on old themes are not the only reasons that economic justifications and management solutions dominate urban school reform talk today. The civil rights movement changed the institutional context of schooling, and those changes have had the collective impact of intensifying the corporate critique while making modern management solutions more salient as reform strategies.

Launched on the 1954 U.S. Supreme Court's validation of two centuries of African American struggles for equality, the civil rights movement uncovered the de facto selectivity and prejudice in Progressive-era versions of equity and citizenship. The movement substituted a different version of equity based on social, political, and economic opportunity: students who suffered from poverty, discrimination, disability, or lack of fluency in English would need greater resources to access the opportunities education was intended to provide. Simultaneously, patriotism and citizenship became broader concepts, encompassing those who rebelled against the actions of the governing regime and those who embraced non-Western traditions and customs.

The federal government responded by expanding its provision of opportunities for economic equality, even as it sought to increase the diversity of community voices in policy making. Twin federal initiatives—targeted categorical programs aimed at compensating for identified disadvantages, and mandated community participation in decision making—institutionalized these new conceptions. Affirmative action, Title I, Title VII, Title IX, court-ordered desegregation, consent decrees, and maximum feasible participation all came into the lexicon of school policy making and changed expectations for school governance while adding federal mandates to a fragmenting education bureaucracy (see Kantor and Lowe, Chap. 7, in this volume).

These laws and ideas also helped to de-professionalize assumptions about how to improve urban schools. As the Progressive-era version of equality lost allegiance, schools became community institutions to be governed by collective, if highly local, values and individuals rather than the centralized hierarchies and corporate values of administrative progressives. Good citizenship now called upon urban dwellers to become engaged in governing their schools (see, for instance, Ravitch 1988; Maynard 1970).

In these same decades, courts imposed desegregation on many of the nation's urban school systems, prescribing changes in everything from attendance patterns to curriculum and hiring guidelines. Non-educators adjudicated the most contentious disputes of urban schooling from outside, using standards that many recalcitrant superintendents and principals debated, resisted, or outright rejected (Cuban 1976; Orfield and Eaton 1996; Wells and Crain 1997). In the process, the moral authority of superintendents and school leaders was weakened. Even when superintendents chose to lead civil rights efforts to rid schools of racism, sexism, and other forms of inequality and limited citizenship, an expanding federal and state bureaucracy with divided loyalties hampered them.

The advent of collective bargaining for teachers further diminished superintendent (and principal) authority while structurally altering the landscape of urban schools. Teachers' organizations in the Progressive era had been predominantly female and often dismissed by their cousins in the trade unions. Tyack and Hansot document a struggle between them and the corporatizers of urban public schools in the Progressive era. Ironically, the intellectual counterweight that the teachers represented then was lost in the process of unionization, half a century later. Today, unions appear fully invested in the existing governance structure of schools, quite willing to adopt any critique of the schools that is based on management failure, and willing, with the exception of vouchers, to support many kinds of economically justified and management-focused reforms (Kershner, Koppich, and Weeres 1997; Gelberg 1997).

These mid-century institutional and governance changes reconfigured the Progressive-era model of school governance and created a constellation of new constraints on the authority and legitimacy of superintendents and school leaders. Between 1970 and 1990, school boards and superintendents lost power to both courts and federal bureaucrats who administered consent decrees and categorical programs. Union negotiations further limited their authority and credibility, as do the remnants of enhanced community participation in the form of district boards and school site shared-governance teams.

Recent recognition of the constraints has not reversed their effects. Although court-ordered desegregation, categorical programs, and trade unionism among teachers are all currently under attack for having created policy gridlock in urban school systems, the combined effect has been to further identify urban school leaders with the lingering problems of underfunded and bureaucratically hamstrung schools. This underscores the corporate critique of school management and encourages reformers to look outside of schools for leaders, reform models, and ideological guidance. In this context, the contemporary insistence on economic rather than political justifications for schooling appears refreshing, holding out the promise of clarity and accountability, if not always substantive improvements.

However, as Tyack and Hansot remind us, "The ideal of a society planned by experts and run by scientific management rested on assumptions not only of how to govern but also about who should govern" (1982, 107). In the Progressive era, educationally trained school leaders sought to wield their power as managers by mimicking the behavior of corporate leaders. Today even this vision of the school leader has diminishing support; business-trained leaders can do the job better. With the benefit of hindsight, the irony becomes clear. The long-term professional status of school leaders may have been eroded by the very strategy they once used to shore it up.

The values of corporate business dominate reform talk with renewed vigor. Urban school leaders are faced with an old choice: to adopt the latest management techniques and affirm the old business values that helped to institutionalize the problems of educational bureaucratization and commodification, or to oppose the already powerful forces that would turn urban schools into ever more efficient engines of economic development.

REFLECTIONS

I began this chapter with a discussion of the themes that mid-century historians drew from urban school reform efforts in the Progressive era. I have sketched out some evidence that suggests a disturbing intensification of those themes in the late twentieth century: we continue to rely on corporate models of organizational efficiency and managerial improvement even as the transmission mechanisms for corporate influence become more numerous and self-reinforcing. We continue to subordinate education to its narrowest economic goals, a process reinforced and strengthened by uncertainty in the new economic context of globalism. And, we continue to elevate corporate executives to the status of moral leaders on educational issues while educators are rapidly losing the moral and professional authority they once commanded.

One result of all this change is the abandonment of many kinds of equality. Neither markets nor business ethics value equality or fairness. If global economies—or even perceptions about global economies—are driving urban school reform, then the process of reform will overlook (in Sassen's words, "evict") a whole range of people who do not fit the prevailing image of what it takes to be competitive (Sassen 1998, 82). Chief among them are immigrants, women, and people of color.

Another result is the anemic citizenship envisioned by economic justifications for schooling. Although corporations may have attained global urban citizenship, neither the customer nor the shareholder—regardless of their increasing numbers worldwide—have access to those global rights. Moreover, it is an impoverished image of civic virtue that values corporate "citizenship" above political citizenship, and a corporate community over the diverse communities in our cities.

Commenting on the current debate about urban education, Clarence Stone sagely counsels that constructing a sustained critique does not reform schools. Relationships must be altered for that to happen (1998, 12–14). At its most basic, a successful school critique must lead to a shared agenda that alters the relationships educators have with their critics.

Admittedly, management solutions have this potential because they appeal to the narrow self-interests of school superintendents, principals, and the university professors who train them. I have little doubt that a renewed symbiosis between these educational insiders and their powerful corporate critics could again realign the management and organization of urban school systems to the image of the modern corporation. If successful—as this process was in the Progressive era—then urban school districts could become more efficient, and school leaders could be at least temporarily relegitimized. They would also be more receptive to market influences like commercialization, privatization, downsizing, and outsourcing. Urban systems could become the large urban businesses, perhaps the holding companies that corporate critics and their political allies sometimes envision.

What would these strengthened relationships do to the common purposes of public schooling in cities? I have tried to suggest that management solutions are built on a narrow range of values: efficiency, bottom-line accountability, customer orientation, and enhanced competition as a method of spurring high quality. They do not seek to build the communities of compassionate empathy or respectful tolerance we so evidently need in our cities. Nor are they likely to help us envision a renewed equity that is more than contemporary social Darwinism. To recreate urban schools today that mimic corporate management and restructuring would affirm Spring's pessimism; there would be little room for goals other than social control in the service of economic efficiency.

Not surprisingly, mid-century historians of the public schools provide insights into the antidotes for these apparent trends. In 1963, Lawrence Cremin had commented on Callahan's *Education and the Cult of Efficiency* with this admonishment:

Ours has not been an era of great ideas in education; it has been an era of technological improvement and administrative reform. And, however much educationists would like to locate the fault in their stars, they had best seek it in themselves. They have cut themselves off from the humanistic traditions that must ultimately provide the basis for their educational judgements and have remained content to concentrate on the narrowest technical and political concerns. (185)

The debates that preoccupy educators and citizens today still rest on potentially unifying educational goals that are, for now, simmering beneath the surface. Written before the current economic Zeitgeist, Diane Ravitch's list once included: reducing alienation, mistrust, prejudice, and misunderstanding; improving the quality of civic and political life; reducing inequality; diffusing the fruits of liberal education; and spreading the capacity for personal fulfillment by developing student's talents, skills, and creativity (1981, 332). Her list, in turn, echoes the sentiments of Horace Mann, America's preeminent common school crusader, who acknowledged salutary schooling effects on productivity but stressed the moral and civic purposes of common schooling for a republican nation (See Reese, Chap. 1, in this volume). In an age of open-ended access to political and social opinions and "data" from electronic media channeled largely by the profit motive, can these civic goals of education be less important than they were a hundred years ago?

Democratic politics have not been pushed off the table, despite protestations of the end of history. They are alive and well in urban schools. Witness recent debates over multiculturalism, religion, language, reading, history, and students' rights. The problem has been that these culturally based political issues divide us more than they unite us. Consequently, they are not likely candidates on which to base a new countermovement to improve schooling. By default, our preoccupation with the economic purpose of schooling and management solutions thrives, becoming the irreducible common ground on which both Afrocentrists and religious fundamentalists can agree.

Perhaps these times require a different critique of urban public school failure, one that acknowledges the common good manifest in the very existence of cities. Urban school failure might be re-envisioned as one outcome of a civic breakdown, rather than as the result of market or management failure. Such a reconception might focus urban residents (corporate and individual) on their common responsibilities as urban citizens and on the benefits of urban life. Rather than focusing on the economic dichotomies that divide (e.g., consumers vs. producers, managers vs. workers, taxpayers vs. welfare recipients), urban citizenship could unite city dwellers through their common interests in the public spaces of urban life, their appreciation of the multiple discourse patterns of diverse peoples, the comforting blend of old and new, and the sensual stimulation and intellectual creativity that dense living in shared space provides.

From this perspective, equity is a common concern rather than an individual responsibility, and the shared infrastructure of urban living (systems of education, transportation, communication, governance, and resource management) is a source of community pride. This view might emphasize the public schools as the primary means to socialize future urban citizens at public expense, aiming to impart collective political values and social responsibility.

For now, the economic justification for urban school reform leads the momentum for change, as it did in the Progressive era. Administrators must change their skills or be overtaken by outsiders who know better how to run big businesses. Rather than grapple with how to provide an equitable education for diverse children who nevertheless expect to spend much of their lives together, or build pathways to citizenship for new immigrants, or reduce the prejudice and mistrust among urban neighbors, or spread an appreciation of diversity in art and culture, or create a safe environment in which school people are free to experiment, create, and take risks—instead, administrators are asked to focus on making schools more productive.

As the next generation of urban superintendents, unionists, and principals cast about for what uniquely qualifies them to be better school leaders than CEOs, MBAs, politicians, or military officers, they can consider embracing the noneconomic goals of education. They might refocus their energies on providing what markets, management mandarins, and economics cannot: a clear-eyed appreciation of the civic benefits of urban life in our democracy; a steadfast determination to provide children with thoughtful and respectful relationships; and values of fairness, equity, and empathy that will allow them to extend the American democratic, multicultural experiment into the future.

PART II

Ways of Seeing the Common Good in Public Education: Social and Political Implications

The four authors in this section, using different ways of seeing, examine critically both contemporary and earlier school reforms to draw out their policy and practical implications.

David Labaree analyzes the contemporary proposal to abandon the common school ideal in the face of manifest failures in implementation, and he concludes that this is a flawed solution. He makes use of the sociologist's concept of strong and weak ties as well as political science categories of exit, voice, and loyalty to compare the likely effects of a range of policy options to ease the current disillusionment with public schools.

Choosing to focus on practical consequences, Labaree argues that strong ties can be divisive to common purposes, that the very diversity of America can be an inducement to build the "weak" ties that link individuals. These weak ties are the glue that holds society and public institutions together, not the strong ties that too frequently divide one tribe from another. Seen in this way, the exit option—leaving the public schools to die if they do not serve individual purposes—is a fundamentally flawed social policy, even when widely adopted by those who can afford to do so. This is because it ignores the essential public purposes of public schooling. Instead, Labaree advocates loyalty to social justice and other public goals of common schooling and urges the voicing of demands for practical improvements. Without identifying winners and losers by race or creed, Labaree's political economy suggests that we all lose when the individual purposes for public schooling overwhelm its public purposes.

Harvey Kantor and Robert Lowe take a contemporary villain among critics of public schools—bureaucracies—and examine earlier and current critiques of this characteristic feature. Kantor and Lowe mourn the loss of a vibrant discourse about public education. They point to the 1960s, when the left's critique of centralization, big schools, and government regulatory bureaucracy challenged the dominant view of improving public schools: redistribution of the benefits of a basically good school system through such reforms as desegregation and programs for the disadvantaged. The system itself, including a vast, impersonal bureaucracy, was deeply flawed. What was needed, left-inclined reformers urged, was breaking up the system, community control, and deregulation.

In the 1990s, however, Kantor and Lowe are uneasy with the technocratic solutions that former leftists propose for the ills of public schooling: vouchers, small schools, etc. They point to the co-optation of the rhetoric (but not the substance) of the left's critique by the right.

What complicates matters at the present moment is that left-of-center critics now defend public schools without examining the role that bureaucracies play in reproducing social inequities. The authors delineate the ideological turnabout but worry whether a revived radical critique of schooling can come to terms with the intractable issues afflicting public schools, such as an impervious bureaucracy, that ultimately constrain a democratic education.

In the last chapter of this section, Larry Cuban examines the ideological conflicts dividing progressive and conservative educators over exactly what constitutes "good" schools. Agreeing with John Meyer (see Chap. 11 in this volume) that these debates look more like religious wars than disputes over which goals public schools should pursue, Cuban suggests that ideologically driven reformers on both the left and the right might make a political accommodation not unlike what occurred in the United States in the past century over the role of religion in politics. Can we as a nation, he asks, agree to set aside pedagogical prejudices in favor of common political values, as we have at least formally agreed to set aside differences in religious observances (or party preference) in favor of individual liberty, legal respect for differences, and equitable treatment?

Specifically addressing himself to long-standing arguments between traditional and progressive methods of teaching and organizing schools, Cuban calls these battles "futile" and asks why there has been so much conflict when there is ample evidence that each ideology can create "good" schools.

Cuban argues that underlying these competing versions of "good" schools are important common beliefs that can serve as the basis for judging the value of schools independent of sectarian differences. In his view, both traditionalists and progressives seek to inculcate in their children the liberal democratic values of respect for others, open-mindedness, and recourse to reason in settling disputes. Judged by these criteria, many kinds of schools are "good." The task is not yet complete, but the resolution he proposes projects a national vision of the common good that is ultimately reconcilable with America's renowned diversity.

CHAPTER 6

No Exit: Public Education as an Inescapably Public Good

David F. Labaree

> Urban schools did not create the injustices of American urban
> life, although they had a systematic part in perpetuating them.
> It is an old and idle hope to believe that better education
> alone can remedy them. Yet in the old goal of a common
> school, reinterpreted in radically reformed institutions, lies a
> legacy essential to a quest for social justice.
> —Tyack 1974, 12

In the closing paragraph of his prologue to *The One Best System*, David Tyack spelled out the basic elements of the philosophy that has guided his writing about American education since his earliest days as a scholar. He acknowledges that public education has long helped perpetuate social inequality in the United States but refuses to blame it for the existence of this inequality. And he argues that public education has within it the potential to support the quest for social justice, without giving in to the temptation to assign education the role of savior. As a result, the story he tells about the history of American education is not filled with saints and sinners, but it nonetheless revolves around a set of principles about what constitutes a good society and a good school. The common school ideal, though never fully realized, still captures for him qualities that are woven deeply into American life and that continue to offer possibilities for a better life. This is not a romantic conception of school and society, but neither is it a vision filled with despair, because the common school represents something basic about who we are as a people and what kind of society we can become.

Over the years, Tyack has defended this vision of public education from the canonizing efforts of many historical triumphalists and from the demonizing efforts of many historical revisionists. As he put it, "I endorse neither the euphoric glorification of public education as represented in the traditional historiography nor the current fashion of berating public school people and regarding the common school as a failure" (1974, 9). This principled position in the middle ground of the debate about public schools is particularly important at the close of the twentieth century, when the rightward drift in American political culture has put all public institutions on the defensive. In an era when markets are triumphant and governments are in retreat, we find that the favored solution to every public problem is to privatize it. Have government get out of the way, we are told, and let markets work things out through the magic of competition (for providers) and choice (for consumers). Words like "common" or "public" for defining school have become epithets connoting drab standardization and relentless mediocrity: public school as public housing project, providing marginal education for the unfortunate and (perhaps) undeserving.

Under such conditions, the temptation is to counter the thunder for all things private with an equal thunder for all things public, to defend the public schools as they are against all comers. To one degree or another, a number of scholars have yielded to this temptation in recent years.[1] In this politically charged setting, Tyack's effort to combine strong support for the principles of public education with sharp criticism for particular practices within this institution presents us with an especially timely and helpful model to follow.

In keeping with the spirit of Tyack's work, my aims in this chapter are to examine the way that implementation of the common school ideal has led to particular forms of educational failure and to examine the negative educational consequences of the alternative put forward by market-oriented reformers, who propose to abandon the common school ideal altogether on the grounds that it is unworkable and counterproductive. This analysis leads me to explore the political economy of public schooling in the United States in an effort to understand the conflict between public and private goals for this institution, to consider the consequences each goal has had on it, for good and ill, and to consider strategies that offer possibilities for dealing with its problems while preserving its essential publicness.

The core of the American conflict over education is the question of whether public education should be seen primarily as a public good or a private good. In the American setting, where markets have long held pride of place and government has long been viewed with suspicion, the sense of education as a private good historically has been a powerful force. This orientation has become especially pronounced since the 1980s, when private solutions have been sweeping the field and the public sector has been in ideological and programmatic retreat. Putting ideology to the side for the moment, it is important to examine the practical consequences for schools as organizations if we treat public education as a public good or as a private good. This issue is particularly important because the free-marketeers have argued that one key reason for adopting a privatized structure for public education is that such a structure would be so much more effective educationally than the current system (Chubb and Moe 1990).

As I have argued elsewhere, there is a growing tendency in the United States to look on education as a private good, the primary purpose of which is to enhance the competitive social position of the degree holder, and this has brought devastating consequences for both school and society (Labaree 1997a). One is that the emphasis on the private benefits of education for individual consumers leaves no one watching out for the public interest in education—no one making sure that education is providing society with the competent citizens and productive workers that the country's political and economic life requires. Another consequence is that this emphasis reinforces the value of tokens of educational accomplishment (grades, credits, and degrees) at the expense of substance (the acquisition of useful knowledge and skill), turning education into little more than a game of "how to succeed in school without really learning."

Here, however, I focus on the impact all this has on the way schools work, in particular on the differences in the way that market mechanisms and political mechanisms influence the organizational effectiveness of schools. The idea is to connect the principles of publicness and privateness that define alternative visions of public schools to the organizational practices of these schools. In keeping with Tyack's clear-eyed democratic vision of the role of public schools, I argue that the principle of public education commands our loyalty while the dysfunctional practices of public education require us to use our voices to demand reform. The peculiar blend of public and private elements within our public schools undermines their effectiveness, but the answer is not to turn them into a purely public good or a purely private good. Instead, we need to recognize that, even though we can exit from public schools as a private good, we cannot exit from public schools as a public good. That is, we can remove our children from urban public schools and send them to private schools or exclusive suburban public schools, but we cannot escape having to live with the social and personal consequences of the public school system we have left behind.

EXIT AND VOICE AS RESPONSES TO ORGANIZATIONAL DECLINE

The best place to start in exploring these issues is with the classic book by Albert Hirschman, *Exit, Voice, and Loyalty* (1970). According to Hirschman, an organization that becomes dysfunctional—unable to satisfy the needs of its customers or members—potentially provokes two kinds of responses that offer hope of restoring the organization to a greater level of effectiveness. One response is *economic*, in which customers *exit* from the organization by choosing to buy the product of another more effective firm; either the offending firm quickly gets the message and makes the necessary adjustments to bring back its customers, or it goes out of business. The other response is *political*, in which members choose not to exit but to stay and exercise their *voice* within the organization, in an effort to bring about the reforms they deem necessary through direct influence.

Of course, neither exit nor voice is the exclusive property of one sector or the other. Consumers often voice their concerns about bad service or faulty products to a company in the hope of correcting the problem, and voters often express their displeasure with one party by exiting and voting for the opposition. But if exit is not exclusive to markets, it is a mechanism for correcting organizational dysfunction that is natural to markets because it is so well suited to market transactions. Likewise, voice is particularly well suited to political interactions. Hirschman puts it this way:

[Exit] is the sort of mechanism economics thrives on; it is neat—one either exits or one does not; it is impersonal—any face-to-face confrontation between customer and firm . . . is avoided and success and failure of the organization are communicated to it by a set of statistics; and it is indirect—any recovery on the part of the declining firm comes courtesy of the Invisible Hand. . . . In all these respects, voice is just the opposite of exit. It is a far more "messy" concept because it can be graduated, all the way from faint grumbling to violent protest; it implies articulation of one's critical options rather than a private, "secret" vote in the anonymity of the supermarket; and finally, it is direct and straightforward rather than roundabout. Voice is political action par excellence. (1970, 15–16)

As a political economist, Hirschman is comfortable in both arenas and sees benefits in both forms of corrective action. But he notes with some alarm that exit occupies a privileged position in American thought and practice. In part this comes from the practical advantages that exit offers over voice. All other things being equal, exit would be the preferred choice simply because it is so uncomplicated and so easy. Unlike voice, it does not require the aggrieved party to gear up for a personal confrontation with anyone in the offending organization. Nor is there a need to spend a lot of time, effort, and money in organizing a sufficient number of people to support your own position or in persuading others to change theirs. Moreover, there is every reason to expect it to produce a quick and satisfying remedy to the problem. All you need to do is drop one stock or product or candidate and pick up another. Case closed, problem solved. In contrast, the voice option brings personal stress, a costly investment of resources, and considerable risk of failure (or of success that is muted by inevitable political compromise).

In part, however, the privileged position of the exit option in American life comes from its close links to American ideology. Founded in market relations (in contrast with European countries, where markets evolved within a feudal setting), the United States has characteristically embraced notions of individual choice with more depth and warmth than most other nations, and exit has long been the preferred way to exercise this choice. After all, most American citizens are descended from immigrants, who voted with their feet by exiting the old country in favor of the new. And, once here, the frontier served as a perpetual exit sign, inviting settlers to leave their current situation in the hope of finding a better opportunity elsewhere. As a result, Hirschman argues, the American character is grounded in a preference for "flight rather than fight" (1970, 108), since, in the words of Louis Hartz, "physical flight is the American substitute for the European experience of social revolution" (1955, 65n, quoted in Hirschman 1970, 107n). In American terms, Hirschman notes, even success—defined as social mobility—requires you to leave the community where you grew up so you can join another that is higher on the social scale.

EXIT, VOICE, AND THE PUBLIC SCHOOLS

In this context, why should schools be any different from other American institutions? It should not be surprising to find that the exit option in recent years has come to be promoted as the preferred solution to educational problems in the United States. Reform initiatives for choice, charters, and vouchers offer educational consumers a variety of ways to leave schools they do not like and move to schools they do like. All of these reforms work by removing governmental barriers to the exercise of the exit option and increasing the responsiveness of schools to their exiting customers. The result, we are told, will be an increase in the freedom of consumer choice and a corresponding increase in the quality of education.

Of course, as Hirschman notes (along with a number of contemporary school choice advocates), some educational consumers already exercise the exit option. Parents who have sufficient financial resources frequently opt to withdraw their children from public schools that do not meet their educational standard and enroll them elsewhere. They do this either by moving to a community where the public schools are of higher quality or by staying where they are and sending their children to private schools. By their actions, these parents are treating education as a private good. That is, they are concerned about the quality of education that their children receive, and they exit one school for another in order to attain a better education for these same children. The aim of their actions, as is the aim of anyone exiting one consumer good for another, is not to improve the organization they are abandoning but to acquire the best goods for themselves. What happens to other consumers who are unable or unwilling to leave the original organization is not the concern of the exiting parties, for in a market setting every consumer and every producer is on his or her own. You make your choices in pursuit of your own self-interest, and you live with the consequences. The impact of your choices on others is irrelevant to your decision.

In theory, when a series of consumers choose to switch to a competitor's product, the original producer either adapts by quickly improving quality or gets driven out of business by competitors who are already providing a quality product. This is a central tenet of neoclassical economics: the accumulated actions of consumers acting in their own self-interest result in a larger public benefit by forcing companies to lower prices and/or improve quality. But here is the catch, according to Hirschman. All too often the exit option actually serves less as a wake-up call than as a safety valve for an inefficient organization, draining off its most quality-conscious and most dissatisfied customers without threatening the existence of the organization itself.

One way this happens is that organizations with similar but not identi-

cal products—McDonald's and Burger King, Republicans and Democrats—just trade customers without either of them suffering a net loss. In
education, such a situation may occur between two private schools or
two public schools that are somewhat different in character without one
clearly being higher in quality than the other. For example, they offer
different curriculum options or different kinds or degrees of religious
training. But there is another way that organizations provoke the exit of
quality-conscious consumers without feeling pressure to improve, and
that involves situations in which there is a disjuncture between the nature
of the organization and the kind of option (exit or voice) that the organization provokes when it grows ineffective.

Consider Figure 1, which is adapted from a table found in Hirschman's
book (1970, 122). In this figure, the vertical dimension represents differences in the degree to which an organization is sensitive to exit or voice,
and the horizontal dimension represents differences in the degree to which
an organization provokes exit or voice in its dissatisfied customers or
members. Characteristically, democratic political organizations are sensitive to voice: politicians watch election results, read their mail, follow
public opinion polls, and talk to their constituents in frequent trips back to
the district. And ideally these same organizations tend to provoke unhappy constituents to express their opinions through the same avenues
that politicians track most closely. Such organizations are found in cell 4
in the figure. Likewise, market-oriented firms characteristically are sensitive to exit: business leaders keep close watch on sales patterns and respond quickly when they see a decline or even a softness in one or another
sector of the market for their products. And ideally when these same firms
fall into a state of decline, they are most likely to provoke the exit response
in their dissatisfied customers, who simply choose to buy a competitor's
product. These firms are found in cell 1 in the figure. Both cell 4 and cell 1
represent efficient systems of signal and response, when organizations and
their customers or constituents are in tune with each other.

The problems arise in the other two cells, when organizational laxity
provokes an ineffective response. In these cases, the organization is free to
continue its inefficient practices without having to pay a significant pen-
alty. Cell 2 is an instance of an organization vulnerable to exit but where
exit is unlikely to occur and voice is the primary response for customers or
members who wish to express dissatisfaction. One example is a company
with a virtual monopoly within a particular market or market segment.
Another is a political organization or voluntary association where alterna-

Decline arouses primarily:

		Exit	Voice
	Exit	Competitive business enterprise	Organization where exit is difficult and dissent is encouraged but ineffective
Organization is sensitive primarily to:		1	2
	Voice	Organization where exit is the prime response and poses no threat	Democratically responsive political organization
		3	4

FIGURE 1

tives are nonexistent or (for reasons of loyalty, identity, tradition) unthinkable. A third is any organization that turns potential leavers into stayers by making a great show of listening to and nominally responding to complaints.

Cell 3 is an instance of an organization vulnerable to voice but most likely to provoke exit among its customers or members who become concerned about a decline in quality. Unhappily, this is the situation with public education in the United States. As a publicly constituted, funded, and governed institution, public education is primarily sensitive to voice in resolving its problems. Consider the wide array of channels through which the public can voice dissatisfaction with public education, the numerous points of vulnerability where people can directly influence their schools: voting for school board members, school millages, and bond issues; speaking out at school board meetings, circulating petitions, and organizing protests; working through parent-teacher organizations; complaining directly to the teacher and principal; bringing to bear the influence of ethnic, religious, professional, and other voluntary organizations; lobbying the state legislature, the governor's office, and congress; and so on. Public schools may be the most politically accessible (they are located in every neighborhood) and politically vulnerable (they are subject to myriad fiscal and popular pressures) of all American institutions.

Yet, for the most quality-conscious and most politically influential educational consumers—those in the upper middle class—the most convenient and effective mechanism for expressing dissatisfaction with public education is exit. In order to meet their educational needs, these families can afford to send their children to private schools or move to a more affluent school district. Such a move provides a simple and immediate solution to the problem by providing their own children with the quality of education that they seek. By contrast, to stay with the original school system and pursue a remedy through the exercise of voice would be messy and time-consuming, and the results are likely to be diluted and delayed in ways that would limit the educational payoff for their children. Better to apply the market solution to the problem by switching to the better product rather than by trying to improve the old product.

This forthright employment of the exit option by upper-middle-class families may solve their educational problems, but it does nothing to enhance the schools they leave behind. One reason is the *effectiveness of voice* for provoking change in these organizations, because, as I have already noted, public schools are intensely political institutions that are primarily responsive to political pressures. Another reason is the *ineffectiveness of exit* for provoking change in these organizations. Why is this option ineffective in reforming schools? Because the loss of customers does not significantly threaten their fiscal base. Parents who send their children to private schools still have to pay taxes for the support of public schools, so the removal of these children reduces the costs of providing public education without reducing the income supporting this education. The case of parents who move from the city to the suburbs in order to send their children to suburban public schools is more complicated, but here too the old school district is buffered against fiscal losses. If enough wealthy families move away, property values in the old district will decline and property tax revenues for the schools will decline temporarily as well. However, two factors protect total school income from the effects of this change: one is that poor districts normally increase millage rates in order to compensate for declining property values;[2] the other is that the state generally intervenes to subsidize district schools with markedly inadequate local resources.

The result is that the school district losing customers has little incentive to change its practices in order to make these customers happy. Unhappy customers are sending a classic market signal of dissatisfaction, but it is not being received because the organization is responsive only to political signals. The loss of these students actually produces a political benefit for these school systems (as well as producing the fiscal benefit of reducing costs), since the families who are leaving are also the ones most likely to use their voices effectively to get results. So these districts in decline manage to get rid of their most complaint-prone and quality-conscious customers without losing fiscal support. The irony, of course, is that in this case exit provokes not the taut competition and rapid corrective response that is promised by the theorists of free-market economics but instead a state of flabby complacency and continuing inefficiency. The existence of the exit option for the most financially able customers actually makes public education worse.

PROMOTING EXIT, CREATING PROBLEMS

Market-oriented educational reformers have a simple and elegant solution to this problem, one that is visually obvious when looking at my adaptation of Hirschman's table: move public education from its dysfunctional location in cell 3 to the functional territory of cell 1. That is, make it so that public schools are vulnerable to the same corrective mechanism they provoke among dissatisfied customers, so if they provoke exit they will also be vulnerable to exit. The result would be to transform this uncomfortable hybrid of politics and markets, of voice and exit, into a purely market institution. This is the solution that is embodied in all of the current proposals to promote educational choice, charters, and vouchers.

One key component of all these market-oriented reforms is that the funding would follow the student. The result is that, if a school loses a customer, it will feel the fiscal consequences because the per-pupil funding for that customer would go with him or her to the new school. In this way, exit would get the attention of school administrators just the way declining sales get the attention of corporate managers, and they would have to adapt to these market pressures in order to win back consumers or face significant cutbacks.

The other key component of reforms pushing the cell-1 option is the elimination of governmental barriers to the free exercise of school choice by educational consumers. Currently, exit is possible but is difficult and expensive. It requires the consumer to move, usually to a higher-cost community, or to stay and pay private tuition on top of public school taxes. Reform proposals call for families to be allowed to send their children to any school they want, without being restricted to the local school or even the local school district. In fact, the logic of the market-based education model would argue that consumers should also have the option of attending private secular and religious schools, and to pay for this with a voucher consisting of each child's share of the tax monies allocated to education.

The consequences of these changes would be to transform public education into a private good like any other such good in the commodity market. Individual consumers rather than political bodies or public regulations would dictate the form and content of schooling, and they would do so simply by freely exercising the exit option. The result would be an array of schools in the educational marketplace competing for students and for the vouchers they bring with them. In the view of John Chubb and Terry Moe (1990) and others in the same tradition, this kind of market discipline, exercised by informed consumers bearing public tuition dollars, would markedly enhance the organizational effectiveness of schools in general. Public schools would have to adopt the same kinds of effective techniques and organizational mechanisms that have allowed schools in the private sector to survive and thrive under competitive market conditions.

One problem with this approach is that the putative organizational benefits of privatization are unlikely to be realized when extended to everyone. What advantages the private sector of American education enjoys over the public sector—organizational leanness and flexibility, greater agreement about educational goals, greater impact on individual students—are currently being realized in a setting where only about 10 percent of the students are attending such schools. When all students attend what in effect are private schools, these schools are unlikely to be able to realize the same leanness, flexibility, homogeneity of purpose, and educational impact that they could attain when they were a small and selective outlet for parents discontented with the public schools. One reason for this is that they would lose the benefit of the selection effect, since they would no longer be able to count on selecting and retaining those students who are the most able, the most motivated, and the most committed to their particular vision of education. Although proponents of the advantages of private over public education claim that they have controlled for these selection effects (Coleman and Hoffer 1987; Chubb and Moe 1990; Bryk, Lee, and Holland 1993), this claim is unconvincing in the face of the fact that only a tiny minority are currently willing and able to avail themselves of this kind of education (Gamoran 1996; Hallinan and Olneck 1982; Labaree 1997a). Another reason is that it has proven notoriously difficult in education to make practices that work for the few work for the many. The history of independent progressive schools in this country provides a cautionary tale of how difficult it is to transfer reforms from a small number of model institutions to the educational system as a whole.

An even bigger problem with the market-based economic solution to the organizational problems in American education—the cell-1 solution— is that it is radically antisocial. By making education entirely subject to the demands of the individual consumer, it leaves no one looking out for the public interest in public education. From the market perspective, the public good is a side effect of the cumulative actions of self-interested consumers, all of whom are seeking to acquire the educational goods that are most advantageous for themselves and their families. But such a perspective assumes that members of the public have no stake in education independent of what benefits it brings to them directly as consumers of educational services—that is, as students themselves or as parents of students.

This, however, is only one way of understanding the goal of education in a modern society, one that looks on education as a private good much like any other consumer commodity whose benefits are limited to the owner. In addition, education needs to be understood as a public good. From this perspective, all of the members of a community (neighborhood, town, county, state, nation) have a stake in the adequate education of other people's children in that community in addition to their own. We all need to make sure that our fellow citizens have the skills, knowledge, and values that are required in order to function effectively as voters, jurors, and public-spirited participants in the political life of the community. And we all need to make sure that our fellow workers have the capacities and orientations that will make them economically productive in whatever occupational roles they may play, in order to promote economic growth and all the benefits that come with such growth—such as jobs, a comfortable standard of living, a broad tax base, and a secure retirement.

This public interest in education is not reducible to the sum of the private interests of all individual consumers, for in the latter situation no one is looking out for the education of other people's children. When the school system is under pressure to provide individual consumers with a private good that will give them a competitive advantage in the race for good jobs, social status, and a comfortable life, it must adapt in ways that undermine the broader public benefits of education. Such a consumer-oriented school system must sharply stratify the educational experience in order to provide its most influential consumers with opportunities to win advantages from the system. It needs to provide educational sorting and selecting mechanisms for producing both winners and losers, for without the latter, winning has no meaning. As a result, we have the following familiar components of the existing, highly stratified educational system in the United States: ability groups in the lower grades (such as the omnipresent high, medium, and low reading groups); curriculum tracks in the upper grades (advanced placement, college prep, general, vocational, and remedial); programs for both the advantaged (gifted and talented education) and the disabled (special education); high rates of attrition at the key transition points in the system (finishing high school, entering college, finishing college, entering graduate school); and sharp differences in the social and educational benefit of graduating from high school in a rich vs. a poor district and from a college with high vs. low status.

Under these conditions, the education of other people's children is undermined by the efforts of the most savvy and empowered consumers to get the greatest educational benefit possible for their own children. We have already seen the consequences of market pressures on American education—giving us a clear look at the nature of education in cell 1—and the picture is not pretty. Treating education as a private good has not and will not provide the community with a system of education that serves the public interest. This system works well for the individual winners, but it leaves most consumers disadvantaged, and it leaves the community without the full complement of competent citizens and productive workers that it requires in order to function effectively (Labaree 1997a). In short, cell 1 is not the answer to the very real problems with the organization of education that we have been examining here.

BARRING EXIT, CREATING MORE PROBLEMS

But there is another solution that is also suggested by Hirschman's table. From this angle, the answer is to move public education from cell 3 to cell 4, transforming it from the current muddled mix of political and market elements into a purely political institution. This would mean reconstructing education in such a way that it provoked citizens to exercise voice rather than exit when they were dissatisfied with the way schools work. By spurring the reaction to which they are most responsive, schools would become more efficient organizationally and more effective educationally. This option is attractive to those who oppose the move by the free-market reform movement to privatize public schooling, because they see public schools as a truly common ground within the community.

In Hirschman's terms, we could accomplish this goal—shifting schools entirely into the political realm—simply by removing the possibility for an easy exit, thereby forcing people to stay and fight for improvement from within. In this view, the problem is not too little exit but too much. The existence of easy exit drains off the very voices that could change education for the better without producing any market pressures that would prompt the system to improve itself. Under these circumstances, then, blocking exit altogether would provide a strong incentive for families and students to do what they can to voice their concerns in a way that will bring about positive change in the effectiveness of educational organizations.

How could this be carried out in practice? For one thing, it would require us to abolish all forms of nonpublic education, thus closing off the possibility of escape from the public sector into the private sector in education. For another, it would require us to standardize the funding of education per student across all school districts in all states, and even perhaps standardize curriculum offerings nationally as well, so that neither wealth nor geographic mobility would allow a family to exit a bad school system in order to enter a better one. If well-to-do families could no longer send their children to private schools or flee to the affluent suburbs, they would have to concentrate their efforts on improving the only educational choice available to them, their local public schools.

Such a solution has a logic to it in theory, but in practice it is unthinkably un-American. If the key problem with the market-based solution to the organizational problems in American education is that it is *radically antisocial*, then the problem with the political solution is that it is *radically illiberal*. By making education a closed public monopoly, it leaves no opportunity for individuals to make meaningful educational choices.

In her book *Democratic Education* (1987), Amy Gutmann defines the elements of a system of education that is supportive of life in a liberal democracy:

A democratic theory of education recognizes the importance of empowering citizens to make educational policy and also of constraining their choices among policies in accordance with those principles—nonrepression and nondiscrimination—that preserve the intellectual and social foundations of democratic deliberation. A society that empowers citizens to make educational policy, moderated by these two principled constraints, realizes the democratic ideal of education. (14)

To deny citizens the right to exit public schools in the manner suggested above—even if a majority of citizens supported this policy—would violate both of her core principles. It would discriminate against minority groups within society that choose to socialize their young in line with the values of that group, and it would effectively repress conceptions of education other than those expressed in the monolithic public school system.

AN ANSWER: THE IMPOSSIBILITY OF EXITING A PUBLIC GOOD

Consider, however, an alternative method for moving public schools from the dysfunctional realm of cell 3 (where they operate without an effective feedback mechanism to correct them when they go astray) into the functional realm of cell 4 (where a political institution of education is responsive to the political feedback from its constituency)—without trampling all over the rights of a heterogeneous citizenry bristling with alternative visions of education. The key is finding a way to balance the public and private interests in education in such a way that the former can be met without unduly limiting the latter. Neither of the options considered so far meets this test. The all-exit market solution discounts and dismembers the public interest in education, and the no-exit political solution does the same to the private interest in this institution.

A viable way out of this dilemma is to recognize that excluding the exit option is unnecessary, since there is really no way for a citizen to escape from being a consumer of public education. As citizens, taxpayers, employers, and workers, people who send their children to private schools must still live with the consequences of public education in their community, and those who send their children to public schools in exclusive suburbs must still live with the consequences of public education in the city they left behind. They cannot avoid the social, economic, and political effects of the system of public education as it succeeds or fails in its effort to provide the political competence and human capital without which society cannot function.

From this perspective, then, the way to convince people to voice their concerns about the failings of public education (rather than to turn their backs on these failings) is to demonstrate to them that they have an irreducible stake in the success of this institution. Since exit is functionally impossible, voice becomes the logical option, with the result that loyalty to the public schools becomes the rational choice for all citizens, whether or not they have children enrolled in these schools.

Note that I am talking about the possibility of exit from the public schools in two different senses here. Thinking of education as a private good, it remains possible for people to exit public education, and, if we are going to honor Gutmann's principles of liberal democracy, as I think we should, then we cannot simply eliminate this option even if such a policy were politically feasible. As a private good, education is a form of personal property, owned by the degree holder and benefiting him or her alone. We cannot ask individuals to ignore their consumer interest in education as a private good, to act as if it did not matter whether they acquired more schooling or less, at institutions that are more prestigious or less so. Neither can we expect parents to ignore the possible advantages that education as a private good can bestow on their children. Education matters in the competition for pay, position, and lifestyle, and no amount of commitment to the education of others can eliminate our own private interest in seeking the consumer benefits that education can grant us.

However, even if people are allowed to exercise choice in education to enhance its benefit to them as a private good and so exit one form of education to pursue another, they still cannot exit education in its guise as a public good. This is not because they have been denied permission to leave but because "no exit" is a property of any public good. Put more positively, a person cannot be denied access to a public good, even if he or she has not contributed to the maintenance of this good. Mancur Olson puts it this way:

A common, collective, or public good is here defined as any good such that, if any person . . . in a group . . . consumes it, it cannot feasibly be withheld from the others in that group. In other words, those who do not purchase or pay for any of the public or collective good cannot be excluded or kept from sharing in the consumption of the good, as they can where noncollective goods are concerned. (1971, 14–15)

Therefore "a state is first of all an organization that provides public goods for its members, the citizens" (ibid., 15). The problem for the provider of a public good, such as the state in providing public education, is that it cannot support this effort "by voluntary contributions or by selling its goods on the market" (ibid.) but must resort to compulsory means such as taxation. Otherwise there would be a large number of people enjoying a free ride at the expense of others.

There are two very important implications of this analysis for our thinking about public education. First, it is perfectly reasonable to tax everyone for the support of public schools, even those who have no children in school or those who have children in private school. In the latter case, parents are not paying double tuition for their children's education (once in tuition to the private school, a second time in taxes for the public schools), as is frequently argued by free-marketeers. Instead they are paying one tuition for education as a private good and a second for education as a public good, whereas families with children in public schools pay only one tuition to cover both. Along the same lines, it is also reasonable to ask families in a wealthy school district to share in the support of public education for students in poorer districts (through redistributive taxation policies of the state or federal government). If we did not have compulsory support along these lines, then we would be allowing people to withdraw from the support of public education while still enjoying its collective benefits; in short, we would be allowing them to hitch a free ride on a public good.

Of course, it is one thing to say that it is reasonable to require everyone to support public education across the entire region, state, or country, even if his or her private interest in education is being met elsewhere, but it is another thing entirely to make this a reality. The problem, of course, is that in a democracy such mandates for the support of public institutions cannot take place without the agreement of a majority of the voters. In the case of families that are currently enjoying the benefits of education as a private good, why should they voluntarily tax themselves to support the education of other people's children across town or in the next city? This brings us to the second implication of our analysis of education as a public good: it is reasonable for citizens to contribute voluntarily to the public education of other people's children (that is, to agree to tax themselves for that purpose), because the indirect benefits they enjoy from this enterprise are real and compelling, and the indirect costs they would experience as a result of the failure of public education would be equally real and compelling. In short, they cannot afford to let public schools fail, even if their own children are gaining consumer benefits from education elsewhere. They cannot afford to live in a society in which large numbers of fellow citizens are unable to make intelligent decisions as voters or jurors, unable to contribute to the economic productivity as workers, and unable to follow the laws or share the values of the rest of society.

The problem with realizing this possibility, however, is that for many citizens their stake in the education of other people's children is not at all obvious. To the extent that many Americans live out their lives at home, work, and play in groups composed of people very much like themselves—in race, social class, values, and social orientation—they may well feel little connection to fellow citizens who are different from them. These others may be experienced as largely invisible, unknowable, and unlikable. The social link between us and them may be very weak, and the walls that separate us from them may be felt as solid and impenetrable, with the result that we can safely ignore what kind of life they lead or what kind of education they receive. Under these circumstances, education as a public good may seem pale and peripheral compared to the robust centrality in our lives of education as a private good. Our ties to others may seem very weak and our ties to our own kind may seem very strong.

A Little Help: The Strength of Weak Ties to the Larger Community

To counter this perception, consider an interesting social anomaly—"the strength of weak ties." The latter phrase is the title of an influential article about social networks by the sociologist Mark Granovetter (1973), in which he argues that weak ties in many ways are more important than strong ties, both to society and the individual. Strong ties are our relationships with the people who are closest to us emotionally and with whom we spend the greatest time and have the largest number of reciprocal interactions. These are our family and our closest friends. Weak ties are our relationships with people that are less intense and less involving in all the same ways. These are our acquaintances, with whom we engage in more limited and functional interactions (at work, store, clinic, etc.). Another, more familiar set of terms for this distinction is primary vs. secondary relationships.

One important characteristic of strong ties is that they tend to be highly correlated: my best friends are closely aligned with the best friends of my best friends. Not only is there a lot of overlap in networks of strong ties, but the people who make up such networks tend to be similar sociologically—likely consisting of people of the same race, ethnicity, social class, cultural orientation, religion, and so on. Networks of weak ties, on the other hand, tend to be much less inward-turning. My network of weak ties is likely to have very little overlap with the networks of others with whom I have a weak tie, and it is likely to be quite heterogeneous socially and culturally.

The social consequences of these differences are striking. Strong ties pull us into a tight community of the similar and like-minded that may well be cut off from the rest of the world and that may encourage us to turn our back on those outside this group. Weak ties connect us outward to the larger community, creating avenues of access and interaction with a wide range of people and institutions that are far from our social-emotional home base within our primary group. In short, whereas strong ties support us emotionally and define us culturally, weak ties are what connect us with social life in its full complexity. Weak ties are what hold societies together in a complex web of connections and interactions, which make up in number and richness what they lack in intensity and duration. In contrast, strong ties are frequently what threaten to dissolve such societies into a collection of insular and defended subgroups based on the indissoluble link of identity rather than the fungible medium of functional interaction.

A rich network of weak ties is therefore the essential basis upon which citizens can construct a sense of public education as a public good. It is not through their strong ties to their best friends—the link of the like-minded—that they will see education as a public good but through their weak ties to acquaintances—the link of the functionally necessary. And weak ties are not only the glue that holds societies together, they are also an essential tool that helps individuals pursue their private interests within society. For example, Granovetter shows that people are most likely to find jobs not through the intervention of their best friends but through the medium of acquaintances in their network of weak ties. Why? Because that is the network which reaches out most widely into the society around the job seeker and which offers the greatest possibility of getting into a situation that is literally and figuratively farthest from the narrow world of family and friends. In these ways, weak ties are very strong and immensely useful, both for a society that has to forge cohesion out of complexity and for an individual seeking to make his or her way within that society.

Weak ties also offer us hope for our ability to establish and maintain a strong public constituency for public education, so that even satisfied consumers of education as a private good will see a reason to support education as a public good. For one thing, their inevitable network of weak ties links them to the larger society in all its variety in ways that cannot be denied or negated by their private life within the gated communities of similarity and strong ties. For another, they have every personal reason to use, extend, and reinforce their network of acquaintance and functional interaction, because it is enormously useful to them in the pursuit of their private interests. Well-educated acquaintances and potential acquaintances are essential if they want to profit and prosper in a highly differentiated modern society. As a result, their link to the larger public that is served by public education is not so weak after all, and their stake in preserving this public arena in a state of good health and social usefulness requires of them a substantial commitment to the education of other people's children.

Under these conditions, there is reason to be optimistic about the prospects for convincing people that they have a stake in the success of public education in its guise as a public good. Loyalty to the public schools is a rational response for citizens to adopt, even if they have chosen to send their own children to private school or to the public school across the city line. They can run from public education, but they cannot hide from its consequences. With no exit possible from this intensely public good, the only reasonable option is to speak up and pay up in order to make these schools better.

CHAPTER 7

Bureaucracy Left and Right: Thinking About the One Best System

Harvey Kantor and Robert Lowe

During the 1960s and early 1970s, criticism of the bureaucratic structure of public schools came chiefly from intellectuals, writers, and activists on the political left. Within educational history, in particular, a number of intriguing studies turned upside-down conventional readings of the past that identified the expansion of public education with the provision of greater individual opportunity and a more robust democracy. These revisionist studies isolated the bureaucratic nature of public schools as the key to an elite-controlled institution that quashed individual freedom, reproduced class inequality, and counterpoised professional expertise to democratic practice and community influence.

Since the late 1980s, however, conservatives have appropriated much of this critique of bureaucracy in an effort to shrink federal intervention and privatize public education. Echoing many of the themes first voiced by critics on the left in the 1960s, these conservatives argue that public schools constitute a calcified, bureaucratic "one best system" that encroaches on classroom autonomy, stifles choice, and frustrates the educational aspirations of parents. Rather than assuming that the establishment of large, professionally managed organizations is the best way to run the schools, they maintain that education should be freed from bureaucratic control so that parents can make their own decisions about what kind of education they want for their children.

Conservatives' conscious invocation of the title of David Tyack's most recognized book fails to acknowledge that Tyack neither advocated the dismantling of public education nor viewed centralization and bureaucratization as wholly negative developments. Much of the left, however, has responded to conservative power by defending the public schools that Tyack viewed as seriously flawed and that radicals themselves formerly labeled bankrupt. In this chapter, we shall argue that discourse about public education has been circumscribed by the left's abandonment of its earlier critique of the way schools are controlled and organized. To a significant extent motivated by the perceived need to defend public education and other public bureaucracies from conservative attack, this abandonment has, ironically, allowed the right to define the main agenda for substantive educational change in cities.

BUREAUCRACY AND SCHOOL REFORM

The left-wing argument about the inegalitarian and antidemocratic character of the public school bureaucracy marked a sharp departure from earlier attitudes about centralization and standardization. Prior to the 1960s, most policy makers and school reformers had typically attributed the shortcomings of public education to excessive localism and the persistence of small-scale, informal organizational structures, and they generally identified educational improvement with more centrally directed systems of school management and the establishment of large, internally differentiated schools (Katz 1987, 126).

This commitment to centralization stemmed partly from the belief that excessively decentralized forms of organization could not ensure an orderly expansion of schooling or equip schools to meet the demands of a more complex, interdependent society. According to this view, the old common school governed by the local lay board of education had been adequately equipped to meet the needs of nineteenth-century students for a basic education in the three R's and civic morality. But an expanded clientele, increased mobility, and a more diversified division of labor had rendered this form of organization obsolete. Adapting schools to deal with the kinds of social and economic problems students faced in the twentieth century, most school reformers and education policy makers believed, demanded more centralized, professionally supervised units of administration and more hierarchical, internally differentiated schools, especially at the secondary level.

If social efficiency was the dominant reason school reformers put their faith in centralization, it was not the only one. More liberal reformers, particularly after World War II, also equated localism and lay control with narrow-mindedness, racial prejudice, class bias, and financial inequities. Consequently, they contended not only that it was socially and economically wasteful but also that it was undemocratic to allow educational aims and educational opportunities to be determined principally by lay officials at the local level. Hoping to universalize what they believed were less parochial, more cosmopolitan values as well as to institutionalize more egalitarian practices, they maintained that centrally controlled and bureaucratically organized schools would eliminate provincialism and optimize opportunity. They would accomplish this by broadening the purposes of education and expanding access to educational services for those who had been denied them because of their class or race or because they lived in the wrong place (see, for example, Warner, Havighurst, and Loeb 1944, chap. 11).[1]

This belief in the benefits of centralization and large-scale, formal organizations was expressed most clearly in two widely read books published at the end of the 1950s. One was James Bryant Conant's study of American secondary schools, *The American High School Today* (1959). Supported by a grant from the Carnegie Corporation to the Educational Testing Service, this study did not recommend any radical changes in the administration or organization of American secondary education. In fact, Conant lauded the basic organizational structure of secondary education for offering a general education to all pupils while sorting out the academically talented from the vocationally oriented and providing specialized training for both of them. Rather, what troubled Conant was that too many high schools failed to conform to this pattern because they were too small to employ sufficient numbers of professionally trained teachers or to offer the kind of differentiated curriculum necessary to adapt students to their future roles in life. Nothing would improve the efficiency of secondary education more or better serve the common good, he concluded, than the implementation of state-mandated plans for school district consolidation so that small high schools might be replaced by bigger ones better equipped to offer the kinds of specialized training needed to accommodate to students' different abilities and prepare them for their different careers (Conant 1959; see also Conant 1961, 1964).

The other book was Myron Lieberman's *The Future of American Education* (1960), parts of which first appeared in *The Nation* and in *School and Society*. An acerbic, often polemical book, *The Future of American Education* contested the idea that local control was the essence of the democratic tradition in education and that the purposes of education should be determined by lay rather than professional authorities. Not only had local control outlived its usefulness, Lieberman argued, but it could not be reconciled with the ideals of democracy or equal opportunity. To the contrary, he maintained that, because it was relatively easy at the local level "for a preponderant group to enforce a policy of intellectual protectionism for its sacred cows," local control was the chief reason for the "dull parochialism" that had overtaken American education as well as for the growing disparity between national needs and local efforts to meet them (Lieberman 1960, 38). In order to limit provincialism and ensure an adequate supply of trained workers, Lieberman concluded, American education needed a more centralized, national system of controls and standards to empower professional educators and protect them from local influences.

This commitment to hierarchical, differentiated schooling had not always dominated twentieth-century thinking about school reform. Earlier in the century, John Dewey had objected to the kind of centrally managed, bureaucratically organized schools that Conant and Lieberman advocated because he believed that they inhibited the introduction of what he and others called the "new" education. Absent small classes, flexibility in the promotion of students and the organization of the grades, and participatory forms of decision making, Dewey argued, schools could not create conditions in classrooms that would encourage teachers to escape from the "inherited and customary" and to experiment with the kinds of methods and subject matter best suited to the "movement of modern life" (Dewey 1902, 19, 22–23; 1916, chap. 7; see also Westbrook 1991, 107–11).

By the 1940s and 1950s, however, such arguments had been drowned out by those who stressed the virtues of large schools and centrally controlled, hierarchically organized systems of education. A few writers, most notably Christopher Jencks, did dissent from the Cold War assumptions implicit in much of what writers like Conant and Lieberman had to say. Jencks complained in an otherwise positive review of the sequel to *The American High School Today* that Conant substituted national security for "the chance to lead the good life" as the main purpose of education (Jencks 1959, 24). But neither Jencks nor most other education writers at the time questioned the premise that more centralized control and bigger, more stratified schools promised to promote a more efficient, cosmopolitan, and meritocratic social order.[2]

THE LEFT CRITIQUE OF BUREAUCRACY

Liberals did not reject these arguments after 1960. On the contrary, throughout the 1960s they continued to look to more centralized, national solutions to the parochialism of local school districts that resisted integration and unequally allocated funds. Consequently, they endorsed policies—most notably, federal aid to education and school desegregation— that multiplied the demands on the federal government and required much greater bureaucratic oversight of local school practices. By the end of the decade, however, an educational left had emerged that did not think it possible to end racism in the public schools or equalize educational opportunity chiefly through national policy legislation and bureaucratic rule-making. Disillusioned by the persistence of educational failure despite the expansion of central power, they rejected the previous generation's commitment to centrally controlled institutions run according to bureaucratic rules of authority. Instead, they located the source of educational failure and injustice in the same structures that up until then had been the preferred vehicle of liberal reform.

These themes surfaced first in several popular exposés that emphasized the bureaucratic ineptitude of urban schools and the racist practices of teachers, administrators, and school board officials. Drawing on their personal experiences teaching in inner-city schools and on research on the politics of school administration in large cities in the 1950s and 1960s, writers such as Jonathan Kozol, Herbert Kohl, Peter Schrag, and David Rogers described how established bureaucratic structures isolated urban school officials from the communities they were supposed to serve and frustrated nearly every attempt at curricular or pedagogical reform. Mostly white, wedded to the norms of bureaucratic and professional authority, urban school officials appeared, according to these writers, more concerned with protecting their personal political ties, diverting challenges to their authority, and preserving established channels of decision making than in making changes to deal with the obstacles children of color faced in the classroom or in opening up the insular system of school governance to encourage community input and involvement (Kozol 1967; Kohl 1967; Schrag 1967; Rogers 1968).

For the most part, these writers attributed the consequences of bureaucratization to the unanticipated outcomes of earlier reforms. In his study of the New York school system, for example, Rogers allowed that there had once been valid administrative reasons for what he called "bureaucratic centralism"—to guarantee uniform standards across the city, to preserve professional autonomy from political interference, and to deal with the sheer complexity of the problems faced by a school system as large as New York City's (Rogers 1968, 272). But, according to Rogers, bureaucratic procedures of administration had been instituted and followed to such an extent that they had outlived their original purpose. Rather, he said, they had created a pathological system whose traditions, structures, and rules subverted their original intent and prevented any "flexible accommodations to client demands" (ibid., 279).

Rogers was especially critical of the Board of Examiners. Instituted to promote professional standards and to protect against patronage through the application of meritocratic procedures in the hiring of teachers and administrators, the board had become the chief obstacle to change; it was more interested in protecting the prerogatives of those already in the system than in hiring or promoting people with imagination and insight. Its licensing system was unnecessarily complex; its examinations stressed local knowledge available only to insiders; and its recruiting policies discriminated against African American applicants, partly because they were excluded from the informal system of coaching necessary to pass the exams and partly because they were ruled out on oral exams because of their Southern accents. Until the board was made accountable and its examination practices changed, Rogers concluded, all attempts at reforming New York's schools were likely to fail.

Rogers remained uncertain about potential remedies. Despite his indictment of centralized control, he acknowledged that in some circumstances the expansion of centralized authority might help break down "provincial customs" and override "segregationist local interests." But neither Rogers nor any of the other writers who documented the failures of urban education believed that such policies could do much to revitalize education in New York or other big cities unless the bureaucratic organization of the school system itself was also reformed by redistributing political power to parents and local communities. Although viable reform would be difficult to implement, argued Rogers, Kozol, and the others, it required some combination of decentralization and community control, or the creation of alternative schools outside the public system.

This critique of centralization and bureaucracy in urban schools did not spring only from the experiences of contemporary school reformers. It coincided with and was reinforced by the work of a group of historians and economists—loosely labeled revisionists—who were engaged in a major reassessment of the nation's educational past. Acutely conscious of inequality and racial prejudice in American society, they too identified the bureaucratic structure of schooling as the key to understanding the anti-democratic and inegalitarian outcomes of public education. But whereas writers like Rogers generally attributed the inegalitarian and repressive nature of school bureaucracies to the unanticipated outcomes of earlier reforms, these scholars argued that there was a fundamental connection between the bureaucratic organization of schooling and the reproduction of a hierarchical social order.

No one articulated this argument more systematically than Michael Katz. In a collection of essays on the origins of public education published in the late 1960s and early 1970s, he directly challenged conventional wisdom about the growth and organization of urban school systems. Urban school bureaucracies were not a recent social phenomenon, Katz said, nor were they an inevitable response to urbanization and modernization, as most social theorists suggested. Rather, they had emerged early in the history of American education and had been just one of many possible ways to organize schooling. They triumphed and persisted, Katz maintained, because they reflected and reinforced the class attitudes and interests of those who constructed them (Katz 1971).

How did bureaucracy do this? Following Robert Dreeben (1968), Katz argued that bureaucratic forms of organization socialized children by teaching them norms of behavior such as universalism, independence, and achievement, which controlled how people were treated in institutions and at work as opposed to within their families. But whereas Dreeben viewed these norms as legitimate principles of conduct that all adults needed to learn in order to function in modern, industrialized societies, Katz claimed that they represented the "crystallization of bourgeois social attitudes" (Katz 1968, xxiii). As a result, he said, the bureaucratization of schooling not only conveyed messages about appropriate norms of adult behavior but it also gave a differential advantage to children from middle- and upper-class families, thereby reproducing rather than altering the existing social structure as the ideology of equal opportunity promised.

Like Rogers, Katz remained somewhat ambivalent about the implications of his analysis for contemporary reform. He acknowledged, for example, that many reforms he favored, such as school desegregation, required an increase in the very same bureaucratic characteristics that he believed had badly served the poor in the past. For the most part, however, the main lesson he drew from his analysis of the origins of public education reinforced the conclusions reached by other left-leaning writers and critics such as Rogers and Kozol that any substantive reformulation of educational purposes and practices could not occur within existing educational arrangements. Such a reformulation, he said, required a "radical restructuring" of the way schools were controlled and organized.

Katz was the first but not the only revisionist scholar to cast a critical eye on the history of class, bureaucracy, and schooling. Others also reexamined the history of school reform and reached similar conclusions. In several essays and books on the history of progressivism in education, for example, Clarence Karier, Paul Violas, and Joel Spring argued that Progressive-era reforms to centralize the control of school governance, inject scientific management into educational administration, and differentiate the structure of the curriculum did little to expand opportunities or to make schools more responsive to the needs of individual children. Rather, by widening the gap between working-class communities and the schools and by encouraging the segmentation of children along class lines, they simply reinforced the kind of centralized, hierarchical form of schooling first put in place in the mid-nineteenth century. Far from democratizing education, they concluded, the history of progressivism in education suggested, as did the history of the common school, that centralized, bureaucratic structures should be abolished because they subordinated individual aspirations to the needs of the state (Karier, Violas, and Spring 1973; Violas 1978; Spring 1972).

Samuel Bowles and Herbert Gintis also made the inegalitarian and repressive nature of school bureaucracies the central theme of their neo-Marxian study, *Schooling in Capitalist America* (1976). In contrast to writers like Violas and Spring, however, Bowles and Gintis argued that it was not the ideology of educational reform or the self-interest of middle-class reformers but the expansion of capitalism itself that accounted for how school bureaucracies emerged and why they operated in the manner they did. Indeed, Bowles and Gintis argued that bureaucratic forms of schooling prevailed not only because they benefited the middle class but because this form of schooling was instrumental to the perpetuation of the capitalist objectives of efficiency, social control, and legitimacy as well.

How did bureaucratic forms of organization help schools meet these objectives? According to Bowles and Gintis, the answer lay in the historical correspondence between the organization of schooling and the organization of capitalist production—what they called the "correspondence principle." For example, in the mid-nineteenth century when production structures were relatively simple, Bowles and Gintis argued, schools were also relatively simple organizations and concentrated on teaching such qualities as punctuality, obedience to authority, and willingness to work for extrinsic rewards—all of which were useful in shaping a disciplined factory labor force. Later, in the early twentieth century, as economic organizations grew more hierarchical and differentiated, so did the schools, mirroring the requirements of the production process and differentially socializing students—according to class, race, and ethnicity—to meet them.

The implications of this argument for conventional notions about school reform could not have been more radical. Not only did it imply that, in order to liberalize education and realize its democratic possibilities, the bureaucratic structure of schooling had to be broken down and school decision making had to be opened up, but, more important, it suggested that this could not happen by focusing on school reform alone. Since the bureaucratic structure of capitalist production was at the root of the problem, capitalism too had to be changed. Less fundamental, more incremental reforms might be possible, but they simply strengthened the capitalist system by making schools and the other governmental institutions that supported it appear more malleable and humane.

Much of this radical critique was overstated. It blurred the distinction between socialization and social control; it assumed that school systems were impervious to community influence; and, as developed by some writers, it failed to recognize that localism often preserved racism and financial inequities that more centralized policies and bureaucratic rules helped to combat. But by demonstrating the connection between the bureaucratic organization of schooling and the hierarchical organization of American society, this critique offered an explanation for the schools' persistent failure to equalize educational outcomes for African Americans and other marginalized groups that more conventional historical accounts tended to excuse because they viewed these failures as idiosyncratic and temporary.

THE RETREAT OF THE LEFT

By the mid-1970s, this critique of bureaucracy had become a standard theme in left-wing analyses of public education. In the 1990s, however, many leftist academics and writers abandoned their earlier arguments about the inegalitarian and antidemocratic consequences of centralized control and the organization of public school bureaucracies. Wishing to preserve the public sphere from conservative attack and seeing public schools as central to this effort, they have argued instead for the basic soundness of the pedagogy and culture of the schools and of public school bureaucracies and for incremental changes in the existing system. Indeed, among the most vocal and visible elements of the left today, schools and other public institutions that not so long ago were attacked for perpetuating educational and economic inequalities are now portrayed as "interrupters of such processes" (Power 1992, 496) and benign buffers against even more repressive agencies.

This transformation is evident in the arguments of Jonathan Kozol and other writers on the left who once were among the staunchest critics of the public schools. Kozol's first book, *Death at an Early Age* (1967), was one of the most powerful critiques of public schools and public school bureaucracies written in the 1960s. Drawing on his experience teaching in the Boston public school system, it described in evocative detail how the public school bureaucracy conspired to devastate educational opportunities for African American children by segregating them in run-down schools, fostering the racist practices of teachers, administrators, and school board officials, and punishing those who made even the most minuscule efforts to transform what was at best an unenlightened curriculum. Fired for failing to get permission to teach a Langston Hughes poem that was not part of the school system's prescribed course of study for the fourth grade, Kozol concluded at the end of this book that it was not hard to understand why the African American leadership in the city had begun to think that the only solution was to set up its own community controlled schools.

Kozol's most recent book on urban education, *Savage Inequalities* (1991), evokes *Death at an Early Age* in its concern with the way schools perpetuate racial injustice. Yet in contrast to this earlier work, *Savage Inequalities* ignores his previous critique of the bureaucratic organization of schooling and does not emphasize the need for change in the structural arrangements of schools themselves. Instead, it views unequal resources as the paramount problem facing the public schools and argues that more funding and more equal distribution of that funding are the key to their improvement. As a result, it suggests an uncritical acceptance of public education as a public good that merely is unequally distributed, instead of viewing it as an institution that cannot be reformed without a major alteration in its basic structure or in the economic and political structures that surround and sustain it.

What is remarkable about this transformation is that Kozol still manages to stake out a position on the left. Although *Savage Inequalities* does not emphasize how the organization of schooling reproduces the inequities of the society at large, it nevertheless makes clear how the broader social and economic context continues to compromise the democratic possibilities of public education. By contrast, many other left-wing educational scholars who previously had been attentive to the reproductive role of schooling no longer talk much about the social and economic conditions or the bureaucratic constraints that make equal educational opportunity difficult to secure. Instead, they assume that the chief problem facing school reformers now is not to transform the structure of public education but to make it work better.

For example, in 1971 Richard Rothstein criticized how schools tracked students to perpetuate structures of inequality, but in 1993 he wrote an essay in *The American Prospect* defending the public schools. Rothstein's focus in the essay is on understanding the jobs/skills mismatch and explaining why the argument that American industry suffers from a lack of skilled workers is an illusion. But his underlying interest is in disproving the contention that academic outcomes have continued to fall while spending on education has increased. Although this myth of public school failure is commonplace, he contends, it has little basis in fact. Marshaling a variety of data, he shows not only that academic achievement has increased and dropout rates have declined, especially for African American youth, but also that little new money has been invested in regular academic improvements since 1965. Per-pupil spending has indeed risen, but, he argues, the additional funds have been used mainly for special education, transportation, nutrition programs, increases in teacher salaries, and marginal reductions in class size—changes that do not have a major impact on school outcomes. That achievement has increased at all, in Rothstein's view, is "to the credit of the public schools and the teaching profession" (1993, 26).

Rothstein allows that bureaucratic structures should be reformed. But, in contrast to the past, this is no longer the main problem facing the schools. Instead, he says, bureaucratic rules eliminate corruption, incompetence, and racial discrimination, and they free teachers to teach by reducing the time demands of administrative tasks that other reforms like decentralization would place on them. He concludes that what schools need most now is not radical reorganization but more money to equalize school funding, further reduce class size, improve teacher salaries, expand

apprenticeship and workplace training, and fund early childhood education so that they can better do what they are already doing right. Anything
else, he believes, would likely do more harm than good.

Rothstein's position is certainly less radical than Kozol's. Whereas Kozol's examination of specific urban school districts uncovers ubiquitous
injustice and failure that require a massive redistribution of resources,
Rothstein's incremental approach to improving public education relies on
soothing aggregate-level data that obscure flagrant inequities on the
ground. As Kozol (1991) and Michelle Fine (1991) have pointed out, in
large cities dropping out and underachievement are concentrated in ways
that tend to be overlooked by the kinds of national-level statistics to which
Rothstein refers.[3] Both viewpoints, however, suppress much of the radical
critique of the organization and structure of schooling that once animated
those on the left (Graubard 1998, 91).

Of course not every left-wing critic has followed this path. Some writers on the left, including Katz (1992), continue to argue that tracking and
other common school practices operate to reproduce inequality and reinforce racial divisions and that schools cannot foster democracy in a closed,
top-down system of decision making.[4] By and large, however, such arguments have been hard to hear. Instead, discussion on the left has been
dominated by those like Rothstein who believe there is nothing wrong
with public education that cannot be changed through relatively marginal
adjustments to its basic structure.

THE LEFT, THE RIGHT, AND THE PRESENT MOMENT IN EDUCATIONAL REFORM

Why Kozol, Rothstein, and others on the left have abandoned their
earlier critique of the repressive and inegalitarian nature of school bureaucracies is not difficult to fathom. In the 1960s, it was easy for leftists
to focus on the unequal and repressive activities of the schools and other
public institutions as well as the inadequacy of the state's redistributive
measures because there was optimism that the entire social order could be
transformed. By contrast, today, when a powerfully resuscitated ideology
of antistatism and privatism has eroded support for public institutions, the
kind of analysis once advanced by radical critics appears likely to do little
but add to the destructive power of conservative attacks on the schools
and other public institutions (Graubard 1998, 94). Rothstein goes so far
as to claim that excessive criticism has undermined support for public

schools among African Americans and other people of color who historically have been the most dependent on them and are the most likely to suffer from their loss of credibility and dissolution (Rothstein 1998b, 96).[5]

It is certainly reasonable to assume that the success of the conservative
agenda would lead to even greater inequality in education. But in abandoning the radical critique of the structure of schooling, leftist discourse
has lost the strong concern for equity and self-determination—both personal and collective—that informed it 30 years ago.[6] Instead, most writers
on the left today have adopted an amelioristic approach to educational
reform that, on the one hand, mimics the technocratic approach to educational change articulated by liberals and conservatives and, on the
other, cedes the initiative for reform to conservatives who urgently advocate changing the structure of public schools.

This is most obvious in the evolution of current debates over the efficacy of vouchers and the left's response to conservative-sponsored efforts
to create an educational marketplace through choice. Milton Friedman
(1955) first articulated the rationale for such proposals in the mid-1950s.
Concerned that government expansion limited individual and family freedom, Friedman proposed vouchers as a way of severing the funding of
education from government control. In his scheme, families would be
given vouchers of equal worth that would provide tuition to the private,
religious, or public schools they chose. "The role of government," he said,
"would be limited to assuring that the schools met certain minimum
standards such as the inclusion of a minimum common content in their
programs, much as it now inspects restaurants to assure they maintain
minimum sanitary standards" (1955, 127).

Responding to potential concerns that his scheme would harm the
promotion of common values by subsidizing parochial schools and exac-
erbating class distinctions by freeing parents to choose schools with students of the same background, Friedman felt that market mechanisms
might diminish the weight of parochial schools as a private school option
and diminish class inequity by expanding private options to all. Yet he
made it clear that, whether or not such consequences followed from
vouchers, the overriding principle was individual freedom. He noted, for
instance, that vouchers were being considered by Southern states as a way
of circumventing *Brown v. Board of Education*. Using vouchers for such a
purpose violated Friedman's personal beliefs, but he did not believe this
invalidated his proposal. "The relevant test of the belief in individual
freedom," he stated, "is the willingness to oppose state intervention even

when it is designed to prevent individual activity of a kind one thoroughly dislikes" (ibid., 131).

Although Friedman's work immediately inspired some Catholic scholarship supporting vouchers (Blum 1958), and vouchers were promoted by a few liberals in the late 1960s (Jencks 1966), they did not emerge as a major instrument of public policy until the publication of John Chubb and Terry Moe's *Politics, Markets and America's Schools* (1990).[7] Chubb and Moe owe a considerable debt to Friedman, but they also expanded on his formulations. Borrowing a page from the earlier leftist critique, they argued that bureaucracy was the central impediment to educational reform and that educational improvement could not be mandated through greater bureaucratic controls but only through their elimination. In contrast to the radical critique advanced in the 1960s, however, they claimed that public schools were necessarily bureaucratic not because bureaucracy is tied to class relations but because bureaucracy is the means through which competing interests institutionalize their influence in the public sphere. The solution to this problem was to substitute the market for politics. This, they maintained, would create autonomous schools that would be organizationally congenial to teaching and learning as well as accountable to the preferences of parents.

Politics, Markets and America's Schools was not the first conservative attack on bureaucracy. But it furthered the conservative agenda by transforming the discourse surrounding vouchers. Prior to its publication, voucher proposals like Friedman's were tainted by their association with the virulent racism of right-wing critics of government like George Wallace, who attacked the federal bureaucracy and court system for interfering with whites' prerogatives through policies like school desegregation and affirmative action.[8] Chubb and Moe, however, couched their argument for vouchers in the technocratic terminology of school improvement, arguing not that an intrusive bureaucracy violated white rights but that bureaucratic interference limited the autonomy of schools and consequently constrained their ability to carry out effectively the tasks of teaching and learning. As a result, their book not only won praise from free-market ideologues and religious conservatives but also legitimated vouchers in the eyes of a broader public by severing them from the language of racial resentment. By representing vouchers as ideologically neutral, Chubb and Moe helped make them central to contemporary debates about urban school reform.

The left has responded to the ascendancy of this technocratic argument for vouchers and the conservative implications of such discourse with a number of critiques of Chubb and Moe and of the other voucher proposals that have proliferated in the 1990s. Some of these critiques address the quantitative underpinnings of the justification for vouchers. They refute the purported academic advantages of private schools and the formulation that freedom from bureaucracy necessarily improves academic performance. Other arguments address the inegalitarian and antidemocratic implications of removing schools from redistributive government policies and treating families like entrepreneurial units. Still others point to the conservative wealth driving "Trojan Horse" voucher plans, like the Milwaukee Parents Choice Program, which are limited to low-income students but are viewed as efforts to expand vouchers to all families. And, finally, there are arguments that voucher plans threaten the wall of separation between church and state and undermine the socially cohering function of a common curriculum (for a summary of these arguments, see Lowe 1992; Lowe and Miner 1996).

All of this strikes us as fundamentally correct. But because the critiques focus chiefly on the problems with vouchers rather than on the bureaucratic structure of public education, they offer few viable suggestions for reforming how schools are organized and controlled. Kozol is right, for example, when he declares that urban public schools are an exercise in compulsory inequality. Segregated, unequal, indifferently attended at the secondary level, graduating fewer than 50 percent of their high school students in four years, and drawing trivial participation in school board elections, urban public schools mock formulations of democratic education and the common good (Kantor and Brenzel 1993). But, like most of those on the left, Kozol opposes choice, leaving the victims of inequality no way out except to hope for a politically unlikely redistribution of resources. In contrast, most younger African Americans respond to the bankruptcy of urban schools by supporting the concept of vouchers.[9]

Of course, reform proposals of educators on the left are not limited to equity in funding. They typically advocate policies like multicultural curricula, bilingual education, authentic assessment, and an end to tracking—policies that are meant to equalize equal opportunity. Yet absent an analysis and critique of the bureaucratic structure of schooling and the social relations that sustain it, leftist educators today have often been unable to articulate how these changes might be achieved so that they become more than technocratic interventions (on this point more generally, see Olneck 1993; Del Valle 1998). Although progressives point to model urban schools to suggest that dramatic egalitarian reform can take place without system-wide change (Peterson 1996; Tenorio 1998),[10] the tiny number of these schools does more to underscore the intractability of the problems faced by urban systems than to suggest how these systems might be reformed.

Most educators on the left disavow market-based reforms, but a few have responded to the intransigence of urban school bureaucracies by arguing for some type of structural and administrative reform. Yet their formulations suffer from the same truncated vision that generally characterizes opponents of choice. Breaking with nearly all of the left, for example, Bowles and Gintis (1996) have come out in favor of vouchers. They differ from conservatives in their advocacy of equal opportunity, racial integration, and multiculturalism. But they reject democratic voice as a viable way of improving schools, and they view parents merely as consumers who hold schools accountable through the threat of exit. Consequently, their proposal relies on government oversight to ensure that equity will result from parents' choices, though this would create many of the same bureaucratic structures and regulations that vouchers are supposed to eliminate.[11]

It is somewhat more common on the left to support choice, so long as it is restricted to public schools. Left-wing educators like Deborah Meier and Allen Graubard, for example, believe that public school choice will free educators to liberate pedagogy and curriculum from the stultifying confines of bureaucratic control (Meier 1995; Graubard 1998). But their interest in circumventing bureaucracy is largely limited to empowering teachers. Presumably teacher-run schools, like Meier's Central Park East Secondary School, have great potential to cultivate democratic practices among the staff and a coherent approach to education that will enable students to become critical citizens. As in voucher proposals, however, parents are essentially relegated to the status of consumers who may choose and depart from options professionals have created and exclusively govern. The layers of bureaucracy are collapsed and power is transferred from bureaucrats to teachers, but teachers and principals alone define the educational good for the children of parents who often differ from teachers in both class and race. In such schools, innovative curricula may flourish, but without a more fundamental transformation in the control of schooling there is little reason to assume that the reproductive functions of education or its cultural biases would be challenged.[12]

A LEFT-WING ALTERNATIVE?

Writing 25 years ago, at a time when radical energies in the United States were waning and the alternative school movement was near collapse, David Tyack (1974) assumed that public schools would continue to be the central vehicle for the education of the young. But he made it clear that "the one best system" needed to undergo serious change. This, he maintained, meant real power sharing, a genuine responsiveness to pluralism, and a commitment to educating the disenfranchised. For the most part, these changes simply have not taken place, and, now that alternatives to public schools are emerging again, they are being seized upon by many of the victims of public schools. As a result, public education in cities today faces a combined and potentially lethal threat from those who want to absolve government of responsibility for "other people's children" and those other people themselves who have been poorly served by public schools.

In our view, the left's proper response to this threat is not simply to point to the shortcomings of vouchers. Nor is it simply to criticize the distortions of the conservative attack on public education and counterpoise public schools as a democratic good to a market-oriented approach to education. Rather, it is to retain an understanding of schools as political institutions that strongly tend to reproduce race and class inequalities; to advocate the dismantling of those bureaucratic structures—spawned by central administrations and teachers alike—that protect the ideologies and practices of public education from community scrutiny and accountability; and to remain attentive to creating opportunities for political organizing and community activism aimed at reviving a democratic politics of education and transforming the social relations of schools.

The foremost large-scale example of this has taken place in Chicago. Leftist leaders of the school reform movement, many of whom were strong opponents of vouchers, organized to secure passage of the Chicago School Reform Act, which trimmed bureaucracy and gave parents a majority voice on policy matters at the school level through the creation of local school councils.[13] Although the results of school reform in Chicago have been uneven and the authority of local councils has become increasingly fragile since 1995 (Shipps 1997), the migration of control from the central administration to the school communities has created the political space for releasing community energies, which in some cases have created schools supporting the aspirations that parents have for their children (Bryk et al. 1998; Katz 1992).[14]

These political spaces, however, often develop outside of public school systems on shoestring budgets that would benefit mightily from vouchers.[15] As we have indicated above, there are many good reasons why people on the left are reluctant to support such a policy, but a resuscitated radical critique of schooling must come to terms with how the intractability and, in the eyes of many who must enroll in them, the illegitimacy of urban public school systems constrain a democratic politics of education. Achieving such a goal may require a tactical flexibility that can be ideologically uncomfortable. It cannot be achieved by merely defending public education as a public good or by applying technical solutions to a political problem.

CHAPTER 8

Why Is It So Hard to Get "Good" Schools?

Larry Cuban

For the entire twentieth century, there has been conflict among educators, public officials, researchers, and parents over whether traditionalist or progressive ways of teaching are best. Struggles over teaching phonics or "whole language" have parallels in math over whether students should learn multiplication tables or the skills of real-life problem solving.[1]

This unrelenting struggle for the one best way of teaching a subject or skill is linked to the enduring search, past and present, for the "good" school. Are schools that effectively prepare students for the workforce "good"? Are schools with high standardized test scores "good"? Are schools that seek to develop the mind, body, and emotions of each child "good"? These questions reveal the competing purposes for public schools that make a label of a "good" school uncertain. As this century draws to a close, passionate analyses of what's right and what's wrong with America's schools again roil the media and educators' journals. Recent book titles capture the persistent quest for "good" schools: E. D. Hirsch, *The Schools That We Need and Why We Don't Have Them* (1996), Gerald Bracey, *Final Exam: A Study of the Perpetual Scrutiny of American Education* (1995b), and Mike Rose, *Possible Lives: The Promise of Public Education in America.* (1995). Progressives and traditionalists, then and now, have sought (and contested) different goals for their schools both in pedagogy and outcomes.

To answer the question that is the title of my chapter, then, I offer glimpses of "good" schools that are clearly different from one another. I argue that all are "good." Based upon these vignettes, I analyze the futile battles between traditional and progressive ideologies during the twentieth century that have in their evangelical fervor, like the religious warfare of an earlier century, constricted the search for "good" schools.[2]

I begin with a verbal collage of three schools. Two are public elementary schools, located in the same middle-class California community and to which parents choose to send their children. Both schools have staffs that chose to work there, and both schools have been in existence for 25 years (Ruenzel 1995).[3] The third school is actually a composite; it describes a high school of about 1,000 students in a working-class neighborhood of a large city.

School A

- It is a quiet, orderly school where both students and parents openly honor the teacher's authority.
- The principal and faculty set high academic standards and demand regular study habits.
- Drill and practice are parts of each teacher's daily lesson.
- Teachers say: "We liked the way we were taught so we teach the same way; we expect kids to adapt to our standards."
- From a first grade classroom: children learn how to spell six new words a day.
- From a fourth grade classroom: children draw up charts on early explorers.
- Report cards with letter grades are sent home every nine weeks. Once a week, teachers send home mini-report cards.
- Parent: "If my kid can truly do something better, I want her to be asked to do it over again until it's done right. That's what they do here."
- Principal of school: "Our kids are happiest when taking a test. The more challenged they are, the better they perform. The harder they work, the better they feel about themselves."
- Banner in the school: "Free Monday through Friday: Knowledge—Bring Your Own Container."
- Parent: "Creativity can't occur until the building blocks are in place. If you are good at sports, you scrimmage. If you're good at music, you practice the scales."
- Alumnus of school: "There was always a standard and a great incentive system that drove you to meet it. . . . I particularly remember the annual awards banquet."

School B

- It prizes freedom for students and teachers to pursue their interests.
- Students call most of the teachers by their first names.
- Banner in a classroom reads: "Children need a place to run! Explore! A world to discover."
- Every teacher encourages student-initiated projects.
- Teacher: "We trust children to make the right choices."
- Most classrooms are multiage (6–9-year-olds and 7–11-year-olds).
- Principal: "We don't compare John with Sara; we compare John with John."
- In this school, there are no spelling bees; no accelerated reading program; no letter or numerical grades. Instead, a teacher describes the personal growth of each student in a 2–6 page year-end narrative.
- Students begin each day by making a schedule of what they will do.
- Teacher: "Learning demands no one skill. It's auditory, social, verbal, visual, and kinetic. So it's our responsibility to respond to the needs of children who have different ways of understanding the world."
- Students in school take only those standardized tests required by the state. Competition among students is discouraged.
- Alumni: "The openness, the freedom. It all taught you to take responsibility for yourself." The school helped us "feel good about ourselves."

On most points, then, Schools A and B are very different from one another. What each group of parents, teachers, and students valued about knowledge, teaching, learning, and freedom differed. Yet each school enjoyed the enthusiastic, public endorsement of their students, teachers, and parents.

The evidence for support is both clear and strong:

- Annual surveys of parent and student opinion have registered high praise for each school.
- Each school has had a waiting list of parents who wish to enroll their sons and daughters.
- Teacher turnover at each school has been virtually nil.
- Moreover, by most student outcome measures, both schools have compiled enviable records. In academic achievement, measured by standardized tests, School A was in the top ten schools in the entire state. School B was in the upper half of the state's schools.

School C

I offer again a verbal collage of images, but they will be taken from a composite of schools, past and present, that have shared these common features (Covello 1958; Lightfoot 1983; Hill 1993; Wood 1992).

This high school of about 1,000 students is in a working-class neighborhood of a large city. The high school had experienced declining academic achievement, poor attendance, and a deteriorating building. High teacher turnover each year created vacancies that had to be filled with inexperienced teachers. The parent-teacher association had dissolved.

A new principal came to the school five years ago and brought with her a cadre of experienced teachers from a previous school, where they had created a community-based school program. Here are some activities and quotes drawn from the school over the past five years.

- A twelfth grade government class prepared a neighborhood map. There were symbols for stores, bars, the police station, city unemployment and housing offices, a park, and trash-filled lots. Students posted the map in the main hallway and had a sign-up list for volunteers to work on weekends to help city workers clear abandoned cars and trash from empty lots.
- A tenth grade science class worked with a retired biologist in the community to test water in the nearby park creek for pollutants.
- A teacher for each grade was released for one period a day to make home visits.
- A half-dozen volunteers provided childcare in school for parents at a school site council meeting.
- Ninth and tenth grade classes spent a half-day tutoring first-graders at nearby elementary schools.
- Principal: "My aim [is] to bring the community into the school, so that our youngsters might better grow into understanding and participating citizens" (Covello 1958, xi).
- Parent: "We asked the principal to do something about a rash of traffic accidents near the school. She got students, parents, store owners, and police officials to pitch in and clear three empty lots for the children to use as playgrounds and re-route traffic. I can't say enough about our principal" (ibid., 251–54).
- School site council and principal hired five community aides, parents of current and former students, to do a housing survey with a neighbor-

hood retired inspector; they reported to the city's director of housing which homes violated the building code.

The evidence for support for School C has been, like Schools A and B, clear and strong:

- The past two years of annual surveys of parent opinion praised the community work of the school and, for the first time, gave high marks to the academic program.
- Student attendance has increased by a third in the past three years.
- Teacher turnover at school has dropped by half.
- For the first time, over 50 neighborhood stores contributed to the scholarship fund.
- The parent-teacher group was resurrected by a few parents and teachers, growing from a membership of 50 the first year to 500 in the fifth year.

Moreover, by most student outcome measures, School C has made substantial gains. In academic achievement, measured by state standardized tests, School C went from 30th percentile in reading three years ago to 52nd last year; in math, the figures went from 25th percentile to 60th.

Can All Three Schools Be Good?

Although the three schools differ dramatically from one another in socioeconomic status, size, and age of students, and although they obviously differ in how teachers organize their classrooms, view learning, approach the curriculum, and connect to their community, the schools possess common features. They have clear and shared purposes; they believe that all children can learn; each school staff has developed a working culture that embodies these common beliefs and enjoys collective action; and parents are deeply involved with the school. Thus, very different concepts of schooling held by parents and teachers can be embraced without sacrificing core purposes of public education. Sufficient toleration, even acceptance, of differences exists to include schools that are dissimilar both in philosophy and practice.

These commonalities evaporate, however, when ideological labels are applied. School A would probably be called "traditional" or "conservative" with pride by supporters and with scorn by opponents of this type of schooling. Schools B and C would be called "progressive" or "nontraditional," also with pride or scorn—depending on the speaker's preferences.

Considering the differences and similarities, are all three schools "good"? Yes, they are.

Notwithstanding such a straightforward answer, my response neglects two important questions. First, what made these schools "good," and, second, why has there been so much conflict, so much intolerance in twentieth-century America among policy makers, academics, parents, and taxpayers over which kind of schooling—progressive or traditional—is best for children?

What accounts for these schools being "good"? Traditional and progressive ideologues would probably argue that their respective beliefs about children, learning, and teaching made the difference. Let me suggest other factors that might explain why these schools became prized as "good" by their students, parents, and teachers.

Schools A and B are in a middle-class community that financially and politically supports public schools. Parents seeking a place consistent with their beliefs about how children should be raised and schooled chose each school. Over 25 years, committed principals and teachers—who chose to be there—worked in tandem with parents to make each school what it is today. School C, in contrast, serves a blue-collar neighborhood, yet it had an experienced (albeit new) principal and teachers committed to a philosophy of making the high school an integral part of a community in what was studied and how academic subjects were taught. They worked together to improve the school for five years. Students learned that where they lived was valued and needed improvement, not contempt.

These may well be the contextual, political, and leadership factors that made the three schools "good," not whether each was labeled traditional or progressive. The century-long war of words over traditional vs. progressive schooling replays familiar if tired arguments filled with charges and countercharges that School A, B, or C is better than the other. Educational leaders who count themselves as either progressives or traditionalists have believed that their way is, indeed, the best way to teach and learn. Moreover, their way is, they believe, both correct and moral. Yet educational researchers have failed, time and again, to prove that one pattern of schooling is superior to another. Consequently, the long-running verbal duel has elevated ideology to the primary factor while ignoring other less obvious but nonetheless important ones.[4]

I doubt, however, whether the faith-based contentiousness will end soon or easily. Even with ample evidence of "good" traditional and progressive schools in inner city and suburban schools, few educators and parents have paused to consider that "goodness" in schools comes in many colors, sizes, and ideologies. No surprise, then, that for the entire century there has been ideological conflict among educators, public officials, researchers, and parents over which pattern of schooling is best for children.[5]

SCHOOL WARS BETWEEN PROGRESSIVES AND TRADITIONALISTS

In the early twentieth century, a version of progressive schooling, drawing from the work of John Dewey and many other school reformers, swept across the country, changing traditional curricula, partially modifying conventional instruction of the day, and greatly expanding the social role of the school to take on duties that families had once discharged. Progressive reformers scorned the schooling of the day with its bolted-down desks, regimented instruction, blind obedience to authority, organizational inefficiencies, and divorce from the world outside of the classroom door. They wanted to focus on the personal and social development of students; they wanted children to be active learners engaged with their teachers in the pursuit of knowledge that was relevant to them and worthwhile to society; they wanted schools to be part of the community rather than separated from it; and they wanted efficient schools to offer many choices to students inside and outside school that would fit their different futures in the world of work and as citizens (Cremin 1961; Tyack 1974).

By the end of World War II, however, progressive educational ideas and practices had declined in popularity, giving way to new programs triggered by national fears of the Soviet Union. The Cold War revived interest in students learning more math and science to become engineers and scientists who could defend the United States against a powerful enemy. The New Math, major science projects, national tests, and programs geared to achieving individual excellence in student performance and increasing respect for school authority—practices usually associated with traditional schooling—replaced progressive programs (Ravitch 1983; Tyack and Hansot 1982).

Supreme Court decisions on race in the 1950s and a growing civil rights movement in the 1960s shifted school policy debates toward matters of equity. Inequalities in buildings, teachers, and curricula between mostly white and mostly black urban schools, along with the neglect of the personal and social development of students, led to a revival of progressive ideas in innovative programs. Head Start, Career Education, "open class-rooms," and "open space schools" became high-profile initiatives in schools where poor children attended. Federal laws created new programs for the poor that served preschool children (Head Start), dropouts (Job Corps), and those preparing for college (Upward Bound) (Ravitch 1983; Kluger 1977; Tyack and Hansot 1982; Silberman 1970).

By the early 1970s, however, with the Vietnam War still dividing the country, declining numbers of students enrolling in schools, and reductions in federal and state funding, enthusiasm for progressive ideas evaporated. Since the late 1970s, as global economic competition increased and periodic recessions reminded Americans that getting and keeping jobs was uncertain, a traditional schooling focusing on higher academic standards, stronger school discipline, a uniform curriculum, and improving standardized achievement test scores returned. Into the late 1980s and early 1990s, the rhythmic oscillation persisted. Progressive reformers urged new curricula based on concepts rather than facts, teaching for understanding rather than acquisition of knowledge, collaborative learning rather than passive listening, and performance-based assessment rather than bubbling in multiple choice items on standardized achievement tests. By the end of the 1990s, however, that progressive moment was overwhelmed by a renewed enthusiasm for traditional patterns in schooling that sought both higher academic standards and higher test scores (Kirst 1988; Cohen and Spillane 1992; Elmore and McLaughlin 1988).

Because of this century-long cyclical rhythm of contentious words about conservative and progressive patterns of schooling, notions of what constitutes a good school in America (unlike most other democratic nations) have become frozen within ideological boundaries. Why has there been this protracted intolerant bickering? I offer two reasons: a deeply rooted political conflict over child-rearing beliefs that has been grafted onto schooling; and a bottom-heavy, dispersed system of schooling where public officials have responded continually to different constituencies who, in turn, have urged schools to adapt to larger social, economic, and political trends.[6]

The Moral Politics of How Best to Raise School Children

In the early nineteenth century, taxpayers, parents, and public officials saw tax-supported schools as places to extend the reach of the family's influence on children. In school, children would become literate (as defined by the norms of the day), God-fearing, morally upstanding, and possessed of republican virtues. Versions of Protestant Christianity steeped in biblical views of parental authority saw children as innately depraved and in need of guidance. Disobedience was a sin. Thus, raising children to respect authority, be self-disciplined, and clearly know right from wrong were essential in the family and expected in their one-room schoolhouses. This model of raising and schooling children was viewed as natural and, of course, "good" (Lakoff 1996; Tyack, James, and Benavot 1987).

Beginning in antebellum reforms and continuing after the Civil War, another view emerged that challenged the religious-based popular model of child rearing and, by extension, of how to properly school students. The onslaught of industrialization, rapid urban growth, immigration, and social upheaval spurred reformers to advocate another, more "progressive" view of how best to raise children. Confined initially to manuals for parents (e.g., Abbott 1899), readers were urged to cultivate the innate goodness of children rather than dwell on their potential for sinfulness. Parents should nurture their offspring through example rather than coerce proper behavior. Parental love would yield respect for authority, self-discipline, and moral rigor in children (Wishy 1968).

To post–Civil War urban reformers who saw immigrant and migrant parents working long hours and living in urban slums, the fabric of traditional family and community life was unraveling before their eyes. Progressive reformers also saw an emerging urban middle class that had the time and money to invest in their children yet worried whether their children would find a proper social niche for themselves. Existing schools, these reformers concluded, were inadequate to cope with either unschooled newcomers or parvenu families. They urged that schools expand their usual duties and take on the nurturing roles that families had once discharged. Schools should offer medical care, meals, explicit lessons to build moral character including respect for civil authority (and cleanliness), and job preparation. Administrators and teachers were expected to develop children's individual intellectual, emotional, and social capacities and, ultimately, to produce happy, civically engaged adults.

The "New Education" at the turn of the century—what historians call "progressive"—extended the ideas generated decades earlier of nurturing children rather than breaking their will. These notions about an expanded social role of public schools converged with the newly emerging science of psychology and growing urban middle class to create a rival ideology of what a "good" child, family, and school were (Cremin 1961, 1988).

By World War I, these competing progressive and traditional ideologies constituted different faiths in the best way of raising children. They were already embedded in educators' language and school programs, thus creating contrasting patterns of schooling children and a platform for subsequent struggles over what "good" schools were. This century-long see-saw struggle of ideas is, then, a much deeper religious conflict over what role schools should play in society writ large and, more specifically, how children should be schooled.

To some readers, labeling the conflict "religious" may be carelessly slipping into hyperbole. I need to explain that I use the word to compare the ideological struggle between progressives and traditionalists with the two-centuries-old contentiousness among rival sects over the role of religious instruction in schools.

Mid-nineteenth-century school reformers, public officials, and religious leaders, anxious to keep competing gospels from aborting the public school movement, had cobbled together a political compromise that enlisted tax-supported public schools in the joint family-church mission of moral teaching without sectarian instruction. The school became a place not only for transmitting core values and gaining literacy but also for perfecting the sin-prone Child. Horace Mann and other reformers, for example, promised that the public school could teach morality. "Educate, only educate enough, and we shall regenerate the criminal and eradicate vice," Mann said. "Through the schools," he added, "we shall teach mankind to moderate their passions and develop their virtues." The idea that whoever has "charge of a young mind should be a moral educator" and that public school teachers were to lead "the progress of Christian civilization" was embedded in the political compromise that removed sectarian religious instruction from public schools (Wishy 1968, 69–70; Tyack, James, and Benavot 1987, 162–68).

It was an ideological compromise, however, that Catholics and some Protestant sects found impossible to accept: a morality divorced from religion. Catholics eventually established a separate private school system. For evangelical and Pentecostal Protestants—rather than modernist co-religionists—who relied upon a literal reading of the Bible and saw public schools as a critical venue for both moral transmission and regeneration, controversies then and since have erupted over Bible reading, prayer, and the teaching of evolution in tax-supported schools. Some evangelical and Pentecostal Protestants, then and now, have withdrawn their children and established private schools. Others have chosen to convert public schools into settings more hospitable to religious teachings. What is (and has been) at stake for such fervent religious advocates of a "best" way of raising children to obey authority, become self-disciplined, and act morally is literally one and only one way of schooling children.[7]

From these sectarian differences in gospels over how best to rear and school children in a proper manner, fiery oral and written exchanges between educational progressives and traditionalists have come to resemble earlier evangelical struggles among religious and secular authorities over morally charged instruction in public schools. Consider the matter of "discipline." Since 1969, public opinion polls on education have asked Americans to identify the single most pressing issue that they see in schools. Every year, parents and non-parents named school discipline as one of the top three problems that schools needed to address. Incidents of school violence such as robberies, attacks on teachers, and drug use became front-page news and television stories. Media amplified the fears of parents and taxpayers that schools were failing to fulfill their primary task of providing security for children and teaching respect for authority (Elam 1989).

How the "religious" merges with the political in patterns of schooling also became evident. Family concerns about how best to raise children easily segued into concerns over children's in-school behavior. For traditionalists, cracking down on students who disobeyed school rules was the best way of teaching respect for authority. Some even sought a return of corporal punishment. Others wanted to expel unruly students and tighten school security measures, including the presence of police (ibid.; Lakoff 1996).

For progressives, a breakdown in school order was a community problem—growing violence in a media-saturated society—that public officials had neglected. Blaming schools for a larger social problem was scapegoating a vulnerable institution, they argued. Moreover, while progressives shared conservatives' concern for respecting authority and the rule of law, they felt strongly that resorting to corporal punishment or imposing more rules and stiffer penalties was counterproductive. Such actions diverted attention from deeper social problems while creating a police-state climate within schools. Progressives were not opposed to punishing unruly students for acts that hurt peers and the school, but they also sought nonpunitive ways of helping children become self-disciplined and respectful of others' rights (Flannery 1997).

Since the late 1960s, there have been few resolutions of these "religious" or ideological differences among progressives and traditionalists over the best way to deal with school discipline. What has remained muted and taken for granted (or perhaps ignored) has been the public's overriding desire for more orderly schools and the common faith, held by progressives and traditionalists, that respect for parental and civic authority and democratic practices are essential. This common faith has been a quiet, unnoticed background to the loud foreground noise over securing discipline in schools.[8]

Frequently expressed concerns over students' behavior underscores the historic common goal of strengthening core family and community moral values. However, defining these ideological struggles over discipline—and I could just as easily have added debates over standardized achievement test scores, using phonics to teach reading, tracking students by their performance, or even school uniforms—as technical educational squabbles between progressives and traditionalists hides the deeper and more pervasive moral imperative embedded in public schooling. Such narrowly defined quarrels over discipline and related school questions have obscured the enduring tension in the United States over which goals for public schools should have priority. Thus, there is a nexus between the religious and political, between the family and the school, between family child rearing and schooling the child. In George Lakoff's terms: moral politics permeate schools.

Yet there are (and have been) other goals that the public expects of its schools. Taxpayers and parents not only expect public schools to develop children's moral character but want schools to honor individual excellence. They expect schools to focus on efficiently preparing students with skills and credentials to get jobs and maintain a healthy economy. They expect schools to do everything they can to develop the personal and social capabilities of each and every child. Over the past two centuries of public schooling in the United States, Americans have viewed building citizens, preparing workers, cultivating each student's potential, and developing moral character as essential and achievable goals. Although these goals for public schools overlap, they are in tension with one another. There are insufficient resources to fully achieve all of them and, equally important, they contain internal contradictions. Experts and casual observers have noted that such conflicts, arising from the inherent contradictions within the very nature of democratic polities have prompted time and again patchwork compromises to reconcile competing values (Paris 1995; Ravitch 1983; Labaree 1997b).

Thus, century-long, stubborn moral politics filled with millennial reform rhetoric about rearing children pervaded national and local debates between traditionalists and progressives over what kind of schooling children should receive. In a democracy where voters can express their opinions about officials and taxes at the ballot box and where authority to govern schools is widely dispersed, the matter of what kind of schools are best has often become contested by rival faiths seeking primacy for one goal over another.

Public School Responsiveness to Constituencies

The second reason for the long-running ideological wars is the permeability of public schools each decade to interest groups from the political right and left. Historians have documented how temperance reformers reshaped public school curricula with mandatory courses on alcohol, tobacco, and drug abuse. Historians have recorded the pervasive influence of business interests in mobilizing public support for vocational education prior to World War I and, since the 1970s, for school reforms calling for higher academic standards, downsized bureaucracies, and greater use of information technologies. The historical record is rich with instances of activists deeply committed to equity and social justice mobilizing support for legislation (e.g., Civil Rights Act of 1964; Education for All Handicapped Children Act of 1975) that required schools to treat underserved children equitably. Finally, historians have noted how elite groups' turn-of-the-century concerns about the many immigrant languages and customs overwhelming the dominant culture were converted into Americanization programs. Similar fears and responses have been noted in the English-only and anti-immigrant legislation that have marked the 1980s and 1990s, when immigration from Latin America and Asia has been heavy (Tyack 1974; Kantor and Tyack 1982; Callahan 1962).[9]

The primary mechanism for schools to respond to larger social changes, of course, is to elect school board members who pursue particular school improvement agendas—singly or as organized interest groups—and then to lobby sitting boards and their appointed administrators in each of the almost 15,000 school districts in the country (down from over 100,000 a half-century ago). A second mechanism of change is the work of local, state, and federal legislators to alter what schools routinely do. Both mechanisms have resulted in many changes within school curricula, organization, and governance.

Why have schools been so responsive to constituents? The answer is uncomplicated: to survive, public schools must have the political and financial support of voting taxpayers. Surely, some very large school district boards and administrators, at different times, have been able to insulate themselves from voter disaffection. But not for long. For the most part, school district governing bodies have responded to coalitions of media, interest groups, and ad hoc parent organizations that pursue certain policies and programs (e.g., more phonics to learn reading, higher academic standards) they believe school boards must embrace. In the early 1970s, for example, amid the winding down of the Vietnam War and the first twinges of an inflationary economy, school boards began to feel the effects of declining school enrollments. Taxpayer groups merged with lobbies for elderly citizens to press school boards across the nation to close schools and save tax dollars. There is a truth about democracy buried in the cliché: when the nation has a cold, public schools sneeze (Wirt and Kirst 1989; Powell, Farrar, and Cohen 1985; Cremin 1990).

BROADENING THE DEFINITION OF "GOOD" SCHOOLS

These two reasons (differences in social beliefs of how best to raise children and the schools' responsiveness to their constituencies) help explain the pendulum-like swings between progressive and traditional schooling over the past century. But they fall short of offering a workable way out of this ideological cul-de-sac.

And that is why I began this chapter with descriptions of the three schools. They represent for me a way out of this impasse over which kind of schooling, which kind of "religion," is viewed as better than the other. I argue that all three schools are "good." One is clearly traditional in its concentration on teaching children the best knowledge, skills, and values in society. The other two are progressive in their focus on personal and social development of individuals and making the community a part of the school's curriculum. Each asserts that it serves different values; each, in its own fashion, puts into practice what it seeks to achieve; each uses emotionally loaded words to describe what it does. Such "good" schools driven by different ideologies and their hybrids exist in urban slums and suburban ghettos. Yet—and this is the important point that I wish to stress—these goals, practices, and vocabulary, different as they appear, derive from a common framework of core values that most parents and taxpayers want their public schools to achieve. Opinion polls and referenda on school issues reveal common values that both progressives and traditionalists want for their children. They want their sons and daughters to become literate, successful, self-disciplined, and self-reliant adults. They want their public schools to inculcate in the next generation democratic attitudes, values, and behaviors (Lakoff 1996; Elam, Rose, and Gallup 1996; Paris 1995).

When writers start using grand phrases like "self-reliant adults" and "democratic attitudes," eyes often glaze over, yawns are stifled, and pages are skipped. This reaction has been especially true in the past quarter century, when the primary responsibility of schools—as so often expressed by public officials and the media—has been equating high test scores with preparation for the labor market. Too often, little notice has been taken of the linkage between public schools and the civic life that Americans holding different educational views desire for themselves and their children.[10]

Within these common beliefs that I claim both traditionalists and progressives share, exactly what do I mean by democratic values, attitudes, and behaviors? A brief, albeit partial, list may help:

- Participation in and willingness to serve local and national communities;
- Open-mindedness to different opinions and a willingness to listen to such opinions;
- Respect for values that differ from one's own;
- Treating individuals decently and fairly, regardless of background;
- A commitment to talk through problems, reason, deliberate, and struggle toward openly arrived at compromises. (Public Agenda 1998; Gutmann and Thompson 1996; Gutmann 1987; Myrdal 1944; Dewey 1916)[11]

Such democratic virtues are learned, of course, in families, at work, and in the community. Most important, however, they are what schools, at the minimum, are expected to inculcate.

What matters in judging whether schools are "good," then, is not whether they are progressive or traditional but whether they are discharging their primary duty to help students think and act democratically. To anyone who has sampled media reports on public schools in the closing years of the twentieth century, however, little time or space is devoted to such matters. Test scores appear on the front pages of newspapers. Pundits wonder whether schools are adequately preparing students to enter a rapidly changing workforce. For the past quarter century, a growing consensus among top policy makers has emerged that ties the fortunes of the United States in the global economy to how well the public schools are preparing the next generation of workers. The gold standard for the adequacy of that preparation has become published test scores (Labaree 1997b; Paris 1995).

How Test Scores Became the Primary Indicator of a "Good" School

If the issue of orderliness in schools is a crude litmus test for distinguishing between progressives and traditionalists, then standardized achievement test scores have also sorted out combatants. Die-hard traditionalists swear by test results because satisfactory scores are proxies for high academic standards, students' acquisition of knowledge, their self-discipline, and equal treatment of minorities—all of which, they argue, will strengthen America's global economic position. Passionate progressives scorn test scores because they fail to capture students' deeper understanding of concepts, their wide range of real-world problem solving skills, and individual changes in attitudes and values. How did standardized test scores become the gold coin of the policy-making realm?

In 1965, when President Lyndon B. Johnson signed into law the Elementary and Secondary Education Act (ESEA), huge sums of federal money flowed into states and school districts to improve schools attended by low-income children. Although federal funds accounted for less than 10 cents out of every dollar spent on education at that time, federal policy makers, fearful of local misspending of funds, mandated that these programs be evaluated to determine whether poor children were improving academically. A federally funded survey (authorized under the Civil Rights Act of 1964) designed by James Coleman and other social scientists used standardized achievement test scores to measure school and individual student performance. From these efforts, another purpose for testing emerged that went well beyond securing a picture of individual students' achievement: holding schools accountable for producing academic results if they receive federal funds (Rotberg and Harvey 1993; McLaughlin 1975; Coleman et al. 1966).

By the early 1970s, the practice of using standardized achievement test scores to assess total school performance, established in ESEA and strengthened by the Coleman study, had swiftly spread. Annual publication of school-by-school test scores became common fare in the nation's newspapers. National reports on large racial inequities in test results and falling test scores began to sink into professional and public consciousness (Coleman et al. 1966; Smith and O'Day 1991; Kozol 1991).

One response to declining student academic performance in the 1970s was a resurgent reform impulse for academic excellence through raising academic standards and increased testing. Most states in those years introduced new tests to make schools accountable for producing graduates who had at least achieved proficiency in basic skills. These "minimum competency tests" identified and measured skills that had to be learned by each grade level and where efforts were needed to improve teaching and learning (Ravitch 1983; Fredericksen 1994; Linn 1994).

Another response to the deep inequities between urban and suburban schools, between black and white student performance, was the effective schools movement. In the mid-1970s, a small number of researchers began working to disprove the new wisdom that what largely shapes students' academic performance—as measured by standardized achievement tests— is family background. Believing deeply in the value of equity and expecting that urban schoolchildren would be especially harmed by such a consensus of opinion among policy makers, this small band of activist researchers identified a handful of big city schools enrolling large numbers of low-income minority children that scored higher on standardized achievement tests than would have been predicted by their socioeconomic status (Weber 1971; Brookover and Lezotte 1977; Firestone 1991).

These researchers-turned-reformers extracted from the schools certain factors (e.g., principal's instructional leadership, concentration on basic academic skills, strong emphasis on maintaining order in school, monitoring academic achievement frequently) that they linked to the students' higher-than-expected academic performance on standardized tests. Within a few years, lists of factors were consolidated into various Effective School models that swiftly spread to many big cities across the country. The factors overlapped traditional approaches to teaching and schooling that also accorded with the wishes of many minority parents and educators in mostly black schools (Edmonds 1979; Ralph and Fennessey 1983; Stedman 1987; Levine and Lezotte 1990).[12]

By the mid-1980s, the national impulse for school reform had accelerated with the publication of *A Nation at Risk* and a barrage of reports about failing American schools. The underlying assumption behind the school reform impulse was to wed schooling to the economy; better schools meant a stronger economy (Peters 1988; Cuban 1992; Levin 1998).

Effective School models spread and became nationalized. Suburban districts and entire states installed programs that identified five, seven, or fourteen factors of effectiveness and laid out careful designs for schools to follow in implementing different models. Amendments to ESEA in 1988 included specific reference to Effective School research. Federal officials directed schools to consider that research when designing their programs and told state agencies receiving federal funds that they had to set aside funds to help schools establish programs based upon the factors researchers had identified (Murphy, Hallinger, and Mesa 1985; Bullard and Taylor 1993).

Few of that hardy band of Effective School reformers in the early 1970s could have foreseen how fears of economic decline would have driven national policy makers to link improved schools to an improved economy and embrace a traditional ideology of schooling. Now, at the turn of the millennium, national goals, performance standards in academic subjects, and tests dominate talk of school reform. Aligning academic goals, curriculum standards, and texts to high-stakes tests has become the challenge.

Since the mid-1960s, then, the conservative idea of a "good" school has been transformed into one in which student performance on norm-referenced achievement tests is the primary indicator of school success. For the past 30 years this concept of effectiveness has become pervasive in federal legislation and school reform agendas. International, national, state, district, and individual schools have been compared and contrasted publicly to ascertain degrees of success. Although other indicators have been used in the United States—such as college attendance, drop-out rates, and numbers of students passing Advanced Placement examinations—standardized test scores remain the signal measure of school effectiveness. A school with high or improving test scores has now become a "good" school (Bracey 1995b; McDonnell 1994).

Recall that, in my description of the three schools, I too had used standardized test scores and other performance measures. I implied that Schools A, B, and C had done well on these outcomes. Therefore they were "good." A careful reader could accuse me of using traditional outcome measures that are really aimed at School A and are generally accepted by the vast majority of Americans in the closing years of this century; such outcomes do not necessarily match what Schools B and C seek to achieve for their students. Such a reader would be correct. I need to return to this point of defining "good" schools and suggest what specific criteria could be used that might melt the ideological deep-freeze imprisoning the search for "good" schools.

Redefining "Good" Schools

To determine whether or not a school is "good," one needs to use standards in making a judgment and holding the school accountable. For schools A, B, and C, I offered criteria like parental satisfaction and staff stability as ways of judging a school's success and thereby being "good." Then, I slipped in test scores and other measures customarily used by policy makers and the media to judge schools since the mid-1960s. All of these criteria would fit the aims of School A and satisfy traditionalists while annoying progressives. Are there criteria to determine a "good" school that might satisfy both traditionalists and progressives while cracking the monopoly that test scores currently have on determining "goodness"? I believe there are.

I have already suggested parent, student, and teacher satisfaction as a reasonable standard to use in determining how "good" a school is. I would go further and add: to what degree has a school achieved its own explicit goals? Traditional School A was a clear success by traditional criteria of students' academic performance, test scores, and obedience to authority.

School B, however, was much less interested in test scores and even report cards. Teachers wrote narratives instead of giving letter grades. What School B wanted most were students who had grown intellectually and socially; students who could think on their own; students who could work together easily with others different from themselves; and students who, when faced with a problem, could tackle it from different vantage points and come up with creative solutions. Parents and teachers had plenty of stories about students reaching these goals, but few tests or quantitative measures exist that capture the behaviors that School B sought.

Similarly, School C had aims that went well beyond the traditional ways of judging "goodness" in schools. The principal and staff sought close connections with the local community by extending academic content and instruction into the neighborhood. Moreover, students and teachers in School C wanted to make a difference in the community by actively working to improve it. Again, there are no tests that can capture to what degree, if at all, the school achieved its goals. There are indirect measures like growing parent involvement, more participation in school life by neighbors, and student satisfaction but, beyond that, very little.

Finally, there is another standard to judge "goodness" in a school that some readers may have already anticipated. I claimed above that the fundamental purpose of tax-supported schooling in the United States has been (and is) to produce graduates who possess democratic behaviors and attitudes. I have argued that this is (and has been) a common framework for public schools in the United States since their founding. It has been lost in the battle of words and programs among public officials and educators who champion traditional or progressive schools. A "good" school, I would argue, is one that has students who display those virtues in different situations during and after their formal education.

But how can educators, parents, and taxpayers ever determine whether or not schools have achieved these outcomes? Certainly, existing standardized tests miss coming close to what I suggest. Schools B and C lack assessments that would capture their worthwhile activities. Previous efforts to do so have faded from the memories of current educators and public officials. Much more would have to be done in constructing such measures, but it is not an impossible task (Smith and Tyler 1942). Here, then, are my criteria for determining "good" schools:

- Are parents, staff, and students satisfied with what occurs in the school?
- Is the school achieving the explicit goals that it has set for itself?
- Are democratic behaviors, values, and attitudes evident in the students?

These criteria contain measures by which schools could be held responsible for achieving desired outcomes. Both progressives and traditionalists, I believe, could declare a truce to this hapless war of words and come to agreement over these criteria.

There are some hopeful signs that the narrow but popular criteria currently used to define "good" schools might be broadening. Beginning in the early 1970s, alternative public schools (magnet schools created out of the desegregation struggles and parental dismay with existing schools) were established that ranged from highly traditional to intensely progressive to hybrids of both. Because parents could choose to which ones they sent their children, no official approval or disapproval was stamped on these alternatives. Since then, alternative schools anchored in the principle of parental choice have survived and, in the late 1980s, expanded into the Charter School movement. As of 1998, state and local authorities had approved over 700 public charter schools of different ideologies in 20 states, enrolling 170,000 students. The idea that there are many ways to school children has become central to charter schools. Finally, the federal government has embraced ecumenism in "good" schools in the Comprehensive School Reform Demonstration program. The legislation authorizing the program offers $150 million to states and districts to improve schools by choosing among a menu of existing school-site programs that include efforts both progressives and traditionalists would applaud (Fantini 1973; Raywid 1985; Wells 1993; U.S. Department of Education 1997; Rothstein 1998a; Consortium for Policy Research in Education 1998).

Let me close by summing up my answer to the question: why is it so hard to get "good" schools? First, notions of "goodness" vary. There is nothing inherently wrong with that, since diverse notions of goodness about schools reflect the national difficulty in defining a "good" society, a "good" person, how to best raise a child, and how to worship God. Democracies are forever reconciling and institutionalizing diverse values through electoral, judicial, and legislative compromises. Respecting different versions of "goodness" has been a political issue in each domain, including education.

Second, these varied notions of "goodness," particularly about rearing children, have been transferred to schools and become politicized. This is neither novel nor surprising. Thomas Jefferson, Horace Mann, and John Dewey pointed out repeatedly the links between education and civic life. What has happened in the past century, however, is that the connections have gotten mired in the old debate between educational traditionalists and progressives over what is "good" teaching and a "good" school. School officials' responsiveness to interest groups pressing for their agendas, and the inability of policy makers or researchers to demonstrate which policies or practices are superior, have kept the ideological warfare alive. Within debates over the direction public schools should take, progressives and traditionalists have contested which pedagogical innovations are better for children, ignoring that there are more ways than one to define "goodness" in schools, and failing to acknowledge openly the mixes of both that have steadily changed schools in this century (Cremin 1990).[13]

That is why "good" schools are hard to get. It is not because of an absence in expertise or a lack of will; parents and educators have created "good" schools often. "Good" schools are hard to get because of an evangelical bias for only *one* version of what "good" is. They are hard to get because few have examined carefully, deliberately, and openly different conceptions of "goodness" and how each view is connected to the essentials of democratic life. Until Americans shed the view of a one-best-school for all, as religious and secular leaders have come to accept in their domain, the squabbles over whether traditional schooling is better than progressive will continue. Such a futile war of words ignores the fundamental purposes of public schooling as revitalizing democratic virtues in each generation and, most sadly, ignores the many "good" schools that already exist.

PART III

Uncommon Ways of Seeing
the Common Good

In this final section, Elisabeth Hansot, Michael Katz, and John Meyer offer unusual ways of seeing the common good in politics, society, and education. These authors, coming from quite different research traditions and
using quite different perceptual lenses, raise provocative questions about
the relationship of ancient traditions to modern democracies, the tensions
between community life and regulatory pressures, and how education has
become a secular religion in the United States.

Elisabeth Hansot deals philosophically with the issue of renegotiating
the common good in public education. She addresses the tension between
the individual purposes of schooling and its civic purposes, drawing on
Aristotle to link the two through the notion of civic friendship. While William Reese (Chap. 1) clarified that the early communal purposes of American public schooling were primarily moral, Hansot seeks to reestablish the
link between those purposes of education and the moral education of the
individual. Civic friendship is the conceptual link.

Civic friendship, in Aristotelian terms, requires some parity among
friends, arenas of common interaction, and constant effort. In modern
terms, it offers a way to bridge the gap between the public and the private
in some civic arenas. Because public schools are locally governed and have
relatively high approval as a social institution, Hansot argues that they
may be fruitful arenas for developing civic friendship, which in turn can
help realign the individual/community imbalance in American society.

A central dilemma she addresses also echoes the worries of nineteenth-century common school founders: do public schools, especially in
cities, have enough parity among the actors to permit civic friendship to
grow? For instance, is the inequality between school professionals and lay

parents too wide to permit civic friendship to flourish? By raising such questions, Hansot presses readers to rethink the very categories of public and private.

So does Michael Katz. From the records of an early-twentieth-century charity agency, he tells a richly textured story of one mother caught in the web of a welfare system in the years following World War I. It is a narrative anchored in the details of agency records and social workers' language. In recapturing the voice of Rose Warrington and her trials with social workers after her husband leaves, Katz presents an implicit critique of theory-driven analysis and a reminder of the ambiguity inherent in representing individual experience as a basis for policies that affect the common good.

This narrative of one mother introduces the human dimension into our understanding of the politics of identity and status. In recounting Warrington's turmoil and struggle in keeping her family together, Katz implicitly displays the conflicts between an individual's assertions of independence and regulation by a private welfare agency. Katz uses the narrative to raise issues of justice and equality, personal agency, and the meaning of bureaucratic involvement in local lives.

In our final chapter to this section and the book, John Meyer offers a theoretical insight to advance an all-embracing supranational and suprapolitical explanation for the purposes of schooling. In constructing a view of public education as the modern secular religion, Meyer suggests that the American sect of the "religion of education" is not fundamentally different than that guiding nearly all the modern world.

Meyer steps back from conflicts over the purposes of American public education and the merits of various solutions to say that the most contentious of the policy debates are not tied to the functioning of our society in any real sense. Instead, they are intensely controversial symbolic issues. For instance, any potential solutions to questions about the teaching of evolution in schools would solve few problems in the real world. The prevalence of just these sorts of debates is clarified when they are understood as cosmological arguments about good and evil in the world, the structure of the universe, and the nature of humanity. Other puzzling features of public schools, such as universal reliance on educational attainment as an accepted and legitimate stratification mechanism even in hereditary societies are also explained by giving education sacred meaning.

CHAPTER 9

Civic Friendship: An Aristotelian Perspective

Elisabeth Hansot

*Friendship seems . . . to hold states together, and lawmakers
. . . care more for it than for justice; for concord seems to be
something like friendship, and this they aim at most of all . . .
and when men are friends they have no need of justice, while
when they are just they need friendship as well, and the truest
form of justice is thought to be a friendly quality.*
—Aristotle, The Nicomachean Ethics

Aristotle held that lawmakers wisely cared more for friendship than for
justice. His claim for friendship (or a friendly quality akin to goodwill) extends beyond justice to encompass other institutions of civic life. It points
us to an understanding of civic friendship as a critical background condition for effective political debate and action (Aristotle 1988, 1287a20–
40).[1] Implicit in this understanding is the notion that institutions like the
judicial or educational system rely, for their proper functioning, on
preexisting dispositions among their constituents—dispositions which
they in turn strengthen. In other words, it is important when thinking
about governing institutions not to focus exclusively on formal
characteristics (whether they are centralized or local, are run by the few or
the many) but to attend also to the dispositions (or habits of the heart) that
support different types of governance. Aristotle's treatment of civic
friendship offers us a rich understanding of the *affective* component in
civic life, as it plays out in different civic settings.

Today many observers of the practice of democracy in America lament a loss of civility, trust, and goodwill. Some would like to see civil society become more associational, more actively engaged face-to-face.[2] Yet others, insisting on a government of laws, not men, want to rid public life of partiality, substituting reasoned agreement and neutral procedures in public affairs.[3] Both of these perspectives are compatible with an understanding of friendship, not as a moral good in itself but as a background condition that enables *associational* life to take place. Although neither party in this debate sees friendship playing a key role in public associations, the likely explanation is that friendship is understood today almost exclusively in personal, intimate terms, not as a condition that enables civic behavior.[4]

Along a somewhat different axis is the debate over the adequacy of the rational choice perspective. This theory argues that people's individual and collective actions are best explained in terms of their self-interest; that is, they seek to maximize gains and minimize losses in social interactions.[5] Cooperation, in this model, would be seen as a strategy based on rational calculation of benefits to the individual or group. Increasingly, however, the rational choice model has been faulted for insufficient attention to social factors such as ongoing interactions with others, group loyalty, and moral socialization. Understanding cooperation, these critics argue, entails paying attention to the social contexts and networks in which individuals act.[6] These two views are, of course, not incompatible; affective, traditional, or group-based loyalties are compatible with rational concerns and may come into play in various combinations in social deliberations.

This chapter is situated squarely within a perspective that seeks to understand how rational and affective behaviors may work in tandem in specific social situations. It draws on Aristotle's understanding of friendship as a rational-affective association of persons who have achieved stable and virtuous dispositions. Friendship is not so much elective as affiliative; one is drawn to others of like character (Aristotle 1991, 1156b9–30).[7] I will use Aristotle's understanding of friendship as developed in *The Nicomachean Ethics* and *The Politics*, to suggest that civic friendship may be a neglected component in our thinking about conditions that sustain civil deliberation and engagement.[8]

Cognate words such as trust, civility, neighborliness, comity, goodwill, caring, amity, and "being well disposed toward" (some of which, such as trust and caring, have generated a considerable literature)[9] capture some of the phenomena I will focus on. I realize that using the word "friend-

ship" in a civic context risks summoning up notions of logrolling, crony-
ism, and machine politics, phenomena far from the one that interests me.
But I want to retain the term "civic friendship" for two reasons, both Aristotelian. The term reminds us that personal friendship and civic friendship
are related behaviors; that is, civic friendship, though different in its practice, is partly anchored in the parallel practice of personal friendship
(Cooper 1990, 237). And the Aristotelian term reminds us that friendship
is a practice, a behavior, as well as a disposition. There is more to friendship than feeling friendly.

For Aristotle, civic friendship prospers best in relatively small and stable communities without too much disparity of wealth or values (1988,
1326b8–25). This chapter suggests that some school communities appear
to be good modern approximations of Aristotle's small and stable communities; they are venues in which civic friendship may flourish. I realize
that linking friendship and school governance may sound counterintui-
tive in a time when education policy is a contentious topic of debate, when
income disparities are widening alarmingly, and when local communities
seem very vulnerable to outside economic and political forces as well as internal dissension. And, of course, local schools and modest-sized school
districts are not freestanding or isolated entities.

That said, my interest in this chapter lies not in this broad societal context but in certain features of schools as institutions that make them
promising environments for the development and exercise of civic friendship. In other words, local school institutions seem to offer an environment in which civic friendship can develop and flourish, and flourishing
civic friendships, in turn, strengthen the local institutions that nurture them.

My basic argument, then, is normative, with some brief empirical illustrations. While considering schools as institutions in which civic friendships might flourish, I also make a claim for their desirability. Civic
friendship is a good in itself as well as a potential source of strength for the
institutions in which it is nurtured. In addition, the notion of civic friendship directs our attention to the *affective* dimension of civic interactions
among groups and individuals engaged in improving educational practice.[10] Here the claim I wish to make is modest: the affective dimension is
by no means the whole of civic deliberation. It does not displace other requirements of civic life such as broad agreements about the rules of fair
play, nor does it preclude other motives for civic life such as the pursuit of
group interest (MacIntyre 1981, 155–56).

Rather, I want to suggest that the practice of civic friendship (the

behaviors and attitudes that constitute it) is a background condition that
supports public communication, much like Aristotle's claim that friendship is a necessary support for justice. Like Aristotle, I would not expect
civic friendship to flourish in communities riven by animosities or large-
scale socioeconomic disparities. At the other extreme, in communities that
are very homogeneous in values and socioeconomic conditions, the ease of
achieving consensus may make civic friendship less important (Aristotle
1988, 1326b8–25). I believe civic friendship flourishes best midway
between these extremes, in small communities not too homogeneous nor
too split by deep-seated antagonisms or social cleavages.

Richard Hofstadter, in a discussion of comity, captures well the middle
ground between these two extremes:

Comity exists in society to the degree that those enlisted in its contending interests have a basic minimal regard for each other. . . . The basic humanity of
the opposition is not forgotten; civility is not abandoned; the sense that a
community life must be carried on after the acerbic issues of the moment have
been fought over and won is seldom far out of mind. (Hofstadter 1979, 454)[11]

CIVIC FRIENDSHIP IN ARISTOTLE

Like our parsing of friendship, our modern understanding of the individual's relation to the state is radically different from the Greek one.[12]
Consequently, any straightforward attempt to transpose Aristotle's understanding of friendship to twentieth-century America is, to say the least,
foolhardy. But three of Aristotle's insights into civic friendship are relevant to modern concerns: that civic friendship is neither just rationally
motivated self-interest nor totally other-regarding, but an amalgam; that
civic friendship needs to be anchored, both in institutions and in behavior;
and that civic friendship is a background condition—or set of understandings—that allows other practices to flourish.

Civic Friendship as an Amalgam of Rationality and Affect

The discussion of friendship in *The Ethics* and *The Politics* presupposes
a continuity between the individual and the community that we no longer
assume. The Greeks understood, in Plato's words, that the *polis* is the
individual writ large (Plato 1961, 615 [II368e–369c]). Indeed, *philia*
(friendship) is a much more inclusive concept than its English counterpart.
In Aristotle it includes, in addition to fellow citizens and tribesmen, friendship between parents and children, men and gods, and husband and wife

(Aristotle 1900, 1161a10–1162a30).[13] Such friendships are understood along a continuum of private and public. This has the virtue of blurring distinctions that moderns often make between private affective and public self-interested behaviors (Aristotle 1988, 1288b1–5).[14]

Friendship in our society tends to be privatized and personalized, an intimate emotional bond based on personal histories or on shared experiences, such as workplace friendships. We also tend to understand friendship as a matter of choice, unlike kin or colleagues. When seen through an Aristotelian lens, personal and civic friendship are much more isomorphic, both entailing complex behaviors and expectations that build on some level of trust (affective), some mutual expectation of benefit (rational), and some understanding of others' needs and constraints (empathetic).[15] Such friendships are both a requirement of morality and a dictate of prudence; they do not neatly separate into one category or another.[16]

The insight that friendship is an amalgam of altruistic and selfish, affective and instrumental, allows Aristotle plausibly to extend friendship from a relationship encompassing a few others to one encompassing a small polity.[17] Political communities in which friendship thrives have a shared set of laws and a shared conception of justice (Aristotle 1988, 1295b, 1262b4–24, 1310a12–20). Civic friendship does not require a personal liking for other citizens; rather, it is expressed through a regard for others' fair treatment, according to shared norms.[18] Such regard benefits all members of the community: the individual or group who acts, and the individual or group who is the recipient of such acts. Neither selfish nor altruistic, this behavior reflects an understanding of interdependency created by shared bonds of affection for fellow citizens mediated through education, common expectations for each other, and a common history of acting together (Schwarzenbach 1966, 105–6).

In a martial society, for instance, where courage is valued, courageous acts benefit the persons who accomplish them, and they are appropriately honored for their deeds. Courageous behavior benefits those who are both protected and instructed by such actions (MacIntyre 1981, 123, 192).

A striking recent description of the importance of the affective component of friendship is seen in a study of a Danish elementary school created by a group of parents with a strong socialist ideology. When a particular curriculum decision in the school arose, it was fiercely debated among parents, teachers, and students. The arguments were "highly elaborated, deeply felt, and passionately expressed." After long and heated debate, a decision was taken. Surprisingly, the decision was never implemented, suggesting that the issue in dispute was really a proxy for something else. The author reporting the incident explains it thus: "In this case, at least, the decision process was much more connected to the generation of reassurance than to the generation of a substantive action" (March 1994, 216–17). In other words, that the school community members' regard for each other could survive such a hard-fought battle was more important than the particular curricular decision. Interestingly, only by *not* implementing the curricular decision did it become apparent what was really at stake.

Anchorage of Civic Friendship in Practice

As I have noted, Aristotle understands civic friendship as grounded, in part, in friendships between persons developed in civic arenas. And of course the reverse is also true: civic friendship in turn grounds the cognate practice of friendship between persons. Common to both is the notion of a settled disposition, the result of education reinforced by habituation in the individual and by custom in the polity (Aristotle 1985, 1179b27–1180a24). And common to both forms of friendship is that its practice is pleasurable in itself (ibid., 1169b30–1170b19).

Because we moderns have a more personal and intimate notion of friendship, it is more difficult for us to see commonalities between private and civic friendship. Let me suggest at least one: the reciprocal character of friendships based on assumptions of equality.

Friendship among equals, Aristotle observes, is the best sort of friendship because neither party looks to gain advantage from the other (ibid., 1158b35–1159a17; Aristotle 1988, 1295b1–25). Although some might claim that modern friendships afford us a greater range, most friendships that are stable over time continue to entail notions of parity. Contributions to "parity" friendships need not be comparable or commensurable but, as Elliot Liebow observed, too great a disparity of status and resources vitiates friendships (1967, 161–207). Friendship entails behaviors as well as dispositions. The wealthy person who commiserates with a friend's undeserved financial misfortune but neglects to help is at best "a fair weather" friend. The poor person constantly succored by a wealthy friend may end up with a benefactor instead. But because to be friendless is seen as a terrible impoverishment, perhaps more cruel than to be without intimates or offspring, vastly unequal parties do at times attempt to maintain a semblance of friendship, an attempt that can be both poignant and distressing (ibid., 206–7).[19]

If the practice of friendship requires a judicious blend of both affections and rational behavior, too great an imbalance between parties tends to skew these practices. If I wish to be wise on someone else's behalf, it is helpful to grasp the other's circumstances in their complexity. I am more likely to come by this knowledge if we are similarly situated. If I wish to sustain my affection for a friend, it helps to have experiences in common. Empathy would seem to be more readily summoned for situations akin to those already encountered. There are practical limits on friendship, less perhaps than Aristotle entertained, but more perhaps than moderns like to acknowledge.

How might the notion of parity among friends ground friendship in the civic arena? As I have noted, a difficulty for moderns, but not for Aristotle, is that we are prone to thinking of friendship in personal terms. Consequently, when we turn to civic friendship or its analogues, we are more likely to ground it exclusively in social institutions and customs.

Aristotle has another advantage: his best polities are typically smaller and more homogeneous than modern counterparts, and hence he is able to assume a certain sort of comity, which builds upon itself (Aristotle 1988, 1326b8–25).[20] Although moderns can make no such assumptions, local institutions such as school districts do seem to offer a partial analogue. While rarely homogeneous, their size and potential agreement about the importance of education (if not the particular form it should take) make them promising sites for the exercise of civic friendship (Schmuck and Schmuck 1992, 147–50).[21] Civic friendship, then, might be viewed along a continuum. At one end, a too-homogeneous community would have little need for such a support; friendships may flourish among the like-minded, but their decision-making processes need little of such lubricant. At the other end, a community riven by class or racial divides may not be able to summon the resources to move beyond this status quo. In between, with all its complexities, is the terrain of groups with different agendas, histories, class, and ethnicities. Amid such complexities, local and familiar institutions such as schools are a potential source of commonalities around which to coalesce, environments in which civic friendships might be nurtured.

Civic Friendship as Background Condition

When I speak of a background condition, I mean a community's shared assumptions about the attitudes and behaviors of others. Such attitudes are not directly expressed in political actions; rather, they constitute the environment within which political actions are interpreted and understood. Sissela Bok captures this background phenomenon when she observes that "*Whatever* matters to human beings, trust is the atmosphere in which it thrives" (Bok 1978, 31n).

These attitudinal and behavioral propensities can be easily taken for granted, so much a part of a familiar landscape that they invite little notice until they change. Akin to Gabriel Almond and Sidney Verba's definition of political culture as "a set of beliefs, attitudes, norms, perceptions, and the like, that support participation" (1963, 33), they are part of the cognitive/emotional frameworks that individuals use to make sense of the world—to organize their reality.[22]

For Aristotle, civic friendship is both a disposition and a practice. Over time, as this disposition/practice becomes customary behavior, civic friendship acquires a third characteristic: it becomes part of the environment, a background condition in which other practices flourish. Hence Aristotle's startling claim that friendship is more essential to the polity than justice. In a climate of hostility or vituperation, just acts will not be perceived as such; even in more benign circumstances, civic friendship counters our tendency to suspect others of attending exclusively to their own political agenda or group (Schwarzenbach 1996, 106–7).

Aristotle's stress on friendship as *praxis* (practice or behavior) usefully signals how differently moderns may value background understandings such as "neutrality." As we encounter the concept in scientific inquiry, it evokes a reassurance that the rules that govern such inquiry are not being bent for personal profit or gain. But in human interactions it may be that neutrality frequently feels closer to being ignored, a tacit form of hostility. Consider walking through a strange neighborhood where its denizens do not respond to a smile or friendly greeting. A detached observer would correctly say that no hostile action has occurred but might also concede that the walker's uneasiness is quite comprehensible—and even prudent. In human interactions, background conditions do not so easily allow of neutrality.[23]

Extreme cases are often instructive. Students of resistance movements, and indeed of war itself, have noted that emergency conditions elicit camaraderie among those involved.[24] Without great confidence in one's fellows, the high-risk activities entailed in resistance might not be undertaken. The disposition to trust becomes inextricably bound up with and reinforced by the requirements of action. Background conditions of trust, thus established, powerfully color the way people relate to each other, the projects they undertake in common, indeed the compelling quality of the public purposes they entertain.

SCHOOLS AS A CONTEXT FOR CIVIC FRIENDSHIP

Tip O'Neill famously remarked that "all politics is local." A politician must pay attention to his own backyard, keeping his folk informed "so that they will like and respect you and allow you to be a 'national' Congressman" (O'Neill 1994, xvi). O'Neill is saying that much of the glue of political life, like loyalty, keeping your word, and not bearing grudges are background conditions, practiced locally. These shared understandings, once cemented, allow one to negotiate ever-present dynamics of power and conflict.

Civic friendship belongs on the same local terrain, because it is most effectively understood as a set of behaviors practiced locally. It is, of course, possible to talk about other forms of civic friendship (the friendship uniting Christians for instance, or the friendship among nations), but if, as Aristotle argued, friendship is a practice as well as a disposition, then its local quality is of the essence.[25] Sara Lawrence Lightfoot observes that "the *unspoken* consonance that the parents and teachers in suburban schools share may be more critical to their understanding of one another than their *spoken* conflicts. In other words, the arguments arise out of some shared and sympathetic understanding of one another, a sense of consonant values and cultural traditions. There is a common language for waging battles and negotiating differences." Lightfoot notes that the greater the difference between family and school norms, the greater the need for such shared understandings (1978, 171–72, 89).

Of the many political settings in which civic friendship might play a key part, school governance—with its tradition of local control—stands out.[26] The school is familiar even when it is disliked. Everyone knows what a school is because everyone has been through one. Other institutions that deal with the young are not so user-friendly. Hospitals are predicated on the expertise of physicians; juvenile justice courts, overcrowded and understaffed, bear the stigma of dealing with deviants; churches and synagogues are, for Americans, private choices where one joins, by-and-large, the company of like-minded people. The school remains a central common institution that incorporates diverse clienteles. With output measured by grades and promotions, by homework and teacher conferences, and by the ubiquitous sports events, its workings are not arcane to the average citizen.

An indication of local commitment to schools is that parents are quite ready to admit that the nation's schools are in a parlous condition, but with astonishing frequency they make exception for their own local school. It is as if, despite newspaper headlines proclaiming that large numbers of schools are flunking, parents maintain a sturdy interest in claiming that their own local institutions are the fortunate exceptions.[27]

The local character of schools has other advantages as well. School issues are often concrete and immediate, as in familiar debates over the trade-offs of cutting one program rather than another in tight budget situations. And in reasonably stable communities, the policies resulting from such debates can be monitored over time, informing subsequent issues.[28]

Embedded in school neighborhoods and districts are powerful incentives for communities to cultivate civic friendship. There are a number of ways citizens might come to such understandings; none, of course, are inevitable. Common values might, for instance, result from citizens coming to understand their stake in good schooling for the next generation: if youth are ill educated as a result of inadequate schooling, the whole community suffers. Common values may be both substantive (agreements about the value of an activity or behavior) and procedural (agreement about how debate or disagreement are handled). The recognition that schooling is a *collective* good might allow participants to acknowledge values held in common with other groups, both substantive and procedural, even as they disagree on particular issues.

Examples of civic friendship are to be found at the often-more-politicized level of the school district as well as the more hands-on level of the school site. The former often uses institutional leadership to connect schools with the broader community; the latter looks to the more immediate school community of parents and teachers. Frank Cody, a fine example of institutional leadership, used the formal powers of his office (school superintendent of Detroit, a position he held from 1919 to 1942) to develop, quite self-consciously and politically, broad friendships within his district.

Cody's remarkably long tenure in the Detroit superintendent's office depended, in part, on his skill in creating friendly background conditions to oil relations among the competing factions that made up the school district landscape at that time. Jeffrey Mirel (1993) notes that potentially the most divisive issue to face the Detroit school board was the expansion of progressive educational initiatives, such as IQ testing, tracking, and junior high schools. Although Detroit enjoyed a tradition of business and labor support of the schools as well as a consensus on expanding the role of schools, Mirel acknowledges how critical Cody's tireless efforts were in nurturing community support for the public schools. Cody himself described this activity in terms that show him to be aware of the importance of friendly civic relations among groups. "Go out and join organizations! The city is full of luncheon clubs, exchange clubs, friendship organizations. Go out and mingle with these men. Find out what they want. Then bring the information back and put it to work in your schools" (Tyack and Hansot 1982, 149).

Even on a trip to Europe, Cody tried to follow his self-imposed rule of making six new friends a day. He counseled graduating students that they could "get along in this world with very little algebra, but you can't get along without friends. . . . The greatest knowledge of the world today is the knowledge of getting along with people" (ibid.). Cody's deputy superintendent, Charles Spain, offered a more restrained description of his boss' activities: "[U]nder [Cody's] leadership every available agency is utilized to bring the schools to the public and the public to the schools. The good will thus generated stands as a bulwark behind the school administration when budgets are under consideration, and when the schools are under criticism" (Mirel 1993, 69; Tyack and Hansot 1982, 146).

Civic friendship, as Cody practiced it, had the great virtue of blurring fracture lines and of avoiding groups becoming entrenched in their positions. What Cody did, admittedly in a district with a history of educational cooperation among competing interests, was to use the visibility and authority of his *office* to forge friendships among potentially divisive factions by approaching them on their turf, attending to their views, reframing those views when necessary and possible, and using his powers of humor and storytelling to make and maintain friends for his enterprise.

Although it is tempting to characterize Cody as a consummate politician whose friendships were merely instrumental (and, indeed, civic friendships *are* politic), I believe Spain captured the sense in which Cody's cultivation of friendships created background conditions that were critical to his successes. Summing up what was most important in Cody's tenure, Spain called it "the 'Era of Good Feeling' in education in Detroit"—an era in which "Public sentiment has been solidly behind the schools and serious obstacles to progress have been entirely wanting" (Mirel 1993, 78).

In contrast to Cody's large-scale view, noted educational reformer Deborah Meier uses her pioneering experience with Central Park East

(1995) to ground us in the texture of the everyday life of that school in all its engaging (and distressing) particularity. Echoing Sissela Bok, Meier notes that trust was the most efficient form of staff development in her school. (Meier entitled her chapter "Trust," but she also uses a variety of words such as affection and camaraderie to describe the phenomenon.) She captures the variety of building blocks of camaraderie among parents, teachers, students, and administrators. The growth of reciprocal understandings involved individual and collective acts of mutual support both on and off the job. Such acts included "helping out when family tragedies struck, organizing the school so teachers could shift their schedules in times of crisis, chipping in when a colleague's purse was stolen or equipment vandalized, and sharing the cost of babysitting so that all staff could attend weekend retreats or after-school meetings" (Meier 1995, 134–35).

When necessary, Meier used external mediators so that those at odds with each other "could really hear each other without . . . having to appear neutral" (ibid., 131). But primarily, the effort to build what I have called civic friendship occurred through prosaic everyday acts. Although not always convenient, loyalty and solidarity are "the products of our increased trust and also the way in which trust is kept alive and healthy" (ibid., 135).

Popular attention often focuses on dissent about education and conflict within schools. But the intensely local and everyday character of schools communities can also produce fertile soil for the cultivation of civic friendship. The clientele is local; many problems are experienced as local; solutions are frequently local, and their efficacy can be monitored locally. Indeed, it is interesting that, for all the discussion about encouraging citizenship in schools, there is comparatively little attention paid to how adults, surely potent role models, might embody it in their local activities.[29] Whether one wishes it or not, the making of school policies are powerful pedagogies. Surely the schools' encouragement of student civic behavior is flawed unless the forums in which adults continue to practice such behaviors are nurtured.

CIVIC FRIENDSHIP: ANCIENT AND MODERN

Civic friendship, as Aristotle clearly saw, needs to be anchored in institutions where broad agreements about values are possible. It needs to be accompanied by well-understood and accessible local arrangements where such values can be made concrete.[30] To the extent that today we understand friendship in personal, psychological terms, we limit it to the sphere of individual choice and practice. Because we tend to believe that notions like neutrality and its close cousin toleration are more appropriate to the civic arena, we are likely to neglect the rich possibilities of civic friendship.

Alexander Aleinikoff, in his discussion of Randolph Bourne's 1916 essay "Trans-national America," captures brilliantly what is powerful in the notion of civic friendship. Aleinikoff distinguishes between tolerance, the politics of peaceful coexistence entailing a live-and-let-live attitude, and mutuality, the politics of recognition that changes the observer. The latter demands active engagement and learning about others in their own terms. To underscore the distinction, Aleinikoff quotes Clifford Geertz: "Largeness of mind" comes from seeing ourselves as a "'case among cases, a world among worlds'; without this recognition of others, 'objectivity is self-congratulation and tolerance a sham'" (Aleinikoff 1977).[31]

Aleinikoff's understanding of mutuality stretches to the limit Aristotle's notion of civic friendship, because, for Aristotle, recognition was more confirmatory than challenging. But if the two understandings are placed along a spectrum of homogeneous to heterogeneous, they give a needed elasticity to the term "civic friendship," appropriate to the variety of social settings where it might be found. Settings where a fair amount of consensus about values obtains, and where economic disparities are modest, allow a more confirmatory, Aristotelian type of friendship to flourish.[32] Societies with a greater range of disparate values and economic conditions, such as Aleinikoff describes, require a greater effort from all parties to engage others on their own terms.

Roland McKean observes that today "we know tragically little about how to produce some of the most important goods in life—mutual respect, friendliness, cohesiveness, a sense of belonging, peace of mind" (1975, 202).[33] Aristotle has illuminated one pathway to civic friendship—one that flourishes in smaller communities that are stable enough to develop a common history and maintain a collective memory. If schools and school districts are one such venue, then we may be persuaded to attend to the conditions in which civic friendship may flourish in such locales.

Devotion and Ambiguity in the Struggles of a Poor Mother and Her Family: New York City, 1918–1919

Michael B. Katz

As we sat around his dining room table about 30 years ago, David Tyack explained that he had tried to write his forthcoming biography of George Ticknor by looking out at the world perched on Ticknor's shoulder.[1] Tyack's metaphor highlighted something important about the writing of history: the shoulders over which historians peer partly define the questions they ask and the ways they read data. Not only their subjectivity—as is often argued—but their angle of vision shapes historians' interpretations of events and ideas.

In historical writing on poverty and welfare, historians usually sit on the shoulders of reformers, legislators, or administrators. They see something of the intentions underlying policy, problems in its implementation, and the politics of reform and resistance. But their view of the subjects of policy remains clouded. Indeed, poor people appear mainly as shadowy figures or abstractions, their lived experience flattened and dissected or distorted by stereotypes. This standard view, which for nearly two centuries has reinforced and reproduced the distinction between the "deserving" and the "undeserving" poor, focuses more on programs and policies than on individuals and families. It produces histories of the Charity Organization Society, mothers' pensions, or the social insurances; it yields current studies of AFDC, Medicaid, and public housing.

But the standard view reveals little about the lives of poor people in their daily struggles to survive. The view over the shoulder of poor people differs because they have contended with multiple and simultaneous sources of assistance and supervision. Every day, poor families have had to locate and combine resources as they respond to the intrusion of well-meaning charity and the punitive, suspicious hand of the state. Poor families daily navigate their way through a complex terrain of potential help and punishment. Charting the course of poor families on this journey defines the frontier of research on both the history and the present-day study of poverty and welfare.

I have tried bringing to light one small piece of this story by reconstructing the experience of very poor families in early twentieth-century New York City from the records of the influential Charity Organization Society, which tried to apply scientific principles to charity through coordinating philanthropy, investigating applicants for assistance, and supervising their conduct. The major source is the detailed case records of the Charity Organization Society, compiled with extraordinary detail by its paid agents, for the most part young women who were among the nation's first social workers.

These case records are imperfect sources. They yield a view over the shoulders of poor families filtered through the perceptions of women of a different class in a position of authority who controlled their access to food, clothing, shelter, and medical care. Nonetheless, no other source I know provides as much intimate and longitudinal detail on the lives and relations of poor families. Much of the material in the case records, moreover, inspires confidence. Assuming the agents did not deliberately falsify their reports, readers can separate evaluative comments from reporting of demographic detail, results of interviews, and accounts of activity. Indeed, the ubiquitous internal contradictions and ambiguities reinforce impressions of agents' candor. Agents faithfully reported contradictory statements about behavior and character from landlords, employers, relatives, friends, and neighbors. Despite their efforts to ferret out a consistent picture, agents filled their reports both with the inconsistencies that reflect clients' successful efforts to hide some of their story and with the contradictions coursing through their public as well as their intimate relations. (In this, their stories are not much different from the stories of any of us subjected to similar inquisition.)

Read closely, these case records reveal a great deal; they bring us as close to the lives of very poor families in the past as we can hope to find ourselves. They certainly do not constitute a statistically representative sample of New York City's poor. They tell us little about Jews, who had their own charitable organization, or African Americans, whom most charity neglected. Rather, the families in the case records should be considered representatives of the city's poor: unelected spokespersons for the great parliament of poverty that composed perhaps half the population of this dynamic, rich city. The case records speak to us of the great themes that ran through the lives of most poor families, if not in exactly the same ways. If we listen to these voices, we learn much we otherwise could not know. We learn even from the story of one family—as in the history of the remarkable family related here.

The historian working with case histories confronts a tension between narrative and analysis. The great power of case records lies in their details: the evocative, moving, tangled stories they tell. I worry that heavy-handed analysis could extract their vitality and value by squeezing them into separate, rather abstract categories. Indeed, the wholeness of experience—the artificiality of single perspectives—emerges as one principal lesson of these stories for historians. For this reason, I have chosen the narrative form for this essay. It is a narrative arranged, to be sure, to highlight themes but, at the same time, not to overwhelm them. The narrative is a text that I read in one way; others may read it differently.

The title of this chapter, "Devotion and Ambiguity," highlights two themes that run through both this family's story and the other case histories. This is partly a story of the love and devotion of a mother for her children and a wife for her husband. It is also an illustration of the ambiguity of all relations, including those within the nuclear family, among the members of an extended family, and in the social relations of charity. Rose Warrington's story speaks to us of experiences peculiar to her time as well as of ones that remain timeless. The contrast between Rose's time and ours points to what we have lost as well as gained in the modern welfare state, and it raises questions about alternative roads not taken. In the end, this story prods us to exchange simple and straightforward accounts about the lives of poor people for narratives that stress contradiction, ambiguity, and the strength demanded for survival. It also forces us to reimagine the welfare state.

On the night of March 1, 1918, Miss Ethel Goldman, 242 West 112th Street, telephoned the Joint Application Bureau of the Charity Organization Society (COS) and the New York Association for Improving the Condition of the Poor (AICP).[2] She reported that Rose Warrington, her family's former laundress, now eight months pregnant, had been deserted by her husband several months ago. Although they could manage overnight, the family needed help, and Miss Goldman asked that a visitor go to them in the morning. Early the next day, the bureau telephoned a request for an emergency investigation to the COS's Harlem District.

When the COS visitor called on the Warringtons at 2451 Second Avenue, "a low grade tenement house," she found them living in three rooms in the rear of the first floor.[3] The rooms were damp, "cold and dark and very dismal and cheerless," with the only window giving direct air opening onto the yard. As early as 1899, twenty families on the rolls of the COS and AICP had lived there, and twelve had dwelled next door at 2449. Together, the two tenements formed the most visible pocket of extreme poverty on their block.[4]

Mrs. Warrington and her four children—Rose, 10; Daniel, 8; Sadie, 5; and John, 4—slept in one bed in a front room; too damp for sleeping, the back room, ventilated only by an air shaft, had been unusable throughout the winter. The apartment contained almost no furniture, and what there was looked "battered and worn." Because Mrs. Warrington worked a few hours a day as housekeeper for the tenement, the family lived rent free. With no options, Mrs. Warrington had not protested when the landlady, unable to rent the ground floor, had moved the family from an apartment on a higher floor into their current rooms. Nonetheless, the landlady treated the Warringtons kindly, promising to replace the gas stove with a coal stove, which would heat and dry the rooms, offering to find someone to do the sweeping during Mrs. Warrington's confinement, and not objecting when Rose left the building to work.

Rose Warrington and her family lived in a microcosm of working-class Manhattan, a neighborhood jammed with tenements, small stores, and saloons that undermines images of New York City as divided into ethnic ghettos.[5] Their five-story, stone-fronted brick tenement, the second building on the block of Second Avenue north of 125th Street, occupied a lot 25 feet wide and 74 feet deep with a store in front. With its lot assessed at only $8,500, or $17,000 including the tenement, it was among the least valuable buildings on a modest block.[6] Unlike many tenements, however, its owner, 57-year-old Ralph Giuliani, an immigrant stonecutter from Italy, lived on the premises with his wife and five children, of whom three worked. As was common in the neighborhood, none of the families in the Warringtons' building included lodgers, servants, or relatives other than parents and unmarried children. Among those in the fourteen families crowded into the tenement a few years before the Warringtons' arrival were an Austrian railroad guard, a German widow, an American widow, an Austrian waiter, an Italian driver, a Hungarian printer, a Russian railway conductor, an Austrian woman who ran a fruit store, an American driver for an express company, a Finnish carpenter, a Finnish stonecutter, an Italian tailor, and an American laborer on the subway. This ethnic diversity and mix of non-industrial working-class occupations reflected the composition of the neighborhood, with the notable exception of the block of East 127th Street south of Third Avenue, where nearly all the residents were black.[7]

Like other tenement districts, the Warringtons' neighborhood compressed people and businesses into crowded streets with little open space. Immediately to the south, separated by a sliver of empty lot, the next tenement, also five stories, with a saloon, faced 125th Street on a narrow, eighteen-foot lot. Another saloon shared the three-story frame house on the corner of 126th Street, and there were stores both in the three-story brick dumbbell tenements attached to the north side of their building and in the five-story tenement between it and the corner, with a small one-story frame dwelling tucked behind it.[8] The elevated railway separated them from the houses across Second Avenue. Between Second and Third Avenues, 125th Street contained six brick tenements, all with stores; on 126th Street in the same block, four of the six buildings, five dumbbell tenements, and a one-story brick dwelling also housed stores. Saloons occupied part of the two- and three-story buildings on the corners of the block of Third Avenue between 125th and 126th Streets, which they shared with four small wooden and a one-story brick building. In each of them was a store.

Institutions of education, religion, charity, and police permeated working-class neighborhoods. A large public school on the south side of 126th Street, between Second and Third Avenues, was the major local institution; a public library occupied a building in the middle of the block's south side. On the north side of 125th were Cook's Auction Rooms and a garage with a 100-foot frontage (the only fireproofed building on the block). Wedged behind them were another one-story frame house and a wooden stable. Also close at hand were the police and charity: the headquarters of the 43rd precinct at 148 126th Street, the Salvation Army at 157 125th, and the Tenth District Office of the COS on 125th near Fifth Avenue. Two Catholic Churches served the district, Holy Rosary on 119th Street, between First and Pleasant Avenues, and Our Lady Queen of the Angels at 228 East 113th Street, with a parochial school attached.

Interspersed with residences and retail were industry and entertainment providing job opportunities, noise, pollution, and fantasy. What working-class neighborhoods lacked, however, was open space. With elevated trains running along Second and Third Avenues, transportation dominated the neighborhood. The freight yards of the Pennsylvania Railroad were across First Avenue, facing the Harlem River; the inspection sheds of the Interborough Rapid Transit Co. were on the north side of 128th Street; and the depot of the Third Avenue Railway Corporation was at 129th Street and Third Avenue. Only a few substantial industries were nearby: Edwin's Cigar Factory on the southwest corner of 127th and Third Avenue; the Goodyear Rubber Insulation Company on Park Avenue between 131st and 132nd Streets; the Mattress Manufactory on the north side of 128th Street near Third Avenue; two ironworks on 122nd and 123nd Streets; a major lumber yard fronting on First Avenue between 126th and 127th Streets; Carolyn Laundry, occupying a 100-foot wide lot stretching between 128th and 129th Street, behind Park Avenue. On Park Avenue, in the same block, Gristede Brothers operated a large (probably wholesale) grocery, and the International Film Company Moving Picture Studio consumed the entire block of Second Avenue between 126th and 127th Streets. With the Palace Theatre on Second Avenue between 123d and 124th Streets, the 125th Street Theatre between Lexington and Third; and Proctor's enormous theater stretching from 124th to 125th Streets on the block between Park and Lexington, mass entertainment was close at hand. The only park, however, was a small patch at 129th Street and Third Avenue in the shadow of a bridge.

Rose Warrington, 40 years old, born to a Catholic family in Jersey City, was "rather large" with black hair and black eyes. Although neither she nor her children were clean, young Sadie and John, with light brown hair, dressed in brown overalls, looked "very cunning," indeed, "like little cherubs." Unable to work any longer because of her pregnancy, Mrs. Warrington had borrowed a little "here and there"; Miss Goldman had given her some money; and the Morningside Girls Club occasionally sent food. Otherwise, she had no income. Until his desertion, she had managed on the income of her husband, Daniel, a plumber's helper, but one morning Daniel went to look for work and never returned.

Daniel Warrington, 50 years old, had been devoted to his children, asserted his wife. Earlier, his drinking had aggravated a chronic heart condition. Warned by doctors at the Lebanon Hospital that his drinking would kill him, Daniel had tapered off. Although he went out evenings with a few men, he always returned early. Out of work for a few months, he and Rose quarreled from time to time, but she had no idea why he had left home. Indeed, she believed him either sick or dead.

Daniel was not her first husband. Rose's parents had died when she was four years old. She then went to live with her only relative, a sister in New York City. When Rose was fourteen, her sister died, and she moved in as a servant in the home of an old woman next door. With almost no schooling, illiterate, unable even to sign her name, she remained there until at the age of 18 she married George Jackson, who worked for the Street Cleaning Department. Together, they had four surviving children and one who died. Then, suddenly, in 1907, after an illness of only two weeks, George Jackson died of "galloping consumption," leaving only a purse collected by his workmates. Within two years, eager to find a father for her children, she married her lodger, Daniel Warrington, a Protestant. Daniel also had been married before. He and his former wife kept a saloon for ten years until his drinking became intolerable and she left him; now, her former marriage a secret from her neighbors, she lived with another man as his wife. Daniel's drinking cost him work, as well. A talented plumber and, when sober, an excellent, reliable workman, he was fired reluctantly by employers no longer willing to tolerate his periodic sprees.

Despite Daniel's desertion, Rose remained devoted to him. She refused to go to Domestic Relations Court to prosecute him for nonsupport.[9] (Her reluctance puzzled the visitor, who asked Miss Goldman "to help us to get at the real reason for her reluctance, for I feel sure there is one.") When someone suggested the child with whom she was pregnant might not be his, Rose's niece replied "She would have nothing to do with anyone else if he were living." She was so devoted to him, said her niece, that "she stood his abuse and ugly ways to such an extent" that she and Mabel, Rose's eldest daughter, "could not bear to go there." Indeed, Daniel's and Rose's relations often had been violent. A succession of former landlords remembered them well. One, an old German woman, hearing their name, "threw up her hands and exclaimed, 'pigs, nothing but dirty pigs.'" They had lived in her house only two weeks, "quarreling and drinking and having company all the time, who drank and swore and she was disgusted with both of them. They went around half clothed and made such an uproar that the whole neighborhood was upset." Another housekeeper recalled that "they had nearly broken her heart, for she had tried to help them and they had treated her 'so mean.' The man was half drunk when he came. . . . For two months things went very well, the people and rooms were clean but after a while they began to drink and things were very bad. They had a great many people in drinking with them and the noise and swearing were frightful. The only word she could call the people were 'bums.'"

At first, the Warringtons lived with her four children and an orphaned niece, who, Rose thought, corrupted Mabel. After the birth of her first daughter with Daniel, according to Rose, she did not want to mix the children from her two marriages because her husband never had cared for his stepchildren. At the time, she had to work, and the children "grew very wild out in the streets, especially the eldest girl Mabel," about 13 years old. "So someone complained and the judge told her she had better commit the children. He told her she was doing wrong to keep [young] Rose but she wanted to have one child left." In fact, in April 1910, Miss Murray from Public School 38 had reported to the AICP that Rose was keeping one child home to care for the younger ones while she went out to work. The AICP's visitor, who found the rooms very dirty, advised her to have her children vaccinated and placed in a day nursery. A follow-up visit found the family evicted for drinking and disorderly conduct.

Convinced of the neglect of the children, the AICP reported the family to the Society for the Prevention of Cruelty to Children (SPCC), which prosecuted the case successfully.[10] The two boys went to Lincolndale Agricultural School and the two girls to the New York Catholic Protectory.[11] Rose reconciled herself to the loss of her children. They were, she said, better off, "getting a good education. William cut off his right thumb when he was seven years old and she was glad to have him educated so he could work in an office." (The name and fate of the second boy are not known.) Mabel, soon old enough to work, left the orphanage to enter service. Florence, four years younger, remained there until she was fourteen, when she was placed with a family who treated her like a daughter. The boys remained in Lincolndale. The niece, Grace, who was older, had married and stayed in intermittent touch with Mabel.

Despite her loosened attachment to the children of her first marriage, Rose remained devoted to the children of her second, afraid, constantly, of losing them to the SPCC. She feared that the real purpose of the COS visit was to snatch her children. When Miss Goldman visited her on March 7, she found her "in a heart broken condition because the children were to be taken away. She said she would die." She refused the repeated advice of the COS visitor to give birth in a hospital or clinic because, despite all the assurances she received, she still feared her children would not be returned from the institutions in which they would be placed during her absence. "I have worked so hard all winter to take care of them," Rose told the COS visitor, "it would break my heart to have them taken away." When the visitor explained the only circumstances that would lead a court to commit them, her relief was "very great," though not sufficient to agree to leave them to enter a hospital. An old woman friend helped deliver her baby at home on April 6 before a doctor arrived. The baby, who appeared healthy, suddenly died in July, again leaving Rose heartbroken.

Despite her history, no COS visitor could fault her care for her children now. One found them "bright and well behaved. They dust off a chair each time for the vis., and [young] Rose seems a very capable child. They mind their mother instantly and seem very fond of her." Nor did her own lack of education leave her indifferent to her children's. In fact, she learned "a good deal from little Rose. Every afternoon after she has played, she comes in at half past four, while it is daylight and she and her mother do the lessons together. The woman was pathetic in her pleasure at learning to spell out a few words." "I know how hard it is to get on without schooling," she told the visitor, "and I don't intend my children shall have to. And it isn't right for children to go to work so young either." Her lack of education and experience had left Rose insecure in dealing with the world outside her home. When the COS visitor took her to a clinic, "She felt badly that she had no hat but brushed her hair neatly and tied a black scarf over her head. She had never been to a clinic before [although she had given birth to nine children] and when she reached the door was shaking with nervousness. She insisted that the visitor sit with her until her time came."

Rose Warrington also cared about her home. One day the visitor found her especially excited. The landlady had said she should move back upstairs so that she could rent the ground floor rooms and the store in front of them together. In the past week Rose had "worked very hard putting up curtains and pictures and straightening out the cupboard." She insisted on showing the visitor the rooms she soon would occupy, which "had all been cleaned and painted." The upstairs apartment consisted of a "fair-sized" front room "with two big windows on Second Ave., a kitchen back of that with a coal range and wash tubs and a bedroom with window opening on an air shaft." They were, in every way, better than the rooms in which she had been living. On another occasion, Rose showed the visitor "all the improvements she had made. The bed was in the front room covered with a red quilt. The mantle shelf had a pink drape with a clock and pictures. Then there were a great many pictures on the walls and the floor was scrubbed clean." Five days before the birth of her child, the visitor found Rose cleaning her home "which looked very well." In July a "change in the rooms" surprised a different visitor, for Rose had furnished and arranged them "very attractively." A departing tenant had left a "couch, a couple of rocking chairs and material for making table covers." She had moved the bed out of the front room and replaced it with the couch. "The rocking chairs and table cover and couch changed the appearance of the room entirely."

Rose was both superstitious and ingenious. Once the visitor found her trembling. A thunderstorm had frightened her "and she was sure the end of the world was coming soon." When she complained of trouble with her eyesight, she recounted for the visitor her brief episode of blindness as a child, cured, she said, when she prayed at a shrine. With little money during the winter, she managed to keep her rooms comfortable: "She had seen in the paper that waste papers wadded up tight gave out a lot of heat, so all winter she had carried in all the waste rags and paper from the barrels and burned them, keeping her rooms fairly warm even when she did not get coal."

Rose Warrington was rarely frank with COS visitors. Worried always about hostile authorities, dependent frequently on arousing sympathy, deception had become a reflex. At one point she and Daniel had tried to evade authorities by living under a pseudonym, Smith, and Daniel apparently had said he would not willingly give his real name to an employer. At the time her husband left, an agent of the "Gerry Society" (the nickname among the poor for the SPCC) had visited Rose at her home, 253 E. 125th Street, and she feared he would try to take away her children. She told him she intended to sell her furniture and use the money to rent furnished rooms. However, after she moved into two basement rooms on 124th Street, two men from the Gerry Society returned to tell her she could not keep her children in furnished rooms. So she "dropped out and told the neighbors not to tell anything about her when the men inquired, so they never found her again." For a while she lived with a friend on the top floor of 253 E. 125th Street; from there she found her current position as a housekeeper at 2451 Second Avenue. At first, Rose tried to conceal both these episodes and, indeed, her former marriage from the COS. Whether Rose and Daniel, or for that matter Rose and her former husband, ever had legally married remained another gray area. COS visitors never could find documentation of either marriage and, despite her protests, refused to believe they had taken place. Nor did they believe she revealed to them all her sources of income. COS visitors also remained deeply suspicious of her relations with Mr. Auclaire, a former neighbor, who visited frequently and gave her money.

Mr. Auclaire, a painter, was working at the School of the Sisters of St. Cecilia, 118 E. 106th Street. There, the "dignified, sweet-faced sister in charge" replied to the COS visitor's questions that she had known him for years as "a quiet, respectable workman whom she often employed when she needed interior painting done." He had told the sister about Mrs. Warrington, asking one day for his pay in order to help her. Summoned by the sister, Mr. Auclaire appeared before the visitor, a "small frail looking man, past middle age. His clothes splashed with white paint. His voice was very low and husky and it was difficult at times to understand him." Until the previous August, he had lived across the hall from the Warringtons with a Mrs. Kathleen Campbell.

During this time Daniel Warrington had been depressed by his lack of work. Although he took an occasional drink, he "never became violently drunk." One morning he asked Mr. Auclaire for carfare to Brooklyn, where he wanted to look for work. Unsuccessful, he returned that night. After another week or so at home, one Monday morning in June he went out, never to return again. Worried about him, Mr. Auclaire called on his former employer, who knew nothing of his whereabouts. Shortly afterward, Mrs. Campbell entered the hospital and died, and, after the funeral, he moved away. Still "exceedingly sorry" for Mrs. Warrington, he continued to give her money many times. "Not a little just five dollars now and then, but more than any one will ever know. Being a single man he did not need so much for himself." Rose Warrington, he stressed, "was devoted to her children and would certainly die if they were taken from her. Any help that was given her was fully deserved."

Although the record suggests only friendship and generosity in Mr. Auclaire's relations with Rose, COS visitors still had reason to question her answers to their questions, for, at the first interview, she lied when she told the visitor that her husband had no relatives. Despite her denials, before long the COS visitor tracked down one of Daniel's former employers, who told her of a brother, Sam, also a plumber, who lived in Yonkers. After a difficult search, the Yonkers COS found Sam and visited him. He was, according to his employer, "of no account, an habitual drunkard, who is willing to work for just enough money to enable him to get drunk when the work is finished." Sam, "very deaf and rather an interesting character," once owned a prosperous plumbing business, which he lost through drink. Returning "the compliment to his employer," he described his brother as always "a tramp, a good-for-nothing ne'er-do-well," roaming all over the country since boyhood. Sam and Daniel had two unmarried sisters and another brother whose address he refused to give the COS without their permission.

Nonetheless, the COS visitor traced the Warrington sisters to 1074 Intervale Avenue in the Bronx and, on her second visit, found one Miss Warrington at home. "She was a slender, hollow-chested woman, past middle age, her face colorless but with clear-cut features, and fine greyish brown hair. Her hands were knarled with rheumatism and her faded blue eyes looked directly at vis., her firmly closed lips showing a resolution not to speak until she knew definitely what was wanted. The room was comfortably furnished with big chairs upholstered in old fashioned silk coverings, the big sofa had a well-made linen slipcover. There were long lace curtains in the bow window, where two American flags were crossed over the blue and white square of membership card. The pictures and ornaments showed the family taste was better than most. Miss Warrington lighted a small oil heater, though the sun was shining brightly into the room. Vis. told of the condition of the Daniel Warrington family. Miss Warrington listened in silence then gave the following facts."

Daniel had been born in New York City; he was one of four brothers and two sisters. He was a fine mechanic whose slide began when he married his first wife, who started him drinking. Contrary to what Sam said, she emphasized, Daniel never had been a rover; Sam simply did not know him very well. At one time, the family set him up as a mechanic in the Bronx, but his drinking lost him the business. They had heard rumors that he had a second family somewhere, but they only learned the truth for certain the preceding April when Rose visited them because Daniel had been missing from home for a week. In that instance, he had been working away somewhere on a job and returned.

About two months later, Rose came back, reporting he had gone again. Miss Warrington had not heard from her since. At the time, the brother who lived with the sisters had been ill with asthma for about a year; their 89-year-old mother had died the year before. "With the sorrow and worry Miss Warrington was so worn out" that Rose's story proved "too much for her and she sent her away saying she could stand nothing more." Like Rose, she was certain something had happened to Daniel: he knew his brother had but a short time to live. The two funerals left the Warrington sisters short of money. They were thinking of moving into a smaller and less expensive place. The second sister worked in an office, and the two of them survived only with the help of a brother in Brooklyn. When the COS visitor suggested that the sisters send groceries or bedding or some clothes, Miss Warrington agreed to talk with her sister that night. "She mentioned that her name was Sarah and blushed with shy pleasure that the little girl Sadie might have been named for her. She said she had thought of it."

Sarah Warrington was a religious enthusiast, interested in the Adventist lectures given daily in the Bronx, whose theories she described to the visitor. Rose Warrington's niece, Mrs. Ghent, did not believe the Misses Warrington were as poor as they protested. They were, she said, stingy and "too strict in their religious views." With this encouragement, the COS visitor once again called on the Misses Warrington to urge them to help Rose. She found the "house uncomfortably clean. They have gathered together all the old Warrington relics, plush furniture and queer old pictures." To her surprise, the visitor found the sisters had been sending food anonymously every two weeks (Rose thought the food came from a nursery); undoubtedly afraid of further demands, they did not want her to know its source, and they refused to visit. "Miss Warrington shuts her mouth very firmly and says that she would not consider for a moment going to see Mrs. Warrington; that her religious views are too strict to permit of this and that she is not her brother's wife anyway." Nonetheless, when she spoke of the children, her manner softened. "She is evidently very fond of them and would love to have the little boy whom she understands is her brother's living image."

Rose Warrington's niece and older daughters remained the only other relatives who could possibly help. The COS visitor found the niece, Mrs. Ghent, at home at 320 E. 157th Street. She had started a garden, and, although her house looked "filthy and in great disorder," she appeared interested in her home. At first she claimed to know nothing about Mabel, the eldest daughter; later she said she thought Mabel lived at service, earning only twelve dollars a month, too little to help her mother, to which the COS visitor replied, "there was no excuse for a girl of her age earning so little." Mrs. Ghent told the visitor more about Rose's history. Her first husband, she said, was "one grand man," sober, steady, always turning in his earnings to his wife. Nonetheless, Rose cared more for Daniel. She would "run to get to him if she thought he was anywhere around." Daniel, she said, had started Rose drinking. Mrs. Ghent had seen Daniel "absolutely insist upon her drinking with him." Had she been allowed to keep her children and not married her lodger, "everything would have gone well and . . . today she would be receiving a widow's pension."[12] Still, Rose was "a hard woman to deal with . . . very quarrelsome." The reason her relations with Mabel had deteriorated reflected "more her fault than the girl's." Mrs. Ghent had meant to visit, but her own girl had been ill.

Although the COS visitor never found her, Mabel's relations with her mother improved. She began to visit her often, sometimes giving her money. The visitor did succeed in tracing Florence, Rose's other daughter from her first marriage, to her home with the Murphys at 1214 St. Lawrence, Westchester. Florence had believed her mother dead. When the COS visitor left Mrs. Murphy no choice but to tell her otherwise, Florence replied that she considered the Murphys her real parents, and they, in turn, offered to adopt her to prevent her return to her mother. Indeed, Mrs. Murphy and Florence had grown as close as mother and daughter. They shared the housework. By two in the afternoon, their work finished, they sat "on the porch sewing and reading together." When Florence had been at Fordham Hospital for an appendectomy in the spring, Mr. Murphy visited her every day, bringing flowers or some other "token of his affection." Mrs. Murphy gave the visitor "many examples of her splendid traits, such as steadfastness, stability, honorableness, sensitiveness, respectfulness, honesty, and her sense of humor." Unable to praise her enough, Mrs. Murphy ended by saying "she had no idea children would ever be as wonderful." When Florence arrived, "looking very neat in her clean white skirt and middy . . . all enthusiasm over a pianist she had just heard," she listened with interest to the visitor's "mission" but could offer no information. She had been only eight when she entered the Protectorate and scarcely had seen her mother since. She only remembered moving frequently, carrying furniture from house to house, and Mr. Warrington's "coming to the house frequently while her father was sick." Her last memory was "her mother's bringing her to the Protectorate where she left her rarely coming to see her again." Florence closed the interview, taking the visitor to the door, "telling what good times 'her' family had picnicking and reading in the woods opposite their home."

As the visitor discovered more about Rose's past, she returned to confront Rose with the inconsistencies in her statements. When the visitor first mentioned the SPCC, Rose's "manner changed, her head moved restlessly and she kept rubbing her hands together." The visitor explained that "so long as she was sober and well behaved nothing could happen" to her children, and, as she talked, "the tension grew much less . . . and visitor felt that woman realized that people were doing their best to help her, and that she had a chance to start over and make good." Later, as she talked about the children from her first marriage, Rose "cried . . . a few hard tears which she rubbed away with her hands." By the middle of June, the visitor knew enough to tell Rose that her "lack of frankness" hampered attempts to help her. She had, said the visitor, heard "pretty damaging things" about Rose, and it would be best for her to tell everything.

At first, "surprised and . . . a little angry," Rose could not understand who had told such stories about her "unless it happened to be a few enemies and she had a number of them who liked to say things that were not so." She had always been a good woman and a good mother to her children, said Rose, as she started to weep. Still, the visitor pressed. She could find no record of Rose's marriages and advised her to admit the truth, which "would not interfere with plans for her in the least." Rose, however, insisted she had been married but had lost her marriage license in the course of moving so many times. The visitor countered with Rose's initial attempt to cover up her first marriage; Rose responded she had done so because she did not want to "drag" her children "into the affair." When the visitor turned to accusations of heavy drinking, Rose denied them. "Some times perhaps a few people were in there and they had a little beer but never enough to become intoxicated." By this point, Rose "was weeping so hard she could scarcely talk." Nonetheless, by the end of the visit she "cheered up," responding "she was glad she had had this talk with visitor."

Whatever they might think of her character, Rose and her children needed help, and the COS orchestrated a campaign of modest support. Its paid visitor enlisted Ethel Goldman as a volunteer friendly visitor to offer advice and support. Told the results of the COS investigation, Miss Goldman replied that Rose was "much to be admired if she has lived thru such a very trying past and is now making such an effort to care for her children." Her family, Miss Goldman said, could afford only modest assistance, though she gave the Warringtons $5.00 from time to time. Ethel, who was 20 years old, also lived in a tenement with her parents and nine siblings, but they were a much more prosperous family as were their predominantly Jewish neighbors. Tenements housed working- and lower-middle-class families as well as the poor. Ethel's father, Siskind, a jobber, had emigrated from Russia in 1875; her oldest brother and sister, still living at home, were schoolteachers; other brothers were a salesman, manager, and jobber, and one sister was a stenographer. Heading the other families in her building (only one of whom contained a lodger) were all men: a German of unspecified occupation, a Russian embroiderer, a Hungarian cutter, an American manufacturer with a live-in servant, a Hungarian restaurant kitchenman, an American confectioner, a Rumanian designer, and a Hungarian in real estate.[13]

The COS also persuaded the local Catholic Church, which paid for the baby's funeral, to give two dollars a week; the society bought milk for the family and agreed to a temporary pension of five dollars a week from its own funds. The visitor figured the Warrington weekly budget as follows: food, $6.50; gas, coal, $1.25; clothing, $1.25; sundries, $1.00. Against this outlay of $10.00 it projected an income of $2.00 from the Church; $2.10 for milk; and $5.00 from the COS for a total of $9.10. The visitor remained silent about how she would make up for the shortfall of $.90, believing as she did, probably correctly, that Rose had sources of income she did not disclose.

When the COS committee voted aid for Rose, it instructed its visitor to tell her that the purpose of the aid, which was not permanent, was to help her "over her confinement . . . and that this is conditional on her complete confidence." After the birth of her child, the committee voted to continue aid "with the understanding that woman would do everything in her power to help us find the man." To help the COS locate her husband, Rose would have to go to court and prosecute him. Throughout the spring, Rose promised to go to court but never could find the time. Finally, in July, the visitor told her she had waited long enough. Either she would go this week, or her allowance from the COS would end. Rose remained "silent for several minutes, looked pensively out the window and finally said she would 'sooner not go to court.'" Her real reason, she said, "was that she considered it a disgrace." She did not want her name in court. When the visitor replied her name was there already, Rose replied that Mabel would consider it a disgrace and had begged her not to go; her niece also had advised against it. Unimpressed, the visitor "urged her to tell the real reason as she felt sure there was something else besides the relatives' opinion." Rose replied that she felt it would do no good; Daniel, she believed, was dead. She started to weep, stopped suddenly, and asked the visitor, "but if you do stop giving aid, you will come to see me just the same, won't you?" The visitor promised and asked Rose how she would manage. Rose replied that she had scraped along some way before and would do the same now. "She appreciated all that had been done for her and would never forget the kindness of the COS."

Rose remained steadfast. A week later she again told the visitor "she would sooner not go" and preferred to manage as well as she could without "bothering about court." She planned to put the children in a day nursery and go to work. Still, the COS persisted, writing to the visitor from All Saints Church to encourage him to persuade Rose to go to court. Throughout the fall, visitors continued to press relatives for information and call on Rose. In early October, when the visitor asked her how she was managing, Rose, though reluctant to discuss her earnings, assured the visitor "that everything was going nicely. She said, 'Look at my children. Do they look starved? You can see by them that they are kept all right.'"

When the visitor paid her December call, she found no one at home. Looking through a crack in the door, she saw the rooms were empty. The landlord told her that Daniel Warrington had returned suddenly and the family had moved two weeks ago. The visitor found her in an "old, but well kept building" at 2487 Second Avenue. The family's new home in a neighborhood close in ethnic and occupational mix, as well as location, to its previous residence was a five-story brick dumbbell tenement, the second house from the corner north of 127th Street, with the ubiquitous store. Eight brick tenements attached to each other composed the block. The six middle ones contained stores, the two on the corner, saloons. Across Second Avenue on the other side of the tracks, the block remained almost empty with nearly no buildings between it and the river. On Third Avenue between 127th and 128th Streets, saloons occupied the two corner tenements and stores the eight tenements between them. Only two stores shared space in the buildings on 127th Street between Third and Second Avenues, which contained five large dumbbell tenements, a series of smaller brick ones, two small frame structures, and a garage with 100-foot frontage on the block.[14]

When the visitor arrived, Rose Warrington cried out, "oh my husband has come home." Daniel was "a tall, well built, jolly, happy-go-lucky-sort of a man with iron grey hair, and twinkling brown eyes." He greeted the visitor "cordially," thanking her over and over for what she had done for his family. He would, he said, "make good"; his "roving days" were over. Not always the "best in the world," now he never would "cause his wife another sorrow." Reluctant to talk of his experiences since he left New York, he insisted on a celebration and "rushed downstairs to buy some cakes." When he had gone, Rose told the visitor that on his arrival in New York, Daniel had gone straight to his sisters' to learn his family's address and "rushed to see her immediately." A couple of days later they moved to their current apartment, "four light rooms, railroad style . . . two stories above the elevated train tracks." Not bothered by noise, they especially enjoyed the lack of buildings across the street and their unimpeded view of the Harlem River.

When Daniel returned, he told the visitor he had been to Illinois and then to West Virginia, where he "worked at his own trade" and earned "quite a stake." Now, he said, Rose could "take it easy." The children were "very fond" of their father, and Rose, "radiantly happy" and "very proud of her husband," watched him "admiringly" as he talked. Again, Daniel repeated how grateful he was to the COS and gave the visitor five dollars. He wanted to know how much had been spent altogether and to pay it back. He invited the visitor "to drop in any time she was in the neighborhood and have a cup of tea." When the visitor returned just after Christmas to check on the family, she found the living room filled with "Christmas presents and toys of all sorts and descriptions." Daniel, undoubtedly prospering from the labor-scarce wartime economy, was working, though Rose did not know where.

While the visitor was there, Daniel returned and "immediately wanted to give visitor some refreshments and brought out some sassaparilla, cake and candy." A man who liked to "talk a great deal," Daniel told the visitor he had left to give his wife "a lesson." Now that he had returned "she appreciates him and does not allow others to interfere." Puzzled, Rose asked her husband whom he meant; she could think only of her niece. He replied, all those people who tried to tell her how "to run her husband. He said she started to take their advice and he got disgusted and left." Although garrulous, Daniel resented being questioned, and when the visitor asked a question, he changed the subject. Not giving his wife "much chance to say anything, every time she protested he silenced her, then added that 'she was the best little girl in the world now,' and that she would never have to work again." Later, in the hall, Rose told the visitor Daniel liked "to talk big" and did "not realize what a struggle" she had waged. Mabel, she said, was coming to visit in a few days, and she wanted her to meet the visitor, who said she would be glad to come. As they parted, Rose told the visitor she "felt so much different" about her "calling to see her now because she . . . was not coming 'on business' but now was a friend."

Friend or not, the visitor reported events to the local Catholic priest, Father Deevy. The COS, she stressed, never had been able to verify the couple's marriage, and she asked him to take the question up with them. Despite her promise, the visitor did not call on the family again for six months. When she did, she found Rose cleaning and the "place in fairly good order." Daniel was working as a plumber, earning about five dollars a day. Nonetheless, Rose "was very angry" that the visitor had spoken to Father Deevy, who had called to talk with the couple about their marriage. She insisted "they were married" and resented "very much the fact that we should believe otherwise." When the former district secretary returned to the COS office in two weeks, she intended to complain. Although she appreciated the COS's efforts and thanked the visitor for coming, this time she did not invite her to return.

By reporting its doubts about the couple's marriage to the church, wrote a member of the district staff, the COS had eroded its previously friendly relations and "destroyed our cooperation with the family so that supervision is difficult." In these circumstances, with the family "about as well off as they have ever been," the district closed the case.

Rose Warrington's story can be read in many ways. Because we cannot know what happened after the COS closed her case, we are not sure that the ending is happy—if Daniel remained at home, a faithful husband and father and steady provider. We do know that Rose had proved herself a woman with a remarkable capacity for commitment and survival, full of grit and determination, never beaten down by circumstances or the pressures of organized charity. Rose defied stereotypes. Everyone, it seems, wanted to put her in a pigeonhole: a former landlady thought she and Daniel were drunken ne'er-do-wells, her in-laws dismissed her as immoral, child-saving agents thought her an inadequate mother. But Rose loved her children and her husband; she took pride in the appearance of her home; she encouraged the education of her little daughter. When the well-being of her children was at stake, she made difficult decisions, even if it meant losing them; she chose giving up aid from organized charity when its agents made relief contingent on following advice she felt was wrong. Somehow she always managed to have food on the table and to pay the rent.

Rose's story is not unlike many others today. When we push through derogatory popular images, real people usually fail to match the stereotypes of "welfare mothers." We find in their lives mixtures of devotion and ambiguity rather like Rose's as well as survival skills that often leave us in awe. The complex relations among clients, charity, and the state in Rose's story also find present-day echoes in the experience of women who, like her, walk the fine lines between compliance and resistance and between candor and concealment, manipulating the system even as they are buffeted and manipulated by it.

Of course, Rose's story seems distant in many ways. In an age when most "welfare mothers" are not married and fathers are reluctant to acknowledge paternity, the concern of the COS and the Catholic Church with the legality of her marriage seems a quaint and offensive example of prying. Today, in most states, Rose could count on Temporary Assistance for Needy Families for five years; she and her children would receive food stamps and Medicaid. When she was pregnant, she would have been eligible for WIC (Special Supplemental Nutrition Program for Women, Infants, and Children). She probably could find public subsidies for daycare, and, if she found a job, she could claim the Earned Income Tax Credit. Nothing remotely like this set of current-day supports—limited as they are—was in place in the early twentieth century. Yet, there were losses as well as gains when the state replaced charity as the primary dispenser of relief. Without eligibility rules, late-nineteenth- and early-twentieth-century charity agents personally determined need on a case-by-case basis and followed clients by visiting them in their homes, not waiting for them to appear at an office. Although an arbitrary personalism suffused organized charity with class and cultural bias, its representatives felt responsible for attending to the needs of clients for housing, medical care, and work as well as food and cash relief.

In the modern welfare state, eligibility rules govern interactions. Clients today receive help not as the result of a personal and comprehensive review of their situation but because eligibility workers decide that they match criteria of need defined and imposed by the state. If they fail to appear for appointments with eligibility workers, clients face losing their benefits.

The modern welfare state has transformed clients into bundles of quantifiable characteristics, not individuals with infinitely varying personalities and circumstances. It would be wrong to wax nostalgic about the days of the COS and "friendly visitors"—marked, as they were, by condescension, moral rigidity, and inadequate material help. Yet, their history does raise questions about what we have developed in their place.

CHAPTER 11

Reflections on Education as Transcendence

John Meyer

It is common, in both social theory and public discourse, to take a realist view of modern education. In this view, education arises from the needs and interests of society, seen as a real functioning system of interdependent power and exchange. And education functions to produce and reproduce the individual components of society, again seen as a hard-wired functioning system. A central theme of this book is that education should and historically does function in this way, though it is at present under threat of serving individual interests independent from the common good of society (see the Introduction). No alternative to a picture of education as functioning for the real-world needs of society is considered.

Many versions of functional models exist, differing in political perspective more than in underlying analytic content. Classic liberal (e.g., American) functionalism imagines that education and changes in education arise from the developing requirements for individuals in the complex and differentiated society: requirements for changing, complex, and diverse skills but also for integrating cultural material. Education then serves, more or less efficiently, to produce these outcomes. In this tradition, much liberal criticism arises about educational inefficiency (the sin of sloth) and inequity (the sin of injustice—especially stressed in the chapters of this book), and much urgent reform is proposed.

Views from the more critical left are also broadly functionalist but imagine that the society for which education functions is fundamentally distorted by exploitive social and especially economic power. Substantively, the arguments do not differ much from the liberal or centrist view.

Education is produced and changed by the interests and forces that domi-nate society, including economic powers but perhaps also the educators themselves as part of an elite structure (see Kantor and Lowe, Chap. 7, in this volume). This highly asymmetric system functionally requires edu-cation to maintain differentiation (vertical differentiation and stratifica-tion are especially stressed), and to provide an integrating legitimating culture (hegemony is the term used). And it functions just so: reproduc-ing elites and providing a legitimating culture absorbing potential resis-tance.

A really critical conservative right is weak in all modern societies, and especially so in the United States (Hartz 1955). What conservatism existed (e.g., in Southern models of society that resisted the extension of education to the peasantry) was practically destroyed in the Civil War (see Mitchell, Chap. 2, in this volume). But the outlines are clear: expanded education is produced by political and market forces that destroy community, and it functions to serve the new leviathan. The argument is essentially the same as the centrist one; it simply involves a much darker view of the new func-tional system.

As a theoretically eclectic historian, David Tyack has always taken very seriously the roots of education in interests and powers and functional requirements of society (and/or some dominating elites). Thus, in his clas-sic *The One Best System* (1974), the functional problems posed (variously for society and for its traditional elites) by urban complexity and mass immigration lead to models of centralized organizational control. These models rationalize education around the needs of society for differentiated personnel and the needs of elites for stable class reproduction. And they maintain the cultural coherence and dominance required in the system.

PERIPHERALIZATION OF THE TRANSCENDENT

All these analyses—and the modern culture that parallels them—em-phasize the real-world significance of education, in both its roots and its consequences. They contrast strikingly with earlier emphases on educa-tion as relating the young to God more than to fallen mankind, and to the spirit of nature more than to the grubby empirical world of action.

The religious origins and nature of education are very striking, both at mass and elite levels. In modern analyses, and in the structure of content of modern education itself, they seem to have disappeared in an avalanche of secularization.

What role does religion now play in our analyses? Principally, it is reduced to one of the multiple factors that may affect the educational system. Religious interests may affect or constrain instruction—creating church-run versions of secularized education and affecting at the margins the content of the curriculum (on issues like evolution, sexual behavior, and artistic depiction). Or, more fundamentally and constitutively, dominant religious values may help motivate educational expansion, infuse it with some special orientations, or affect its structure.

In these respects, religious influences are given continuing and careful attention in Tyack's work. American Protestant notions of gender equality encourage coeducation (Tyack and Hansot 1990). Protestant ministers and values, particularly in this country, create an emphasis on the Kingdom of God in the common school (Tyack 1966b). These forces play an important role in the spread of education in the American West (Tyack 1978; Meyer et al. 1979), and religious values pervade the nineteenth-century American school (Tyack 1970, 1971; Tyack and James 1985). Catholics evolve their own emphases (Tyack 1967a).

Most of this work takes an underlying functionalist or realist model of education and adds to it a variety of religious influences and pressures. Out of the panoply of interests in society that shape education, one subset is religious in character. Real historical forces shape education, and religion is part of the history.

But in the work of Tyack, as in many other analysts of education and its history, a stronger model appears in which religious and transcendental components are not simply social influences on education but are rather more constitutive of it. In Willard Waller's famous phrase (and Tyack has taken a strong interest in Waller's thinking, as in Tyack 1989), education is a "museum of virtue," not just of real-world interest and function. American educational leaders, historically, are depicted as heroic religious "managers of virtue" (Tyack and Hansot 1982). The reforms of the "one best system" (Tyack 1974) are triumphs of moral and scientific transcendence, not simply social control strategies (see also Shipps, Chap. 5, in this volume). And the vision of the Kingdom of God does not simply affect the American common school; the common school is an embodiment of it (Tyack 1966b).

Education can usefully be conceived as a transcendental or religious institution. In the famous phrase, it is the secular religion of a modern society. The discussion below pursues this idea, and as a good deal more than an analogy. I consider the implications, for understanding modern educational systems, of a conception of education as making up a religious system.

EDUCATION AS RELIGION

In order to pursue this theme, I need not torture the definition of religion but can placidly follow along with convention. By religion, I mean two standard components: a cosmology, or overarching "sacred canopy" depicting a universalized larger environment of human activity; and doctrines or rules providing meaningful linkages of humans and their activity to this cosmos (Berger 1967).

Since mass education has its roots in Protestant (and then Counter-Reformation) religion, and since the university was transformed with the enlightenment outcomes of such religion, we need to further specify the kind of religion we are talking about. To simplify, the relevant components of the cosmology involved include the presence of a high God who creates a lawful and rationalizable Nature that functions on its own and who acts, not directly, but through ties to human actors. These human actors include principally individual persons (though in some versions national states and other organizations). Empowered by ties to God that confer legitimated agency, these human actors have the capabilities to engage in legitimate social action and the capacity to comprehend the lawful character of both natural and spiritual environments (Thomas et al. 1987; Meyer and Jepperson 2000).

This system obviously constitutes modern education in all its forms, though some forms more than others. The two relevant principles not only follow from their religious roots but themselves directly transcend immediate and mundane experience and functioning: (1) education contains and transmits knowledge of the rationalized and universal cosmos, including analyses of physical, social, and human nature, and analyses of the moral order; and (2) individual persons are empowered to act properly in this (physical, social, moral) cosmos and can understand its lawful structure. Briefly, a lot of transcending material is rational enough that people can be educated about it, and people have the capacity to be educated. Neither of these principles makes much sense in terms of practical experience and social functioning, and neither is likely to have been derived from experience and functioning. The principles make sense only in a transcendent universe and are likely to have been developed only out of the contemplation of such a universe.

Reflection on these themes can make clear why education and educational reform are of special importance in American history and current society. The American tradition downplayed any other link between the transcendent and the real world of action than the individual. It was hostile to the expansion and charisma of the putatively corrupt state, which in Europe played a strong mediating role between God and the individual. It was even more hostile to the idea of natural community as linking individuals and God: attacks on every sort of aristocracy were central to the American tradition. Individual persons—not communities and states—are to be the carriers of the common good; this makes education and its reform very central.

Further, the American tradition located the proper human individual in a highly rationalized and lawful natural, social, and moral universe (Thomas 1986). History and tradition were less important than intelligent analysis, in the perfected society (Tuveson 1968), and education was thus a very central good.

The chapters of this volume repeatedly stress the centrality of education and reform in American history (see especially the Introduction and the chapters in Part I). They emphasize less strongly that this centrality lies not in the functional importance of education in America but in the foundations of American culture in a rationalized and individualistic religious system (but see Thomas 1986).

EXPLANATORY IMPLICATIONS: STANDARDIZATION OF UNIVERSALIZED EDUCATIONAL FORMS

Many features of the modern educational system make more sense if one sees schooling as constituting a religious system rather than an instrument of concrete social functioning. These include the universalism of its rules of participation, the universalistic rationalism of its core content, the standardization of both forms and content, the cosmological character of the knowledge involved, and the weak linkages of educational knowledge and participation to the practical and differentiated roles of actual social life.

Universalism of the Rules of Participation

In actual social life, people play very differentiated roles, some of which would seem to require much school knowledge, and many of which do not. But modern educational systems are built on norms and aspirations of universal participation: all children are to participate, and for years on end. Education is not—especially in America—to be principally linked to differentiated roles. Most education for the great majority of young persons is in fact standardized compulsory, and rules (and often practices) of compulsory education characterize most modern national societies (Ramirez and Ventresca 1992). As the chapters of this book make clear, the aspiration to a universal education, without much differentiation or stratification, runs through the whole history of mass education, perhaps especially in the United States. Threats to this universality are seen as extremely destructive.

Unusual among modern social rights, education is at once an entitlement of young persons, a compulsory obligation, and the obligation of the state to provide (and parents to permit). In this, educational participation is very distinct from rights to vote, to receive welfare protections, and to be treated with due process. It is much more similar to the status of baptism in a Universal Church: a badge, initiation rite, or ceremony of compulsory personhood, linking the ordinary individual to wider truths and laws.

Note how odd this is, given modern emphases on individual freedoms and rights. Without due process, or any demonstration of the failure or incompetence of children, we feel free and obligated to imprison them in state or public institutions for many years: a practice that, applied to any other category of persons, would be in gross violation of elementary human rights standards. The right and duty to do this to the young reflects the transcending status of education, which is constitutive of proper personhood and relates the child properly to universalized knowledge.

Increasingly, with the globalization of world society, norms of universal participation transcend nation-state boundaries and become enshrined in world-level models of general human rights. Thus, the recent "education for all" movement explicitly made it a world goal to universalize participation: a goal to be assisted by all, regardless of national boundaries (Chabbott 1996). Education goes with human rights and the universal social status "human."

Universalized Standardization Across Status and Role

Further, the education to which the young are universally to be exposed is itself very highly standardized (in principle or aspiration, though by no means in practice), exactly as characterizes the ceremonial efforts of a Universal Church. The young vary greatly in present capacities and in future prospects. Modern systems make great efforts, nevertheless, to provide standard educational programs for all. Remedial efforts are made for those with limited capacities. And standard programs are designed for all, regardless of likely future outcomes: it would be a violation of fundamental principles of human equality to do otherwise.

The most extreme example, here, is gender. Despite the historical inclination of all modern societies to design radically different adult roles for males and females, the great tendency has been to design common educational programs for the two groups. Historically, men participated in politics, women did not; men played substantial roles in a variety of organizational and economic elites, women did not. The occupational activities, including family responsibilities, differed greatly for men and women. Despite all this deeply rule-laden differentiation, the Western (and later world) inclination was to provide essentially identical mass educational circumstances for boys and girls (see Ramirez and Cha 1990 for data on the intensification of this over time). David Tyack and Elisabeth Hansot (1990) give sustained attention to the puzzle involved.

It is indeed a puzzle if education involves preparation for real-world social participation. Why would we so consistently have provided common basic education for males and females if the two groups are going to play radically different roles? The puzzle disappears if we see education as essentially religious, relating initiates to the wider cosmos rather than relating ordinary boys and girls to their functional futures. In modern thought and culture, persons are ultimately similar and equal, and they are constituted as entitled and obligated to have a direct and equal relation to the wider natural and moral cosmos.

The sociological literature on education attends with vengeance to the obvious fact that aspirations to effective standardization are often unrealized; this theme is evident in the chapters of this volume (e.g., the Introduction and the chapters by Mitchell, Donato, Shipps, Labaree, and Kantor and Lowe). Children differing in class, ethnicity, or gender in fact receive different experiences, opportunities, and resources. There is much to study here. But this research tradition takes for granted the underlying standardized-equality norm, which should be the object of explanation. It does not seem surprising that, in real, modern societies, higher status people give personal advantages to their children or that later in life the empowered can pay the disempowered to tend their gardens, hair, and toes. Should it be so surprising that they similarly gain educational advantages? Is it not more surprising that there is a sustained worldwide effort, built on the strongest norms, to create standardized ceremonial equality? In the argument here, such norms reflect the transcendental aspect of education. It is understandable if stratification happens in mundane society; it is unacceptable if it happens in the Kingdom of God.

Universalized Standardization Across Societies

With the contemporary worldwide spread of models of the rationalized national state and society and of the empowered human person, the aspiration to universal and standardized education has also gone global. Despite enormous differences among national societies in resources (the inequalities run a hundred to one) and economic structure, in political form, and in traditional cultural values, great efforts are made to create a standard universalized educational system. This describes the form of education, which expands to universality in all types of countries and which extends to the extremely rapid expansion of universities everywhere (Meyer, Ramirez, and Soysal 1992; Riddle 1993). It also turns out to describe the content of education, with highly standardized models established essentially everywhere (Meyer et al. 1992). The topics and fields to be covered are remarkably similar, and they change in the same broad directions. Doctrines of instructional methods seem also to be quite homogeneous and to change in common directions. At the university level, the same sets of fields of instruction are laid out.

Thus, enrollment levels tend toward vastly greater homogeneity worldwide than do economic resource levels, economic structures, political forms, or cultural traditions. And the content carried by educational systems is clearly much more isomorphic than the obvious differentiations might suggest. Again, we find universalized standardization around common principles, in a world of the greatest actual or mundane diversity. The young are going to play very different roles in different countries: why then are educational models and aspirations so similar?

The puzzle disappears if we see education as a religious system. Models of constitutive and ritual personhood—though by no means the actual roles persons play in society—are remarkably similar around the world. And while actual forms of society vary greatly, all societies are understood to operate in the same transcending natural and moral context. If education is about personhood, and about relating initiates to the universal forms of truth, then it makes perfect sense that its ideals would be similar everywhere. Ideas of this kind motivate massive standardizing educational aid programs from many core countries (especially the United States), official intergovernmental associations (e.g., the World Bank, UNESCO), and a great many nongovernmental and professional associations.

The standardized character of ideal educational models produces a taken-for-granted quality about most possible issues of educational content. There are bitter conflicts at a few margins, having to do with sexual instruction, the theory of evolution, or the interpretation of a civil war. But, for the most part, the content of educational curricula is now a matter of a social silence, delegated to professionals. The point is that this happens because education is mostly about a widely shared ideal world, not the noisy and diverse and differentiated real one. This can help us understand why the chapters above, though devoted to the reforms and improvements in education and doubtful about many current trends, rarely discuss matters of educational content. The issues are mainly about social equality and integration in access to educational virtue, not in the definition of what this virtue is (see Cuban, Chap. 8, for a parallel discussion).

Cosmological Content

I have discussed above the ceremonial standardization and universalization of the educational form within and between societies. I turn now to the actual cultural content carried and transmitted by these educational forms. Clearly this content has been standardized a great deal and universally applied. What is the nature of the content involved?

The hopes and fears of traditional realist analyses, celebrating the relation of education to a real social system, can serve as "straw men" here. Throughout modern history, the hopes of the liberal centrists and the fears of those on the left (and sometimes right) have been that educational content might be tightly linked to the actual role structure of the modern system. There would be some integrating cultural material, to be sure, but much training (often differentiated) for role performance. The centrist liberals have seen this sort of education as a functionally required part of the societal machine; the right and left take the same view but see the machine involved as an alienative and exploitive leviathan cut loose from more natural human community.

As seen in the discussion above, a main prediction from this line of thought—that educational content would vary dramatically by socioeconomic conditions—is a renowned failure. Educational content tends to be much the same in agricultural rural settings and in the industrialized town. It tends to be similar (in aspiration, in any event) in Third World peasant societies and in developed postindustrial ones.

A second prediction—that the possession of schooled knowledge would predict (and be designed to predict) successful role performance for individuals—is also a rather clear failure. On the empirical side, many studies show that schooled persons are allocated social roles appropriate to their schooling. But holding constant educational status, few studies can show much benefit in role performance from variations in measured student achievement, whether this is assessed by teachers (as in "grades") or by standardized achievement tests (see, among many others, Berg 1971). It also seems true that the mental qualities or abilities that underlie successful educational achievements themselves play weak roles in directly affecting later adult role performance (though the tests are commonly used to select those who will be allowed to enter particular adult roles).

This disconnection from effective role performance seems to be a characteristic of the intended design of modern education, not just of its empirical outcomes. We deliberately segregate students from society, rather than integrating them in apprenticeship relations. We construct an educational knowledge system designed to link the student to great truths, not to routines of role performance. The students are not practiced at being consumers, family members, workers, and managers. Rather, we teach them general principles about the nature of things that are thought to underlie the world in which they will function. The students are tested in terms of their understanding of such principles and their ability to use them in dealing with abstracted questions, not in terms of any effective social role performance.

A social world that is really concerned with, say, training young women to act effectively in the town market does so with mechanisms of apprenticeship and direct role performance: girls accompany older women in the marketplace. This may produce reasonable performances, though it certainly would not help the trainees perform well on school tests about the issues involved. Modern educational systems keep the child out of the marketplace and cover the topic with instruction in abstract models and principles, producing better answers to tests and little marketplace skill.

It is possible, and sometimes conventional, to see all this as a mistake— an educational regime disconnected from its putatively real purposes. It is a better idea to see it as a highly purposive part of the logic of a modern, standardized, rationalized, universalistic system. The aim is to link the child as a developing person directly with the lawful universal natural, social, and moral cosmos, not with particular role performances (though in modern thinking, this should naturally follow). The child is to become an active agent and empowered individual, (1) carrying the high human spirit linked to the Mind of God, and (2) informed about the natural and social environment in terms of the laws of this Mind. The God in question is inert ("dead" is the conception), but Nature (both physical and social) carries the laws, and humans carry the legitimated capacity for action and for an understanding of the laws.

Modern education carries this cosmology far more than it carries training for role performance. Role performances are particular and mundane. The underlying principles of human agency and of a lawful and universalized nature are cosmic and transcendent. This is why a universal and standardized education makes sense, and this is why, whenever universal education arises, it tends to take a cosmological form.

Thus, in social science, the contemporary student is less exposed to information on the history or geography of local or national society than to "social studies," which encompasses a general understanding of human society across time and space (Wong 1991). Courses of study may also include some psychology, economics, or sociology, which take the same approach. The student is to acquire a general understanding of general principles, not particular knowledge about local circumstances. Civics instruction similarly covers general principles of public life and individual centrality in this life, not detailed knowledge of local (or national) structures of power and authority; even in countries with authoritarian regimes, instruction emphasizes the principles of democracy and human rights (Rauner 1998). The twin emphases involved are those of the modern cosmology: the universality of general principles of social life, and the central location of the comprehending and participatory individual person within this scheme.

Science and mathematics too carry this story (McEneaney 1998). Detailed knowledge and competence give way to a dramatic emphasis on individual participation in these enterprises (every child can learn to think scientifically) and to a translation of specialized knowledge into general universal metaprinciples. It would be reactionary to mainly teach the student the names of trees or the parts of the leaf—the point is to produce an understanding of the internal and external interdependence of the forest and the individual person's responsibility to help preserve it. The student does not learn the names or lengths or volume of rivers, or the types of clouds, let alone detailed principles of hydrology: the aim is to produce an understanding of rivers and rainfall in general, and of the relation of these to a responsible society and individuals.

Art, music, and literature are similarly disconnected from particular canons or historical traditions, and increasingly treated eclectically, as texts enabling general understanding (and as texts in which the individual student can directly and legitimately participate and engage in interpretation). Critics sometimes complain about the subjectivism involved, but this is, in reality, subjectivism under the constraints of (1) individual responsibility to relate to (2) the broadest range of possible cultural materials. The student as interpreting person is central, but is to respectfully and tolerantly interpret the whole range of human culture.

Language itself remains relatively national, though even this is universalized compared with societies in which most actual communication is more local: many countries emphasize a more universal cosmopolitan language than those actually spoken domestically. But the sacred and traditional authority of national language is weakened, and the student is to learn to use it as a medium of personal expression and communication, not so much as a series of canonical rules. There is also an increasing emphasis on instruction in metropolitan languages—almost always in the contemporary period, English (Cha 1991). The really primordial classical languages disappear, as do efforts at instruction in languages of authoritative high culture (French, German). And local languages are being killed off at a very high rate, in good part through education.

The modern curriculum, thus, can be understood as a celebration of two great principles of the modern cosmology. First, the wider universe—physically, biologically, socially, and psychologically—can be seen as constructed out of coherent, lawful, universal, general principles. Local empirical realities, which are often practically inconsistent with such principles, are less important than understanding the principles. And, in the long run, comprehension of the basic underlying principles will be the route to decoding and improving local realities. Second, the individual person can comprehend these principles and can choose and act and participate freely in behaving in light of them. The constraints of local familial and power structures may make this practically very unreasonable, but education should ignore most of this and focus on the ideal model in which the intelligent and educated person is a free and empowered actor.

In educational practice, many concessions are made, as in all religious systems. Principles turn into metaprinciples, so the student may be taught to think "scientifically" without much scientific content or without anything by way of concrete scientific lawful structures. Participatory involvement may be mostly ritualized, rather than carried out in substance. And many problems of coverage of cosmological content are resolved through the competing principle of individual choice: all students should learn to think scientifically, but they may make many choices within this constraint.

The Celebration of Individual Intelligence

The combination of the two cosmological principles—that the universe is rational and orderly and that individuals can and should comprehend it—produces an enormous modern emphasis on education, which has rapidly expanded everywhere. The emphasis is on education as oriented cosmologically, not toward ordinary social practices and roles.

This combination also explains a peculiarity of the modern system, particularly its liberal American variant. There is an enormous emphasis on individual intelligence, in contrast to knowledge and performance skills. In the United States, young persons take tests to be sorted in elementary and secondary schools, to be admitted to higher education, and even to enter postgraduate training. The tests are aptitude tests, at least in intention, not tests to assess knowledge and performance. The test-construction effort is to find items that are sufficiently unrelated to experience and training in the real world so as to be appropriate indicators of a very abstract intelligent rationality.

This all makes little sense in functional practice, where assessments could most usefully take a very different form. In admitting persons to medical school, for example, it might be most sensible to let the decision rest on sixteen years of school performance or on direct measures of performance skills. Nevertheless, even after all these years, an intelligence test is employed. Obviously, a very great faith in the abstract rationality of the universe, and in the measurable capacity of individuals to comprehend this rationality in ways that supersede experience, is involved.

Further, schooling tasks are effectively designed so that measured intelligence is in fact a dominant predictor. In other words, tasks are designed to fit a rational universe and rationally choosing individuals, rather than the real world and socially embedded ones. In both the tests and schooling tasks, the universe is quite a strange place, unlike most of social experience. All questions have answers, the answers are the same for everyone, the answers can be figured out by individuals, and these individuals can and should do it alone. Nothing in social life quite parallels, in purity, the constructed world of the test and the school. And, as noted above, tested and schooled abilities usually turn out to be rather poor predictors of the competence of individuals in playing their roles in society.

The Education-Based Stratification System

Around the world, modern stratification systems turn out to have a great deal in common. As in all societies, young persons from socially advantaged families tend to end up in advantageous positions. But in modern societies, this is channeled mainly through the educational system, not through the direct assignment of experience, role activities, or wealth. So once one has taken educational attainment into account, the further advantages of those from favored backgrounds tend to be rather small. Educational attainment, in other words, is the main—and increasing—basis of status allocation. This turns out to be true on a worldwide basis. And education-based meritocratic assignment is generally, in the modern cultural system, taken to be virtuous and proper—clearly more highly legitimated than other forms of status transmission and allocation.

A further commonality lies in the very definition of social status, an issue addressed in much social research. Theories, rooted in nineteenth-century thought, tend to be functionalist and realist. They imagine that, in a functioning modern society, status would be allocated in terms of power and money, since the state and the market are understood to be the two main arms of the modern leviathan. The main public roles people play in the modern system are occupational, and occupations should naturally be sorted out in terms of their political/organizational or market control and resources.

Such matters are important, indeed, but it turns out—and on a worldwide basis—that by far the most important dimensions of status have to do with educational attainment. The educational attainment of individuals predicts more important consequences than do the other dimensions, from marital prospects and fertility through political participation to the advantages transmitted to children. And it of course predicts occupation. Moreover, it turns out that the most important status property of occupation does not have to do with income or power; the core measurement dimension is the education characteristic of its incumbents. The occupations that come out on top on status measures, worldwide, are those of the educated professionals—the doctors, lawyers, scientists, professors, and so on.

As I have stressed above, the education involved is not training for immediately relevant knowledge, skill, performance, and social function. It has a more transcendent character. Thus, the point is that the modern stratification system is built, not on social functioning, but on a ceremonial assessment of persons in terms of more transcendent criteria. As parents around the world know, the crucial path to success is education, and education turns out to be about (1) the possession of rather cosmological knowledge and (2) the creation of individuals empowered by their close relation to this wider cosmos.

In medieval society, only the clergy, among the elites, were educationally rooted. The military and political elites, and the landowning and merchant economic elites, were not. In the modern, supposedly secularized, society, it turns out that essentially all the elites are. Those who dominate the state and the military apparatuses do so with educational degrees, as do the managers of the modern economic system. And these degrees are organized around knowledge (and empowerment in relation to this knowledge) far removed from functional requirements of practical society. The core virtue is closeness to the Mind of God, not skill in the mundane functioning of secular society.

The Nature of Conflicts Between Education and Older Religious Forms

As many observers have noted, the rise of modern educational systems is associated with many conflicts with older religious arrangements. These conflicts run from organizational questions about how education is controlled through questions about the appropriateness of common education for different groups (especially males and females, but sometimes over the peasantry) to all sorts of issues about educational content (especially science, but also many other areas).

The issue is usually seen as involving secularization. Older and traditional religious arrangements come in conflict with the new functional requirements of the expanding secular society. Thus religion is at war with a realist and functional educational system. It may be more useful to see the conflicts as taking place between two religious cosmologies, rather than a replacement of religion by something else. Both sides of the conflicts, in other words, have transcendental bases. This helps explain the intensity of the conflicts, since both sides are fighting over the same turf.

It also helps explain the substantive nature of the conflicts, which tend to be curiously unrelated to real social functioning and very closely related to transcendent matters. The field of battle lies in this arena, befitting the conflict between two religions.

On content: The classic starting point is Galileo's conflict with the Church. Note that this conflict was not over any matter of concern in real functioning society (the principle of usury, for instance; or the status and rights of women or peasants; or the authority of kings). It was about the moons of Jupiter (an area of current excitement in science and education, too). The concrete functioning of society was not at issue. Another classic conflict is over evolution and the prehistoric meaning of various fossils. This conflict goes on into our own time and is profoundly insignificant to the functional operation of the interdependent parts of the social system. Still other conflicts occur over what is to be taught about human sexuality; again, these are seldom about role performances and relationships in functioning modern society, and very much about ontological questions.

On organization: There have been great and continuing conflicts between more secular educational authorities and religious ones over who is to manage the schools. These have a notably abstract character and are about authority rather than functional issues. Despite much research effort, there has been little demonstration that it matters to any measurable outcome who runs the schools: students come out about the same from either structure. And, indeed, in the current period, schools operated by religious bodies seem to have about the same immediate curricula and purposes as those operated by nominally secular authorities.

In short, the educational system differs from the traditional religious one less in its model of society than in its model of the trans-social cosmos—the character of a wider reality, not the domestic one. This clearly follows from our arguments about the core nature of education as an institution linked to a transcendent universe more than a local or functional one.

CONCLUSION

The entire modern social stratification system rests heavily on education and on the abilities that underlie it. As we have stressed, this system is focused on a religious cosmology—about both the wider universe and the individual human's relation to it—that seems to be a core component of the modern system. The universalistic rules of participation, the worldwide standardization, and the rationalistic curricular content all follow from this.

All of this is much criticized, throughout the modern period, as lacking in immediate social "relevance." Enormous reforms are devoted to making education more relevant: much archaic knowledge is eliminated, and more rationalistic and contemporary forms substituted. But relevance is a very unclear concept. Under its umbrella, a modern cosmology comes into place. It is apparently relevant for students to follow a social studies chapter (or literary account) on life in some present or past society they will never contact, or to examine theories of the distant origins of the universe, or to inspect the skulls of ancestors of the human race, or to practice mathematical forms they are unlikely to ever utilize. Relevance thus seems to mean linkage to universalized logics and rules, to understand that immediate conditions and experiences can properly be interpreted in terms of such rules, and to feel and be invested with a close linkage to them. The sensibility involved is clearly religious in character: what changes with the rise of modern education is the nature of the religion involved.

Dorothy Shipps and Larry Cuban

This collection of essays questions several assumptions that make up the conventional wisdom about our public schools, and particularly about ways to improve them in the new century. One common assumption about the process of improving the public schools is that any break with the past frees our expectations for the future. Many current school reformers argue that the existing system is so flawed that any innovation is an improvement. More temperate critics aver that recreating schools is a risky process that may produce its own problems but that current needs demand, at the very least, a conceptual laissez-faire.

Yet, compared with the nineteenth century or the early or middle decades of the twentieth century, contemporary notions of the common good in American public education look anemic. Whether reexamined through the records left by nationally influential educators like Horace Mann, William T. Harris, George Counts, and other school reformers, or through the perspectives of earlier historians, the purposes of public schooling being pursued today appear both less optimistic and less encompassing than they once were.

As enticing as the term "radical reform" has lately become, there is very little new in proposals to improve schooling by privatizing them. Market metaphors and solutions draw on deep reservoirs of experience that have seldom been as salutary as proposed. Vouchers, only the most obvious of the current forms of privatization, already have a history not much different from many other kinds of governance change, beginning in loud claims and ending quietly in small adaptations. David Labaree reminds us that such market-oriented exit options are rooted in longstanding political expectations. Leaving is simultaneously easier than staying to fight and, in the American experience, an act of social rebellion. Forbidding exit is both "unthinkably un-American" when applied to individuals and unnecessary when applied to the institution of public schools. There is no other way to affect the collective social consequences of public schooling than voicing complaints, hearing others, and collectively seeking improvements.

The adoption of private sector management in the public schools, a more common form of privatization, has a century-long history. When management reforms cross the divide between private businesses and public schools, they bring with them market assumptions that require commitments to indirect and narrowly defined measures of success or failure. One set of narrow definitions of the good school gives way to others, and it appears as though radical reform requires blinkered vision, permitting no other perspectives. For example, pedagogical ideologies and narrow definitions of the good school become "protracted intolerant bickering," in Larry Cuban's straightforward terms. Yet history suggests that no single definition of the good school has been able to supplant all others indefinitely. The bickering happens more readily when the moral and religious undertones of the debates ignore essential agreements about the importance of schooling to the development of common democratic values and disciplined respectful behavior toward one another.

As the essays in this volume have clarified, however, to seek the good old days of common schools would also be a mistake. American individualism is a cornerstone of public education; the private benefits of schooling have always been central. Reconceptualizing the common good has been the repeated task of a succession of public school reformers (and movements) since the founding of our system. Each has responded to different historical circumstances while building on a legacy just as real as individualism: our shared democratic and egalitarian values.

Another popular, but unexamined, assumption about the current ills of public schools is that governance reform can be dismissed as a superstructure of perpetual turmoil largely unrelated to the improvement of education for children, and therefore relatively unimportant. This is a professional and technocratic argument that reinforces a dichotomy between private purposes and opposing common goals. It suggests that the private provision of skills is more central to the core purposes of schooling than the common creation of community. It is also shortsighted.

Seminal periods in the struggle for equity and dignity in public education in the mid-nineteenth and mid-twentieth centuries reveal that school governance has been central to the community and nation-building aspirations of African Americans, Asian Americans, and Latinos. These periods of more inclusive expectations for educational governance demonstrate that public schools do not easily nor necessarily include minorities in the calculus of the common good.

Inquiry into these periods also clarifies how specific governance arrangements can hinder or facilitate an inclusive concept of the common good. The essays by Ted Mitchell, Rubén Donato, and Harvey Kantor and Robert Lowe each describe a link between specific governance arrangements and the varied purposes of public schooling. All trace patterns of governance and decision making that affect the inclusion of minorities into the school system: federal support of schooling for former slaves, rural Hispanos controlling their own schools, or the left's abandonment of its mid-century critique of bureaucratically run schools. Collectively, they suggest that inclusiveness and flexibility in the governance structures and organizational arrangements of public schooling may be necessary, if manifestly insufficient, conditions for recreating the common good in our fragmented and stratified society.

Their essays also highlight the radical contingency inherent in the governance dilemma of balancing central oversight—to ward off racism and other forms of pernicious parochialism—against the democracy-enhancing opportunities of local governance and decision making. Not only are governance arrangements crucial to inclusive visions of schooling that widens the space held in common, but, disconcertingly, they also may require regular adjustment.

Adopting a philosophical lens can provide a different view of the link between governance and the purposes of schooling. It draws attention to the larger framework in which specific public school governance arrangements are embedded. If public schooling functions to reproduce stratified social and economic relationships, it also provides a near-ubiquitous opportunity to develop common values and a civic identity. In one response to such dilemmas, Elisabeth Hansot points to the Aristotelian notion of "civic friendship" as an important "background condition" for all types of local school governance arrangements. In doing so she also balances the rational expectations we have of school governance—to provide multiple forums for debate, to clarify rules and procedures for decision making, and the like—with the affective conditions needed to develop and sustain a collective sense of the common good.

A third common assumption about the public schools and reforms to improve them is their essential functionality. When debates about public schools occur, there is no shortage of rational arguments for how things got so bad. Nor is there much delay before reformers pose supremely logical and, lately, quite systematic prescriptions for improving things. Most of the chapters of this book assume that a dialectical, causal relationship exists between how we envision our public schools and what sort of society and nation we have. John Meyer challenges this modern, realist paradigm in his essay. Adopting a comparative international perspective, he suggests that the assumptions we make about public schools and the importance of reforming them might be better understood if we take seriously the notion of schooling as a belief system—a secular religion. Rather than the working out of specifically defined sets of more or less useful responses to circumstances of success or failure, inclusion or exclusion, schooling embodies the sacred.

The motive behind this book is that contemporary notions of the common good embodied in the institution of schooling need reconceiving, perhaps resuscitating. This is not for lack of political treatises or communitarian prescriptions calling for greater awareness of democracy, community, and the whole child's needs in the schools. It comes, we think, from forgetfulness.

We already have a public school system that embodies, as no other American institution does, common values about what it means to be a good citizen and a good person. We might think of reconstructing the common good in public education as an act of (secular) religious reformation. The participants in that reformation will have a significant hand in determining what the new governing regime will be and, hence, who will be legitimated as interpreters of the creed. Will corporations have the same status as parents? Will nonparenting adults and children themselves be permitted a voice? Will this reformation require a new set of credentials for entry into the educational professions? As transmitters and translators of the creed, how will teachers and administrators respond? We do not need to break radically from the past to realign schools with their mission as carriers of common values and moral content, but that begs the question of the urgency that spurred this book. That urgency is nowhere better reflected than in our urban schools.

The harshest and most unforgiving dilemmas of reconstructing the common good in public education are concentrated in urban settings. Although social links between people in cities are probably no weaker than elsewhere, the daily interactions among unlike urbanites are more tangible and direct. Michael Katz's narrative clarifies how easy it is for people of different classes, national origins, religions, languages, and cultural expectations to encounter one another in cities. In the city, the common shared space is of necessity larger and more salient than elsewhere, and city residents are often made most aware of sharing that space when they see others using it differently. For instance, no one living in a city fails to be regularly reminded that her neighbors may be puzzled by, indifferent to, or even hostile to her most cherished beliefs. These daily encounters can serve to sharpen feelings of individuality, tribe, and difference, or they can be occasions for empathic, common understanding of the other.

It is no surprise then, that urban education is at the heart of the current critiques of public schooling. City schools are often the places where children and their parents encounter difference in a sustained way. Without a strong sense of the common good in urban schools, and simultaneously the common good that schools can help to foster, these institutions are especially vulnerable to the charge of being dysfunctional providers of private credentials and individual life-skills.

William Reese reminds us of the ironies in the urban school plight. American public schools were shaped in the mid-nineteenth century as a "panacea" for a crisis of confidence in political and social life brought on by rapid economic change, especially in cities. Urban schools, in particular, were expected to build a sense of community, lower crime rates, rectify incivility in the streets, and provide a social ladder that would make local and national leadership available to all regardless of the social class he or she was born into.

Today, urban public schools suffer a crisis of confidence. Contemporary reformers challenge the ability of urban schools to provide basic literacy to a diverse population, and many appear to have given up hope that city schools can ameliorate the social disruption and inequities that result from economic change. Instead, the goals of urban schooling seem to have been reduced to preparing urban children to compete with one another in an increasingly polarized economic environment, one in which they are no more likely to receive social or economic rewards than before. As several authors in this volume have observed, many powerful and sometimes sympathetic people reply to this disjuncture: "how better to improve them than to demand that schools, teachers, and children compete more fiercely with one another?" Thus, where urban schools were once conceived as the government-sponsored antidote to the evils of unfettered capitalism and free-market disruption, competitive markets are now the antidotes to the evils of government-sponsored schooling.

Embedded in this larger irony are smaller tragedies of American urban life that children must suffer. To make urban public schools attractive to the rich who already sent their children to private academies, nineteenth-century public school advocates convinced elites to construct public school cathedrals and provided public school teachers with both higher wages and fewer students than their private counterparts. Today, these same urban schools are community eyesores suffering from decades of deferred maintenance, and public school teachers typically teach more (and more varied) students than their private school counterparts. Although some urban public school teachers still earn higher salaries, it is often characterized as "combat pay," precious little compensation for the low status and the workplace indignities they suffer.

Although fraught with ambiguities and enduring tensions, reconstructing the common good in city schools (as elsewhere) seems to require both moral and intellectual commitments to recognize the other as different but nonetheless filled with potential and worthy of dignity. Rebuilding school cathedrals will not be sufficient, neither will recasting public school governance suffice, but if current arguments over markets and governments in schooling really do reflect religious warfare, then openly examining assumptions and debating the underpinnings of our commitments are a sensible, as well as a principled, response.

REFERENCE MATTER

NOTES

CHAPTER 1: Reese, The Elusive Search for the Common Good

1. My understanding of Harris's life and educational career was strengthened by reading the William T. Harris Papers at the Missouri Historical Society.

CHAPTER 2: Mitchell, Turning Points

1. The Mexican War and the ongoing war of domination in the West certainly count as experiences with occupation, yet the practices of ignoring Mexican settlements in the Southwest and of extermination or forced migration of Native Americans were not acceptable options in the South, making Reconstruction an experience with few models for the United States.

2. Du Bois, in *Black Reconstruction in America*, made this argument in 1935 at a point when, as he said about white reformers during Reconstruction, historians "listened without ears" (727). In the 1960s, shaped by the Civil Rights Movement and efforts by African Americans to recover their unique past, historians began not only to uncover elements of agency by African Americans but also to place these efforts into a broader theoretical framework of class formation and class struggle. Herbert Gutman's *The Black Family in Slavery and Freedom* (1976) marks a path-breaking step in the identification of a unique history of blacks in America as well as an integration of that distinct history into the struggles of working people in nineteenth-century American society. Leon Litwack's *Been in the Storm So Long* (1979) captures brilliantly the social history of Freedmen during the first decade after emancipation. Ex-slaves' voices carry Litwack's narrative and create a portrait of participation and agency that has not been equaled. Eric Foner's *Reconstruction* (1988) is the ablest synthesis of both the new, more complex view of white attitudes and efforts during Reconstruction and the restored view of blacks as powerful agents in determining the Reconstruction agenda. In regard to education, two books epitomize this new movement. Ronald Butchart's *Northern Schools, Southern Blacks, and Reconstruction* (1980) provides a revised view of the work of the Northern

missionary societies. Butchart's analysis presents a compelling case for the importance of black as well as white attitudes and actions. James Anderson's *The Education of Blacks in the South, 1860–1935* (1988) is an excellent treatment of the development of schooling for blacks, emphasizing black "self-activity" in Gutman's phrase, in contrast to white efforts to first deprive blacks of schooling and later to shape that education in the most restrictive of ways.

3. Richard Bensel, in *Yankee Leviathan* (1990), argues that the Civil War saw the creation of the centralized modern state in America. For Bensel, the war itself provided the impetus for the creation of a vast new administrative apparatus, including the draft board, that rapidly became institutionalized. Similar arguments are made by William Nelson in *The Roots of American Bureaucracy* (1982).

CHAPTER 4: Donato, "No One Here to Put Us Down"

1. Consider the order of time: Spain began to colonize the area in the seventeenth century, Mexico won its independence from Spain in 1821, and the New Mexico–Colorado region became an "American territory" in 1848 (see Rosenbaum 1981, 18).

2. Los Fuertes, for example, was organized in 1853; San Pablo in 1854; San Luis, Garcia, and Old San Acacio in 1856; Chama in 1860; Mesita in 1909; and New San Acacio and Jaroso in 1910.

3. Edna Vigil, Simonita Salazar, Josephine Pacheco, Sara Martinez, Edna Gallegos, Virginia Marquez, Mrs. Julian Candelaria, Patrick Jaquez, Mary Medina, Joe Garcia, Josephine Sandoval, and Madeliene Vigil were all employed as teachers during the 1920s and 1930s (San Luis School District, Teacher's Register 1920–29).

4. At Centennial High School, Silver Jaramillo was superintendent; Abie Duarte was principal; Ben Jiron taught algebra II, geometry, and trigonometry; Joseph Martinez taught geography and English; Chris Martinez taught biology; and Val Sena taught algebra and physics.

CHAPTER 5: Shipps, Echoes of Corporate Influence

1. The unity of corporate America has been a hotly debated topic. However, both pluralists and their critics seem to agree that it is not a question of whether corporate America is politically unified, but when. Business historian David Vogel (1989) argues that corporate power varies according to the U.S. position in the global economy and internal growth rates. At the other extreme, James Lamore (1988) identifies six circumstances that drive corporate involvement in social policy making. These include economic crisis, politicians' efforts to discover business preferences, conflicts between corporations, conflicts between corporations and other interests, corporate efforts to advance a particular

business goal, and neo-corporatist policy-making arrangements. Despite such differences, analysts of business influence frequently acknowledge that corporations often cede to a few among them the role of spokesperson on public policy issues. In some places these spokespersons have been self-appointed executives, at others they have been leaders of business associations with substantial resources focused on influencing public policy.

2. Callahan's basic arguments about the impact of corporate and economic change on the public schools seemed to some "irrefutable" (Cremin 1963, 185). To others, he had painted a "caricature" (Cartwright 1963, 723), envisioning abrupt historical changes midway in the Progressive era that were actually much more complex, conditional, and gradual processes (Smith 1964) and ignoring many other simultaneous and prior social forces (Cuban 1976).

3. For commentary on these distinctions and their relationship to management debates, see Stephen P. Waring, *Taylorism Transformed* (1991). Pages 13–16 clarify the distinctions between Taylor's bureaucratic scientific management and the corporatist critique of "worker anomie" fostered by psychologist George Elton Mayo in the early years of the twentieth century.

4. For instance, Spring could dismiss Progressive-era dissenters like George Counts because they focused on control of schools or curriculum, not on the inherent weaknesses of a public school system in a corporate state (Lazerson 1973; Troen 1974; Fields 1972).

5. Although they disagree on points of emphasis, reviews of Tyack's work typically note that, as historical synthesis, both *The One Best System* and *Managers of Virtue* walk a fine line between revisionist historians like Callahan and Spring and an earlier generation who extolled the achievements of mass public education to American society and democracy (Cohen 1975; Mattingly 1976; Clifford 1975; Lazerson 1975; Kirp 1982).

6. In one memorable passage he quotes the opening prayer for the 1910 annual convention of the National Association of Manufacturers: "O Thou Great Manufacturer, Greatest of all, Maker of trees and flowers, of soils and mountains and worlds, we take Thy material into our hands, and try to make it more marketable among men" (Spring 1972, 42).

7. For commentary on this view, see Bloom et al. 1989.

8. John Gray argues somewhat more strongly that the current phase of globalism pits *democracy* against free markets. Agreeing with conventional wisdom that socialism is dead, he is not confident that its successors will be free markets, which are themselves inherently unstable. Until now, he points out, its successors have been a variety of forms of capitalism, some dominated by criminal activity, others more by kinship and corruption. He further argues that globalism itself is a gradual process that has been occurring over two centuries and should not be confused with the political collapse of socialism from within. (See Gray 1998.)

CHAPTER 6: Labaree, No Exit

I am grateful for the comments by Bob Lowe and Michael Mintrom on an earlier version of this paper; for better or worse, I chose to keep the argument largely intact despite their well-voiced cautions and concerns.

1. For example, David Berliner and Bruce Biddle (1995) and Gerald Bracey (1995a, 1996, 1997) at times have fallen into this trap. At times, so have I (Labaree 1997a).

2. Poor districts in the United States have notoriously high school-millage rates whereas wealthy districts have notoriously low millages, since high property values in the latter districts allow them to produce higher tax revenues with lower tax rates.

CHAPTER 7: Kantor and Lowe, Bureaucracy Left and Right

The authors would like to acknowledge the support of the Joyce Foundation for their research on this article

1. On the liberal commitment to cosmopolitan values more generally, see Pells 1985, chap. 3.

2. In an exchange of letters that raises questions about conventional political labels, Thomas A. Bledsoe of the conservative Council for a Basic Education took issue with Conant's unsubstantiated position that 85 percent of students in high school could not do serious academic work. The liberal Jencks defended Conant's estimate (see *New Republic* 1959).

3. For a recent report on dropout rates in urban schools, see Education Week 1997.

4. We would like to thank Frank Margonis for clarifying this point.

5. Similar arguments were made earlier by liberals who criticized radicals like Kozol for undermining the support of public education, thus lending weight to conservatives' argument that public schools did not need more money (see, for instance, Donley 1976, 220).

6. Much of the radical critique was concerned with ways that education stifled individualism. But this individualism, which stressed an antimaterialistic and a noncompetitive ethos, was quite different from the competitive individualism that today conservatives hope educational choice will nourish (see Farrell 1997).

7. For conservative caution about categorically embracing vouchers before the 1990s, see Wilson 1989 and Doyle 1992.

8. On Wallace and the politics of racial resentment, see Edsall and Edsall 1991 and Carter 1995, 1996.

9. To the query, "Would you support a voucher system where parents would get money from the government to send their children to the public, private, or parochial school of their choice?" 66.4 percent of 18–25-year-old African

Americans and 86.5 percent of 26–35-year-old African Americans said "yes." In contrast, this was true of only 31.3 percent of African Americans who were 51–64 years old and of 19 percent of those older than 65 (see Bostis 1997, table 7).

10. One example is La Escuela Fratney School in Milwaukee.

11. For the difficulty of achieving an egalitarian voucher policy, see Hausman 1996, 345-46, and Brighouse 1996, 472-75.

12. Despite the high praise bestowed on Central Park East Secondary School, for example, Frederick Wiseman's documentary of the school (1994) records what we view as paternalistic behavior of staff toward students and parents that suggests a colonial relationship.

13. G. Alfred Hess, Jr., for example, called Donald Moore of Designs for Change "the chief of the 'architects' of the reform legislation" (1995, 37). Designs for Change (1995) also was a major opponent of vouchers.

14. One such school, Roberto Clemente High School, is overtly political and embattled with public officials who want to reduce the power of the local school councils (Ramos-Zayas 1998, 190).

15. Ana Ramos-Zayas (1998) devotes the bulk of her article to Pedro Albizu Campos High School, which charged tuition of $500 during 1994-95.

CHAPTER 8: Cuban, Why Is It So Hard to Get "Good" Schools?

1. The words "traditionalist" and "progressive" are variations of common terms used to characterize different ideological positions on learning, teaching, knowledge, curriculum, governance, and organization of schools. As with "conservative" and "liberal" in the political world, each term carries the baggage of positive and negative connotations, depending upon the reader. Those who use the dichotomy have often been criticized for simplistically dividing the world into halves and obscuring much variation; nonetheless, the dichotomy has survived in popular and scholarly discourse (see, for example, Dewey 1900, 1938; Gage 1985; Silberman 1970; Hirsch 1996). Other writers have tried hard to avoid the educational labels, even coining new ones (Jackson 1986), but have still used the notion of competing patterns of education.

Acknowledging the risks for readers that accompany using these familiar terms, I need to note one in particular and clarify what I mean. In using each word, I recognize that there is a range of positions taken by progressives (or traditionalists) on any given issue. Traditionalists, for example, vary in their views on the use of phonics in teaching reading, removing books from the school library, prayer in school, and vouchers. In short, there is no monolithic traditionalist (or progressive) view on each of these issues.

For continuing controversy over the teaching of reading, see National Research Council 1998. For similar controversy over math, see Cheney and Romberg 1997 and Loveless 1997. For bilingual education, see Bronner 1998b.

2. I recognize that there are prior conditions essential to securing any version of a "good" school: parents sufficiently attached to public schools to enroll their children and support the school's goals; committed (and qualified) professionals; adequate facilities; and minimally sufficient resources to get a school running and sustain its operations. When these prior conditions are absent, securing "good" schools of any type is even more difficult to attain.

3. I have visited both schools over the past two decades.

4. A recent example is the Effective Schools movement that began in the late 1970s and has continued under different names (see, for instance, Edmonds 1979; Bullard and Taylor 1993). For previous efforts to prove one pattern of schooling better than the other, see Bennett 1976 and Aikin 1942 as well as the federal government's major evaluation effort of early childhood models of teaching and learning called Follow Through (see Elmore 1975; House 1978).

5. Some readers may question whether there are, indeed, configurations of ideas and practices that can be safely labeled "progressive" or "conservative." Two criteria can be applied to determine whether such patterns have existed and are present now: (1) There are sufficient features such as concepts and practices held in common over time that cohere into a tradition. From notions of what constitutes good teaching and learning to report cards and daily classroom practices, one can easily construct parallel columns that make clear the differences between the two patterns. (2) There is sufficient evidence that each of the patterns was put into practice at different times. I have cited some sources already that have offered such evidence. Based upon these criteria, I have argued that these patterns exist in both words and practice.

For recent works prizing traditional patterns in schooling, see Bennett 1988, Hirsch 1987, and Ravitch 1984. For works prizing progressive forms of schooling, see Wood 1992, Bastian et al. 1986, and Featherstone 1971.

6. The two reasons I offer for the protracted ideological wars over different patterns of schooling are anchored in institutional and political conflict models that are elaborated in my previous work and drawn from other theorists. I see public schools as political entities heavily influenced by a web of social beliefs in the larger culture (e.g., ideas about child rearing, what is appropriate knowledge to be taught in schools) and utterly dependent upon taxpayers and parents for fiscal and political legitimacy. Although institutional and political factors do shape organizational behavior, they do not mechanistically determine schools' responses. Schools, as institutions, have had discretionary room to adapt to these environmental demands through political processes and leaders' actions. I have used these models in my work (Cuban 1993, 1999). For elaboration of the theories I use here, see Lakoff 1996, Meyer and Scott 1992, DiMaggio 1992, and Wirt and Kirst 1989.

7. George Lakoff's argument is that the linkage between politics and family-rearing practices permeates all arenas of American life. Public support for prayer

and moral education in schools has been evident in opinion polls for decades (Lakoff 1996, 228–36; Elam 1989, 7). For a discussion of evangelical and Pentecostal Protestants and their struggle with modernist Protestants, see Brinkley 1998, 266–76.

8. I could just as easily make the point on academic standards. Although progressives and traditionalists argue at length over who should set the standards, and exactly what those standards will be and in what areas, there is general agreement among both groups, white and black, that academic standards should expect more from students (Elam 1989, 8; Public Agenda 1994; Public Agenda Online 1998).

9. In California, where heavy immigration from Mexico and Asia since the early 1980s has affected the schools, voters have approved referenda that ban public services to illegal immigrants and bilingual classes in schools (Los Angeles Times 1998).

10. In 1989, President George Bush convened the nation's governors in an educational summit. The outcomes were national goals that President Clinton has endorsed and expanded. Goal 3 aims to have all students who leave grades 4, 8, and 12 by the year 2000 demonstrating proficiency in academic subjects; goal 5 states that, by the year 2000, American students will be first in math and science on international tests (National Education Goals Panel 1995). Most school districts now have press releases when state and local test scores are published. Media list school-by-school scores with comparisons to state and national averages, where appropriate. For typical examples of these articles, see Strauss 1998 and Aritani 1998.

11. This partial list I offer of democratic behaviors and attitudes could easily be labeled a liberal credo. There has been (and continues to be) acrimonious division over whether liberal and conservative ideologies have dominated political thought in the United States. Rather than enter the fray, I chose this partial list from those liberal and conservative intellectuals who share basic modernist, secular values. I have, in other words, excluded the fundamentalist wing of conservatism that is generally anti-secular and has established separate private schools. For a discussion of these common values, see Brinkley 1998, 277–97.

12. For educator and parental support of traditional forms of teaching and schooling for black children, see Delpit 1988, Foster 1995, Ladson-Billings 1994, and Public Agenda Online 1998.

13. The evidence of hybrids of traditional and progressive practices is strong in this century and often ignored by partisans of each ideology. For example, small-group work in elementary and secondary schools—a progressive innovation at the turn of the century—is standard fare in schools that prize traditional practices. Movable classroom furniture, field trips, physical education, and community-oriented schools are other innovations that derived from progressive ideology and have become embraced by parents, administrators, and teachers in

traditional schools. Inattention by the faithful of either side to these changes in schools over the decades has helped prolong the futile war of words. Although this is not the place to make the argument, I would point out here that few teachers and principals are progressive or traditionalist ideologues; they have learned that hybrids have been most practical in educating children, who bring so much diversity with them into classrooms.

CHAPTER 9: Hansot, Civic Friendship

1. See also Aristotle 1985, 1107a33–1122a17, 1160a28–30. Amy Gutmann and Dennis Thompson (1996, 79) observe that mutual respect (a requisite of their central principle, reciprocity) "requires a favorable attitude toward, and constructive interaction with, the persons with whom one disagrees."

2. The communitarian view is represented by Taylor 1989, Putnam 1993, Sandel 1978 and 1996, and MacIntyre 1981. To some extent, Hannah Arendt's account (1958) of the public realm can be claimed for this tradition. According to Margaret Canovan, Arendt's conception of the political realm, influenced by Aristotle, entailed a notion of friendship as "constant talk between citizens about the common political world lying between them, a discourse which itself humanizes this common world." Political thinking required one to have a "firm hold on the many-sidedness of reality that comes from sharing a world with others" (Canovan 1988, 186, 191).

3. Rawls 1973, Nagel 1970, Dworkin 1978, and Macedo 1999 represent the liberal view. For a discussion of the multiple ways theorists define "civil society," see Schmidt 1998. As an interesting attempt at using a notion akin to civic friendship to bridge some of the key differences between liberals and communitarians, Susan Mendus suggests that, for the liberal language of strangers and the communitarian/socialist language of brotherhood, one might substitute the language of neighbors. The language of neighbors, she argues, better captures the conception of the agent as self-constituted (capable of forming one's identity anew) yet bounded by ends that are not freely chosen (a product, in part, of one's community).

4. For a description of modern assumptions about friendship, see Parlee et al. 1979, Bensman and Lilienfeld 1979, Friedman 1989, Williams 1992, and Cocking and Kennett 1998. For a discussion of the importance of proximity and like activities for friendship, see Gladwell 1999, 56. For a discussion of the appropriateness of civic friendship to the liberal society, see Spragens 1999, 1–17.

5. For rational choice theorists, see Eisenhardt 1989, Olson 1971, and Axelrod 1984.

6. For criticism of the rational choice model, see Etzioni 1988, Selznick 1992, and Wilson 1993.

7. For an excellent discussion of Homeric and Aristotelian concepts of friendship, see Stern-Gillet 1995, 3–10.

8. Recent major studies of Aristotle on friendship include Schollmeier 1994, Schwarzenbach 1996, Cooper 1980, Rorty 1980, Price 1989, Kraut 1989, Sherman 1989, and Stern-Gillet 1995.

9. On trust, see Baier 1990 and Fukuyama 1995. On caring, see Gilligan 1982, Noddings 1984, Held 1993, and Tronto 1993.

10. Francis Hutcheson, the Scottish Enlightenment thinker, used the term "affection" to denote a middle-distance relationship akin to civic friendship (Hutcheson 1971). See also Hume 1939 and Smith 1902. A similar term, "social affection," is used by Dickens, Carlyle, Ruskin, and other nineteenth-century re-formers to describe behaviors that cannot be accounted for by political econo-mists (Ruskin 1967, x, xi, 15). The critical need for "cohesive sentiments" amid "incommensurable realms of discourse" is powerfully restated by Martin Marty (1997, 69, 157). He stresses that cohesive sentiments involve both rational claims and sentiments or affections (ibid., 69, 164–78).

11. Alternately, the "middle ground" might be thought of as midway be-tween the state and private sectors, a space, in Benjamin Barber's terms, that is simultaneously voluntary and public and that aims at "consensual, integrative, and collaborative action." More specifically, however, Barber defines civil soci-ety as the "*non-governmental*" public spaces we create for our common civic purposes. To the extent that his quarrel is with the "excessive, elephantine, and paternalistic" character of government, many local school sites and districts could certainly claim exemption (Barber n.d., 1–2).

12. Steven Lukes notes that the idea of the independent, rational citizen is a central presupposition of classical liberal democratic theory, one version of which, anchored in contractarian theory, postulates a civil society made up of "independent centres of consciousness" (Lukes 1973, 139–40; see also Schneewind 1986; Frohock 1990).

13. In his discussion of civility, Stephen Carter captures well this more inclu-sive notion of friendship, observing that "our duty to be civil toward others does not depend on whether we like them or not" (1998, 279).

14. For a discussion of the socially constructed and shifting understanding of public and private, see Pateman 1989, 118–40. For a discussion of the merits of locating altruistic behavior along a continuum, see Monroe 1994. For a discus-sion of the difference between emotion and feeling (emotion, unlike feeling, en-tailing a *pattern* of attention), see Elgin 1996, 161–65.

15. Concepts such as mentoring or perhaps networking do seem to combine both affective and rational elements, but they are very individual oriented (*my* mentor, *my* network) and somewhat instrumental (one cultivates a network or attends to a mentor because of the benefits to be derived). But see Parks et al. 1996, 81–101, 154–69, for a discussion of mentoring as key to social engagement

with others from different cultural and class backgrounds. The authors emphasize the importance of compassion and of a felt, empathic connection with others for a commitment to the common good (ibid., 67–72).

16. For a discussion of the mind as a consuming organ with two distinctive
capabilities—that of information processing and reasoning and that of pleasure
machine or consuming organ—see Schelling 1985. For a discussion of the affective and rational component of toleration, see Mendus and Edwards 1987, 1–16.

17. "Koinonia," the Greek word for community, is derived from the adjective
"koinos," which refers to anything shared or held in common and means literally a sharing or partnership (Aristotle 1988, 1280a8–1281a10; see also Schwarzenbach 1996, 104–5).

18. Gutmann and Thompson, in their discussion of reciprocity as background behavior for deliberative democracy, similarly emphasize the importance
of shared understandings (1996, 55).

19. See Aristotle 1988, 1253a27–33; 1900, 1234b33; and MacIntyre 1981,
135.

20. For a discussion of the size of Greek city-states, see Ober 1989, 32–33.

21. In answering one of their guiding questions—whether small districts encourage cooperation and collaboration (better than urban and suburban school
districts do)—the Schmucks give a mixed message. In economically depressed
communities, few professional or business leaders are willing to run for the
school board because of the risk of controversial decisions for their businesses.
Moreover, tightly interwoven kinship networks are, on balance, an additional
hindrance to communication. Although the Schmucks conclude that the school
districts they studied "lack a sense of everyone pulling together," the recommendations they offer for changes in practice suggest some optimism (1992,
176).

22. See also McKean 1975, 30, 34–35. For a critique of the notion of civic
culture, see Pateman 1989, 182.

23. For an extended discussion of the limits of neutrality as impartiality in
civic discourse, see Gutmann and Thompson 1996, 52–94.

24. See Gray 1959, Scott 1990, and Simmel 1955. See also Hansot 1994.

25. Exactly what the purview of Aristotelian friendship might be is subject to
debate. Sibyl Schwarzenbach notes that Aristotle's use of practical reason (integral to his understanding of friendship) rests on the "'educated perception' of
concrete particulars . . . grounded on a prior training and habituation of the
emotions . . . because, in Aristotle's view, the emotions are 'ways of seeing': they
create salience in the environment and thus have cognitive power and content"
(1996, 125). I agree with Schwarzenbach's understanding of Aristotle's use of
practical reason, but I would interpret "salience in the environment" to require
a local context in which specific features of the environment are recognized and
weighed. Schwarzenbach, to the contrary, argues that friendship, though nur-

tured in the concrete circumstances of everyday life, is capable of being extended to a wide range of fellow humans. The example she offers is the Swiss army, reformed into a sort of civil service and thus capable of becoming a part of the training ground for the citizen of the future (ibid., 126-27).

26. Alasdair MacIntyre notes that the Greek idea of a political community as a common project is alien to the modern, liberal, individualist West and suggests schools and hospitals as rough modern approximations to the Greek *polis* (1981, 156).

27. Being local is quite an advantage. In 1985, according to the Gallup polls, parents who had children in public schools tended to rate public education much more highly than the average respondent, and those polled had a higher opinion of local schools than they did of schools in general. Forty-three percent of all respondents rated local schools as A or B, compared to 27 percent who gave those grades to the nation's schools. And a startling 71 percent of parents gave A or B ratings to the school attended by their oldest child (Tyack and Cuban 1995, 30-31).

28. Hegel contrasted "concrete morality" (conscientious consciousness), in which concrete moral decisions are made after considering a feasible number of practical circumstances, to "abstract morality" (pure morality), in which general standards of duty, like the Kantian categorical imperative, invite irresponsible and even capricious behavior because the practice is at a distance and bears on unfamiliar situations (1961, 647-48; 1942, 76 para. 108). Concrete morality might not involve us, for example, in the poignant drama of starvation in Somalia, but it also would not risk "compassion fatigue" precisely because its strong suit is in the ordinariness and the localism of the issues dealt with.

29. *The National Educational Goals Report* (1997) is a case in point. An eighth goal was added that conceptualized adult school roles almost exclusively in terms of their benefits to children's learning or performance in schools. "By the year 2000 every school will promote partnerships that will increase parental involvement and participation in promoting the social, emotional and academic growth of children" (National Education Goals Panel 1997, 3). David Mathews (1995) deals at some length with some of the conditions for strong civic activity in a community, noting particularly the importance of intangibles such as a sense of community and norms of cooperation. For a discussion of the critical role of community in the moral and, by implication, civic education of youth, see Damon 1997.

30. Robert Wuthnow (1998) emphasizes the importance of local organizations in helping to define the conditions under which trust can be exercised, a gray area for many communities.

31. Michael Walzer (1970, 73) similarly distinguishes between a facile empathy that aims at feeling with another person and the more rigorous exercise of joining intellectually and imaginatively in another's situation and choices.

32. Aristotle was well aware of the problems of the "unitary" or homogeneous state; it was part of his criticism of Plato's "Republic": "[A] state is not
made up only of so many men, but of different kinds of men; for similars do not
constitute a state" (Aristotle 1988, 1261a15–25).

33. McKean goes on to discuss the social conditions that support altruistic
behavior. Altruism is understood, in Kenneth Arrow's terms, to be behavior in
which the welfare of each individual depends both on his/her own satisfaction
and on the satisfaction obtained by others, including the satisfaction of *oneself*
contributing to the welfare of others (Arrow 1972, 348–49).

CHAPTER 10: Katz, Devotion and Ambiguity

This narrative is based on material in the case files of the Community Service
Society Archives, Butler Library, Columbia University. Unless otherwise noted,
all details are in the family's case history. All names of private individuals have
been changed.

1. "I have tried to look, with the reader, over Ticknor's shoulder at his
world, to see the moral questions of his time as much as possible from his perspective" (Tyack 1967b, 3).

2. The AICP, founded by Robert Hartley in 1843, was the city's largest voluntary relief organization. The COS was created in 1882 to eliminate fraud and
duplication in relief by investigating applicants for other societies and to reduce
dependency by offering support and advice through friendly visiting. By the
early twentieth century, it also gave relief. To coordinate their efforts, in the
mid-1890s the AICP and COS established a Joint Application Bureau, which received requests for help and parceled them out to the appropriate society. In
1939, the two organizations joined to form the Community Service Society. The
COS divided New York City into districts. Each district had its own office,
headed by a district secretary, with a staff of paid visitors or agents. Visitors had
authority to offer emergency assistance, but the District Committee, composed
of district residents who volunteered their time, made decisions about long-term
care. Committees generally met weekly and contained representatives of the
principal professions and religious denominations. The COS central office maintained a registry of cases and performed other functions, including organizing
specialized committees to consider citywide problems. It also sponsored social
research and the first social work training in the city.

3. At this point in its history, all "visitors," unless designated "friendly visitor," were paid employees of the COS. In cases where the agency thought long-
term support and advice were required, it attempted to assign a volunteer
friendly visitor with the family.

4. Lawrence Veiller, "Map [#16] Showing Over-Crowding of the Buildings
on the Lots and the Consequent Lack of Light and Air Space also Strong-Holds

of Poverty and Agencies for Betterment in the Tenement House District Bounded By . . . 3rd Avenue–12st Avenue. 130th–110th Streets" (original in New York Historical Society).

5. Neighborhood descriptions are based on Bromley and Bromley 1914. On the emergence of tenements as the dominant form of working-class housing in New York City, see Blackmar 1989.

6. Other improved lots on the same side of Second Avenue between 125th and 126th Streets were valued at $26,000; $12,000; $19,000; and $18,000. Values on 125th Street between Third and Second Avenues, on the north side, were $16,000; $18,000; $65,000; $100,000 (a quadruple lot); $13,000; and $19,000. Properties on Third Avenue between 125th and 126th Streets were worth considerably more than their counterparts on Second Avenue: $80,000; $25,000; $25,000; $21,000; $28,500; $27,000; and $40,000 (*Annual Record 1918*).

7. Occupation, ethnic background, and family composition are from the manuscript of the New York State Census, 1915, in the office of the New York County Clerk, 60 Chambers St., Room 141b.

8. An 1879 amendment to New York City's weak 1867 Tenement House Act permitted the construction of dumbbell tenements, so-called because of the distinctive shape of the air shaft that separated buildings joined together at the front and back. The standard source on housing reform in New York City in this period is Lubove 1962.

9. New York City established a separate Domestic Relations Court in 1910. It was located at 57th Street and Third Avenue. Magistrates also heard complaints involving nonsupport and desertion.

10. The SPCC, organized first in 1876 in New York City, investigated complaints of child neglect and abuse. Its quasi-police powers permitted it to charge parents in court and to apply to have children committed to institutions. It also served a quasi-penal function, incarcerating children awaiting trial for crimes, removed temporarily from their homes, or waiting for institutional placement after trials.

11. The New York Catholic Protectory was incorporated in 1862, Westchester, New York City. Its branches were the Lincoln Agricultural School in Lincolndale (formerly Somers Centre), New York, and St. Philip's Home for Industrious Boys, 417 Broome St., New York. The General Office was at 415 Broome Street, New York City. "For destitute and delinquent Catholic children under 14 years of age, entrusted for protection and reformation. 2d. Those between 7 and 16, committed as idle, truant, vicious, or homeless by a Police Magistrate. 3d. Those of a like age transferred by the charge of the Brothers of the Christian Schools. The boys are educated and taught trades in male department at Westchester, and agricultural, dairy work etc., at Lincoln Industrial School. Positions are found for them at St. Philip's Home. Girls' Protectory in

charge of the Sisters of Charity of Mt. St. Vincent. The girls are educated and taught industrial employments. Supported by voluntary contributions and per capita allowance from city. Cared for 4,310 [in 1912]. Receipts, $552,355.94, of which $351,945.88 were from public funds; expenditures, $543,745.11" (Miller 1913, 166–67).

12. New York City first granted pensions to widows under the state's widows' pension law in 1915. The pensions were administered by a new Board of Child Welfare composed of citizens who served without pay. Its executive secretary was Harry Hopkins. Pensions were limited to the widows of citizens and carried other restrictions, including certification of acceptable behavior by an investigation. Pensions were $8.14 per month for each child under sixteen; the first group of widows awarded pensions had an average of 3.13 children, bringing their monthly allowance to $25.48. Because of an ambiguity in the law, New York City at first permitted the Department of Public Charities to conduct investigations. This infuriated the law's champions, who, wanting to distinguish the new pensions from charity, quickly introduced an amendment to the bill (Loeb 1916a, 1916b).

13. New York State Census, 1915.

14. Although they apparently were more desirable, lots and buildings on this block were assessed at a somewhat lower value than the ones on the block where the Warringtons previously had lived (Bromley and Bromley 1914; *Annual Record 1918*). In 1915, 2487 Second Avenue contained twelve families, only one of which housed a boarder and one extended kin. As at 2451, the nativity and occupations of families reflected the makeup of New York's working class. Two women, one from Norway and the other American born, headed households, supported by working children. Male household heads were a Russian laborer in a market, an Austrian shoemaker, an Irish laborer, an American barkeeper, an American interior painter, a Russian paperhanger, an American employee of the New York–New Haven Railroad, an American stenographer, an American driver and truckman, and an American house painter.

REFERENCES

Abbott, Jacob. 1899. *Gentle Measures in the Management and Training of the Young*. New York: Harper.

Abbott, Lyman. 1864. "Southern Evangelization." *New Englander* 23 (Oct.): 244–53.

Adams State College. 1935, 1945–50, 1955–62, 1964. *El Conquistador*. Alamosa, Colo.: Nielsen Library, Archive Room.

———. 1945. *South Coloradan* (Mar.). Alamosa, Colo.: Nielsen Library.

———. 1951–52. *Catalog Bulletin*. Alamosa, Colo.: Nielsen Library, Archive Room.

———. n.d. *South Coloradan*. Alamosa, Colo.: Nielsen Library, Colorado Room, Clip Files.

Aherns, Earl H. 1968. "A Socioeconomic Study of a Spanish-American Barrio in Monte Vista, Colorado," Master's thesis, Adams State College.

Aikin, Wifrid. 1942. *The Story of the Eight Year Study*. New York: Harper and Brothers.

Alberthal, Les. 1999. "Corporate Policy on Community Outreach and Philanthropy," *Executive Speeches* 13, no. 5 (Apr./May): 1–5.

Aleinikoff, T. Alexander. 1977. "A Multicultural Nationalism." *The American Prospect: A Journal for the Liberal Imagination* 36 (Jan.–Feb.): 80–86.

Allen, Jean, ed. 1989. *Can Business Save Education? Strategies for the 1990s*. Washington, D.C.: Heritage Foundation.

Almond, Gabriel A., and Sidney Verba. 1963. *The Civic Culture: Political Attitudes and Democracy in Five Nations*. Princeton, N.J.: Princeton University Press.

Alvord, John. 1867a. *Third Annual Report of the Commissioner of the Bureau of Refugees, Freedmen, and Abandoned Lands*. Washington, D.C.: GPO.

———. 1867b. *Fourth Annual Report of the Commissioner of the Bureau of Refugees, Freedmen, and Abandoned Lands*. Washington, D.C.: GPO.

———. 1868. *Fifth Annual Report of the Commissioner of the Bureau of Refugees, Freedmen, and Abandoned Lands*. Washington, D.C.: GPO.

―――. 1870. *Tenth Annual Report of the Commissioner of the Bureau of Refugees, Freedmen, and Abandoned Lands.* Washington, D.C.: GPO.

American Historical Association. 1934. *Conclusions and Recommendation of the Commission on Social Studies.* New York: Scribner's.

Anderson, James. 1988. *The Education of Blacks in the South, 1860–1935.* Chapel Hill: University of North Carolina Press.

Annual Record of Assessed Valuation of Real Estate, Borough of Manhattan, The City of New York, 1918. 1918. New York: New York Public Library (Map II, Sec. 6, Vol. 5).

Annual Reports of the Board of Education. 1838–50. Boston, Massachusetts: Board of Education.

Annual Reports of the St. Louis Schools. 1868–80. St Louis, Mo.: Board of Education.

Arendt, Hannah. 1958. *The Human Condition.* Chicago: University of Chicago Press.

Aristotle. 1900. "The Nicomachean Ethics." In J. Burnet, ed., *The Ethics of Aristotle.* London: Methuen.

―――. 1985. *Nicomachean Ethics.* Trans. Terence Irwin. Indianapolis: Hackett.

―――. 1988. *The Politics.* Stephen Everson, ed. Cambridge, Engl.: Cambridge University Press.

―――. 1991. *The Nicomachean Ethics.* Trans. David Ross; rev. by J. L. Ackrill and J. O. Urmson. New York: Oxford University Press.

Aritani, Lori. 1998. "On Test Scores, Is It OK to Be Average?" *San Jose Mercury News* (July 2): 1.

Arrow, Kenneth. 1972. "Gifts and Exchanges." *Philosophy and Public Affairs* 1, no. 4: 343–62.

Ashwell, Andrew, and Frank Caropreso, eds. 1989. *Business Leadership: The Third Wave of Education Reform.* New York: The Conference Board.

Axelrod, Robert. 1984. *The Evolution of Cooperation.* New York: Basic Books.

Baier, Annette. 1990. "Trust and Antitrust." In Cass Sunstein, ed., *Feminism and Political Theory,* 279–308. Chicago: University of Chicago Press.

Banks, Nathaniel (Comdr.). 1864. *Report of the Board of Education for Freedmen, Department of the Gulf, 1864.* Washington, D.C.: Daniel Murray Pamphlet Collection, Library of Congress.

Barber, Benjamin R. n.d. "The Search for Civil Society." *Parties and Partisans.* [www.cpn.org/sections/partisans/perspectives/new_democrat/rebuild_search. html]: 1–6.

Bastian, Ann, Norman Fruchter, Marilyn Gittell, Collin Greer, and Kenneth Haskins. 1986. *Choosing Equality: The Case for Democratic Schooling.* Philadelphia: Temple University Press.

Bean, Luther E. 1927. "An Educational Survey of Costilla County Colorado with a Historical Introduction." Master's thesis, Colorado Agricultural and Mechanical College.

Beatty, Jack. 1998. *The World According to Peter Drucker*. New York: The Free Press.

Beinart, Peter. 1997. "The Pride of the Cities." *The New Republic* (June 30): 16–24.

Bennett, Neville. 1976. *Teaching Styles and Pupil Progress*. Cambridge, Mass.: Harvard University Press.

Bennett, William. 1988. *James Madison High School*. Washington, D.C.: U.S. Department of Education.

Bensel, Richard F. 1990. *Yankee Leviathan: The Origins of Central State Authority in America, 1859–1877*. Cambridge, Engl.: Cambridge University Press.

Bensman, Joseph, and Robert Lilienfeld. 1979. "Friendship and Alienation." *Psychology Today* (Oct.): 56–66.

Berg, Ivar. 1971. *Education and Jobs*. Boston, Mass.: Beacon.

Berger, Peter. 1967. *The Sacred Canopy*. Garden City, N.J.: Doubleday.

Berlin, Ira. 1992. *Slaves No More*. Cambridge, Engl.: Cambridge University Press.

Berliner, David C., and Bruce J. Biddle. 1995. *The Manufactured Crisis: Myths, Fraud, and the Attack on America's Public Schools*. Reading, Mass.: Addison-Wesley.

Blackmar, Elizabeth. 1989. *Manhattan for Rent, 1785–1850*. Ithaca, N.Y.: Cornell University Press.

Bloom, Allan, Pierre Hassner, Gertrude Himmelfarb, Irving Kristol, Daniel Patrick Moynihan, and Stephan Sestanovich. 1989. "Responses to Fukuyama." *The National Interest* 16 (summer): 19–35.

Blum, S. J. Virgil. 1958. *Freedom of Choice in Education*. New York: Macmillan.

Bode, Boyd H. 1938. *Progressive Education at the Crossroads*. New York: Newson.

———. 1940. *How We Learn*. Boston, Mass.: D. C. Heath.

Bok, Sissela. 1978. *Lying*. New York: Pantheon Books.

Borman, Kathryn, Louis Costenell, and Karen Gallagher. 1993. "Business Involvement in School Reform: The Rise of the Business Roundtable." In Catherine Marshall, ed., *The New Politics of Race and Gender: The 1992 Politics of Education Association Yearbook*, 69–83. Washington, D.C.: Falmer.

Borrego, Eva. 1946. "Some Educational Aspects Affecting Acculturation of Spanish-Culture Background Students in the San Luis Valley." Master's thesis, Adams State College.

Borrego, Thomas. 1947. "Suggested School District Reorganization in Costilla County." Master's thesis, Adams State College.

Bostis, David A. 1997. *Joint Center for Political and Economic Studies 1997 National Opinion Poll: Children's Issues*. Washington, D.C.: Joint Center for Political and Economic Studies.

Bovard, Bernadine. 1941. "A History of the Progressive Education Association, 1919–1939." Ph.D. diss., University of California, Berkeley.

Bowie, Norman. 1995. "New Directions in Corporate Social Responsibility." In W. Michael Hoffman and Robert E. Frederick, eds., *Business Ethics: Readings and Cases in Corporate Morality*, 3d ed., 597–607. New York: McGraw-Hill.

Bowles, Samuel, and Herbert Gintis. 1976. *Schooling in Capitalist America*. New York: Basic Books.

———. 1996. "Efficient Redistribution: New Roles for Markets, States and Communities." *Politics and Society* 24, no. 4 (Dec.): 307–42.

Bracey, Gerald. 1995a. "The Fifth Bracey Report on the Condition of Public Education." *Phi Delta Kappan* 77, no. 2 (Oct.): 120–36.

———. 1995b. *Final Exam: A Study of the Perpetual Scrutiny of American Education*. Bloomington, Ind.: Technos Press.

———. 1996. "The Sixth Bracey Report on the Condition of Public Education." *Phi Delta Kappan* 78, no. 2 (Oct.): 149–60.

———. 1997. "The Seventh Bracey Report on the Condition of Public Education." *Phi Delta Kappan* 79, no.2 (Oct.): 120–36.

Bradley, Ann. 1993. "The Business of Reforming Cincinnati's Schools." *Education Week* (May 19).

Brameld, Theodore. 1935. "Karl Marx and the American Teacher." *The Social Frontier* (Nov.): 53–56.

Brighouse, Harry. 1996. "Egalitarian Liberals and School Choice." *Politics and Society* 24, no. 4 (Dec.): 457–86.

Brinkley, Alan. 1998. *Liberalism and Its Discontents*. Cambridge, Mass.: Harvard University Press.

Bromley, George, and Walter Bromley. 1914. *Atlas of the City of New York, Borough of Manhattan*, vol. 4. updated and revised. Philadelphia: G. W. Bromley (Plates 14 and 23).

Bronner, Ethan. 1998a. "Better Schools Is Battle Cry for Fall Elections." *New York Times* (Sept. 20): 1.

———. 1998b. "In Bilingual Schooling Setback, Educators See Another Swing of Pendulum." *New York Times* (June 10): B11.

Brookover, William, and Lawrence Lezotte. 1977. *Changes in School Characteristics Coincident with Changes in Student Achievement*. East Lansing: Michigan State University, College of Urban Development.

Brothers, Theresa, ed. 1992. *School Reform: Business, Education and Government as Partners*. New York: The Conference Board.

Bryk, Anthony S., Paul Hill, and Dorothy Shipps. 1998. *Decentralization in Practice: Toward a System of Schools*. Chicago: Consortium on Chicago School Research, University of Chicago.

Bryk, Anthony S., Valerie E. Lee, and Peter B. Holland. 1993. *Catholic Schools and the Common Good*. Cambridge, Mass.: Harvard University Press.

Bryk, Anthony S., Penny Bender Sebring, David Kerbow, Sharon Rollow, and John Q. Easton. 1998. *Charting Chicago School Reform: Democratic Localism as a Lever for Change*. Boulder, Colo.: Westview Press.

Bullard, Pamela, and Barbara Taylor. 1993. *Making School Reform Happen*. Boston, Mass.: Allyn and Bacon.

Butchart, Ronald E. 1980. *Northern Schools, Southern Blacks, and Reconstruction*. Westport, Conn.: Greenwood Press.

Callahan, Raymond E. 1962. *Education and the Cult of Efficiency: A Study of the Social Forces That Have Shaped the Administration of the Public Schools*. Chicago: University of Chicago Press.

Canovan, Margaret. 1988. "Friendship, Truth, and Politics: Hannah Arendt and Toleration." In Susan Mendus, ed., *Justifying Toleration: Conceptual and Historical Perspectives*, 117–98. Cambridge, Engl.: Cambridge University Press.

Carter, Dan. T. 1995. *The Politics of Rage: George Wallace, the Origins of the New Conservatism and the Transformation of American Politics*. Baton Rouge: Louisiana State University Press.

———. 1996. *From George Wallace to Newt Gingrich: Race in the Conservative Counterrevolution, 1963–1994*. Baton Rouge: Louisiana State University Press.

Carter, Stephen L. 1998. *Civility: Manners, Morals and the Etiquette of Democracy*. New York: Basic Books.

Carter, Thomas. 1970. *Mexican Americans in Schools: A History of Educational Neglect*. New York: College Entrance Examination Board.

Cartwright, William H. 1963. Review of *Education and the Cult of Efficiency* in *The Mississippi Valley Historical Society* 49 (Mar.): 722–23.

Centennial High School. 1960–62. *The Rambler*. San Luis, Colo.: Centennial High School Library.

Cha, Yun-Kyung. 1991. "Effect of the Global System on Language Instruction, 1850–1986." *Sociology of Education* 64, no. 1: 19–32.

Chabbott, Colette. 1996. "Constructing Educational Development." Ph.D. diss., Stanford University.

Chamberlain, D. H. 1864. "Reconstruction and the Negro." *North American Review* 128, no. 267: 161–73.

Cheney, Lynn, and Thomas Romberg. 1997. "Creative Math or Just 'Fuzzy Math'?" *New York Times* (Aug. 11): A13.

Chicago Tribune. 1988. *Chicago Schools: Worst in America*. Chicago: *Chicago Tribune*.

Childs, John L. 1956. *American Pragmatism and Education*. New York: Henry Holt.

Chubb, John E., and Terry M. Moe. 1990. *Politics, Markets and America's Schools*. Washington, D.C.: Brookings Institution.

Clapp, Elsie Ripley. 1932. "Learning and Indoctrination." *Progressive Education* 9, no. 4 (Apr.): 269–72.

Clarkson, Max B. E. 1995. "A Stakeholder Framework for Analyzing and Evaluating Corporate Social Responsibility." *Academy of Management Review* 20, no. 1 (Jan.): 92–117.

Clifford, Geraldine J. 1975. Review in *Science* 188 (May 23): 832–34.

Cocking, Dean, and Jeanette Kennett. 1998. "Friendship and the Self." *Ethics* 108 (Apr.): 502–27.

Cohen, David K., and James P. Spillane. 1992. "Policy and Practice: The Relations Between Governance and Instruction." In Gerald Grant, ed., *Review of Research in Education*, vol. 18, pp. 3–50. Washington, D.C.: American Educational Research Association.

Cohen, Ronald. 1975. Review in *Thought* 50, no. 199 (Dec.): 458–60.

Coleman, James S., E. Q. Campbell, D. J. Hobson, J. McPartland, A. M. Mood, F. D. Weinfeld, and R. L. York. 1966. *Equality of Educational Opportunity*. Washington, D.C.: GPO.

Coleman, James S., and Thomas Hoffer. 1987. *Public and Private High Schools: The Impact of Communities*. New York: Basic Books.

Conant, James Bryant. 1959. *The American High School Today*. New York: McGraw-Hill.

———. 1961. *Slums and Suburbs*. New York: McGraw-Hill.

———. 1964. *Shaping Educational Policy*. New York: McGraw-Hill.

Consortium for Policy Research in Education. 1998. "States and Districts and Comprehensive School Reform." *Policy Briefs*, RB–24 (May): 1–11.

Cooper, John. 1980. "Aristotle on Friendship." In Amelie Rorty, ed., *Essays on Aristotle's Ethics*, 301–46. Berkeley: University of California Press.

———. 1990. "Political Animals and Civic Friendship." In Gunther Patzig, ed., *Aristotle's "Politik."* Göttingen: Vandenhoeck und Ruprecht.

Costilla County Free Press. 1949. "Costilla County Education Directory, 1949–1950." San Luis, Colo. (Sept. 30).

———. 1954. "Primary Election Notice to the Electors of Costilla County." San Luis, Colo.: *Costilla County Free Press* (Sept. 3).

———. 1961. "Honor Roll, Centennial Union High School." San Luis, Colo. (Mar. 17).

Counts, George S. 1922. *The Selective Character of American Secondary Education*. Chicago: University of Chicago.

———. 1927. *The Social Composition of Boards of Education*. Chicago: University of Chicago.

———. 1929. *Secondary Education and Industrialism*. Cambridge, Mass.: Harvard University Press.

———. 1930. *American Road to Culture*. New York: John Day.

———. 1932. "Dare Progressive Education Be Progressive?" *Progressive Education* 9, no. 4 (Apr.): 257–63.

———. 1938. *The Prospects of American Democracy*. New York: John Day.

———. 1939. "Whose Twilight?" *Social Frontier* 5, no. 42 (Feb.): 135–40.

———. 1941. *The Education of Free Men in American Democracy*. Washington, D.C.: National Education Association.

———. 1951. *American Education Through the Soviet Looking Glass*. New York: Teachers College Bureau of Publications.

———. 1962. *Education and the Foundations of Human Freedom*. Pittsburgh, Pa.: University of Pittsburgh Press.

———. 1971a. "A Humble Autobiography." In Robert Havighurst, ed., *Leaders in American Education: The Seventh Yearbook of the National Society for the Study of Education*. Chicago: University of Chicago Press.

———. 1971b. "International, Intercultural, and Interracial Education." *Viewpoints* 47 (Sept.): 1–18.

———. 1978 [1932]. *Dare the School Build a New Social Order?* Carbondale: Southern Illinois University Press.

Counts, George S., et al. (Committee of the Progressive Education Association on Social and Economic Problems). 1933. *A Call to the Teachers of the Nation*. New York: John Day.

Covello, Leonard. 1958. *The Heart Is the Teacher*. New York: McGraw-Hill.

Cremin, Lawrence A. 1957. *The Republic and the School: Horace Mann on the Education of Free Men*. New York: Teachers College Press.

———. 1961. *The Transformation of the School: Progressivism in American Education, 1876–1957*. New York: Knopf.

———. 1963. Review of *Education and the Cult of Efficiency* in *Teachers College Record* 65, no. 2 (Nov.): 184–86.

———. 1988. *American Education: The Metropolitan Experience, 1876–1980*. New York: Harper and Row.

———. 1990. *Popular Education and Its Discontents*. New York: Harper and Row.

Cronin, Joseph. 1973. *The Control of Urban Schools: Perspectives on the Power of Educational Reformers*. New York: Free Press.

Cuban, Larry. 1976. *School Chiefs Under Fire*. Chicago: University of Chicago Press.

———. 1992. "The Corporate Myth of Reforming Public Schools." *Phi Delta Kappan* 72, no. 2 (Oct.): 157–59.

———. 1993. *How Teachers Taught*, 2d ed. New York: Teachers College Press.

———. 1999. *How Scholars Trumped Teachers: Change Without Reform in University Curriculum, Teaching, and Research, 1890–1990*. New York: Teachers College Press.

Curry, Jabez Lamar Monroe. 1885. *National Education Association Journal of Addresses and Proceedings*. Madison, Wis.: National Education Association.

Curti, Merle. 1935. *The Social Ideas of American Educators*. Totowa, N.J.: Littlefield, Adams.

Cutler, William III. 1976. "The Systematization of American Education." *History of Education Quarterly* 16, no. 1: 79–92.

Daily Delta. 1862. "Our Schools." *Daily Delta* (Sept. 18): 3.

Daley, Herman E., and John B. Cobb, Jr. 1989. *For the Common Good*. Boston, Mass.: Beacon Press.

Damon, William. 1997. *The Youth Charter: How Communities Can Work Together to Raise Standards for All Our Children*. New York: Free Press.

Del Norte High School. 1951. *El Rio*. Del Norte, Colo.: Del Norte Administrative Office.

Del Norte School District. 1924. "Census List for School-aged Children Between Six and Twenty-One." Del Norte, Colo.: Del Norte High School Archive Room.

———. 1950. "Census List for School-aged Children Between Six and Twenty-One." Del Norte, Colo.: Del Norte High School Archive Room.

Delpit, Lisa. 1988. "The Silenced Dialogue: Power and Pedagogy in Educating Other People's Children." *Harvard Educational Review* 58: 280–98.

Del Valle, Sandra. 1998. "Bilingual Education for Puerto Ricans in New York City: From Hope to Compromise." *Harvard Educational Review* 68, no. 2 (summer): 193–217.

Designs for Change. 1995. *Voucher Myths and Realities: The Chicago School Voucher Legislation*. Chicago: Designs for Change.

Dewey, John. 1900. *The School and Society*. Chicago: University of Chicago Press.

———. 1902. *The Educational Situation*. Chicago: University of Chicago Press.

———. 1916. *Democracy and Education*. New York: Free Press.

———. 1934a. "Can Education Share in Social Reconstruction?" *Social Frontier* (Oct.): 12.

———. 1934b. *Education and the Social Order*. New York: John Day.

———. 1935. "Liberty and Social Control." *Social Frontier* (Nov.): 41–42.

———. 1938. *Experience and Education.* New York: Macmillan.

DiMaggio, Paul. 1992. "Interest and Agency in Institutional Theory." In Lynn Zucker, ed., *Institutional Patterns and Organizations,* 3–21. Cambridge, Mass.: Ballinger.

Donato, Rubén. 1999. "Hispano Education and the Implications of Autonomy: Four School Systems in Southern Colorado, 1920–1963." *Harvard Educational Review* 69, no. 2: 117–49.

Donley, Marshall O. 1976. *Power to the Teacher: How America's Educators Became Militant.* Bloomington: Indiana University Press.

Doyle, Denis P. 1992. "The Challenge, the Opportunity." *Phi Delta Kappan* 73, no. 7 (Mar.): 512–20.

Doyle, Denis P., Bruce S. Cooper, and Roberta Trachtman. 1991. *Taking Charge: State Action on School Reform in the 1990s.* Indianapolis, Ind.: Hudson Institute.

Doyle, Elisabeth Joan. 1960. "Nurseries of Treason: Schools in Occupied New Orleans." *Journal of Southern History* 26, no. 2: 161–79.

Dreeben, Robert. 1968. *On What Is Learned in School.* Reading, Mass.: Addison-Wesley.

Drucker, Peter F. 1998. "Civilizing the City." In Frances Hesselbein, Marshall Goldsmith, Richard Beckhard, and Richard F. Schubert, eds., *The Community of the Future,* 1–6. San Francisco: Jossey-Bass.

Du Bois, W. E. B. 1975 [1935]. *Black Reconstruction in America.* New York: Atheneum.

Dworkin, Ronald. 1978. "Liberalism." In Stuart Hampshire, ed., *Public and Private Morality,* 120–43. Cambridge, Engl.: Cambridge University Press.

Eaton, John. 1907. *Grant, Lincoln, and the Freedmen: Reminiscence of the Civil War.* New York: Longmans, Green.

Eaton, William Edward. 1975. *The American Federation of Teachers, 1916–1961: A History of the Movement.* Carbondale: Southern Illinois University Press.

Edmonds, Ron. 1979. "Effective Schools for the Urban Poor." *Educational Leadership* 37, no. 10: 18–24.

Edsall, Thomas Byrne, and Mary D. Edsall. 1991. *Chain Reaction: The Impact of Race, Rights, and Taxes on American Politics.* New York: W. W. Norton.

Education Week. 1997. *Quality Counts: A Report Card on the Condition of Public Education in the 50 States.* Washington, D.C.: *Education Week.*

Eisenhardt, Kathleen. 1989. "Agency Theory: An Assessment and Review." *Academy of Management Review* 14: 57–74.

Elam, Stanley, ed. 1989. *The Gallup/Phi Delta Kappa Polls of Attitudes Toward Public Schools, 1969–1988.* Bloomington, Ind.: Phi Delta Kappa Foundation.

Elam, Stanley, Lowell Rose, and Arthur Gallup. 1996. "The 28th Annual Phi Delta Kappa/Gallup Poll of the Public's Attitudes Toward the Public Schools." *Phi Delta Kappan* 78, no. 1 (Sept.): 50–65.

El Democrata del Condado de Costilla County. 1927. "Costilla County Teachers for 1927–1928." *El Democrata del Condado de Costilla County* (San Luis, Colo.) (Oct. 8).

———. 1928. "Notice of Primary Election." *El Democrata del Condado de Costilla County* (San Luis, Colo.) (Oct. 13).

Elgin, Catherine. 1996. *Considered Judgment*. Princeton, N.J.: Princeton University Press.

Elmore, Richard. 1975. "Lessons from Follow Through." *Policy Analysis* 1, no. 3: 459–84.

Elmore, Richard, and Milbrey W. McLaughlin. 1988. *Steady Work*. Santa Monica, Calif.: Rand Corporation.

Etzioni, Amitai. 1988. *The Moral Dimension: Toward a New Economics*. New York: Free Press.

———. 1995. *Rights and the Common Good: The Communitarian Perspective*. New York: St. Martin's Press.

Fantini, Mario. 1973. *Public Schools of Choice*. New York: Simon and Schuster.

Farrell, James J. 1997. *The Spirit of the Sixties: Making Postwar Radicalism*. New York: Routledge.

Faust, Drew Gilpin. 1988. *The Creation of Confederate Nationalism*. Baton Rouge: Louisiana State University Press.

Featherstone, Jay. 1971. *Schools Where Children Learn*. New York: Liveright.

Fields, Jack. 1972. Review of *Education and the Rise of the Corporate State* in *Teachers College Record* 43, no. 4 (summer): 460.

Fine, Michelle. 1991. *Framing Dropouts: Notes on the Politics of an Urban High School*. Albany: SUNY Press.

Firestone, William. 1991. "Educators, Researchers, and the Effective Schools Movement." In J. Bliss, W. Firestone, and C. Richards, eds., *Rethinking Effective Schools: Research and Practice*. Englewood Cliffs, N.J.: Prentice-Hall.

Flannery, Daniel. 1997. "School Violence: Risk, Preventive Intervention, and Policy." *Urban Diversity Series No. 190*. New York: Teachers College, Columbia University, ERIC Clearinghouse on Urban Education (Dec.).

Foner, Eric. 1988. *Reconstruction: America's Unfinished Revolution*. New York: Harper and Row.

Ford Foundation. 1989. *The Common Good: Social Welfare and the American Future*. New York: Ford Foundation.

Fosler, R. Scott. 1990. *The Business Role in State Education Reform*. New York: National Business Roundtable.

Foster, Michelle. 1995. "African American Teachers and Culturally Relevant Pedagogy." In James Banks, ed., *Handbook of Research on Multicultural Education*, 570–81. New York: Macmillan.

Fowler, Francis. 1995. "The International Arena: The Global Village." In Jay P. Scribner and Donald H. Layton, eds., *The Study of Educational Politics: The Politics of Education Association Yearbook, 1994*, 89–102. Washington, D.C.: Falmer.

Fredericksen, Norman. 1994. *The Influence of Minimum Competency Tests in Teaching and Learning*. Princeton, N.J.: Educational Testing Service.

Freedman's Second Reader. 1865. Boston: American Tract Society.

Freedman's Third Reader. 1865. Boston: American Tract Society.

Friedman, Marilyn. 1989. "Feminism and Modern Friendship: Dislocating the Community." *Ethics* 99 (Jan.): 275–90.

Friedman, Milton. 1955. "The Role of Government in Education." In Robert Solo, ed., *Economics and the Public Interest*, 123–44. New Brunswick, N.J.: Rutgers University Press.

———. 1970. "The Social Responsibility of Business Is to Increase Its Profits." *New York Times Magazine* (Sept. 13): 32 (4 pp.).

Frohock, Fred. M. 1990. "Conceptions of Persons." *Social Theory and Practice* 13, no. 1: 12–22.

Fukuyama, Francis. 1989. "The End of History?" *The National Interest* 16 (summer): 3–18.

———. 1995. *Trust: The Social Virtues and the Creation of Prosperity*. New York: Simon and Schuster.

Gage, Nathaniel. 1985. *Hard Gains in the Soft Sciences: The Case of Pedagogy*. Bloomington, Ind.: Phi Delta Kappa.

Gamoran, Adam. 1996. Review of *Catholic Schools and the Common Good* in *Teachers College Record* 97: 483–86.

Garnett, William. 1865. "Education of the Freedmen." *North American Review* 101, no. 209: 529–49.

Gelberg, Denise. 1997. *The Business of Reforming American Schools*. Albany: SUNY Press.

Gilligan, Carol. 1982. *In a Different Voice*. Cambridge, Mass.: Harvard University Press.

Gladwell, Malcolm. 1999. "Six Degrees of Lois Weisberg." *The New Yorker* (Jan. 11): 51–63.

Gonzalez, Gilbert. 1990. *Chicano Education in the Era of Segregation*. Philadelphia: The Balch Institute Press.

Goodenow, Ronald, and Wayne Urban. 1977. "George Counts: A Critical Appreciation." *Educational Forum* 41: 166–74.

Granovetter, Mark. 1973. "The Strength of Weak Ties." *American Journal of Sociology* 78: 1360–80.

Graubard, Allen. 1998. "On the Defense of Public Schools." *Dissent* 45 (winter): 90–94.

Gray, J. Glen. 1959. *The Warriors: Reflections on Men in Battle.* New York: Harper and Row.

Gray, John. 1998. *False Dawn: The Delusions of Global Capitalism.* New York: New Press.

Greer, Colin. 1972. *The Great School Legend.* New York: Basic Books.

Griffin, Alan. 1942. "Teaching in Authoritarian and Democratic States." In Walter Parker, ed., *Educating the Democratic Mind,* 79–94. Albany: SUNY Press.

Guinness, Ralph. 1934. "Teach—Don't Indoctrinate." *High Points* 16 (Jan.): 67–71.

Gutman, Herbert. 1976. *The Black Family in Slavery and Freedom, 1750–1925.* New York: Pantheon.

Gutmann, Amy. 1987. *Democratic Education.* Princeton, N.J.: Princeton University Press.

Gutmann, Amy, and Dennis Thompson. 1996. *Democracy and Disagreement.* Cambridge, Mass.: Harvard University Press.

Hacker, Andrew. 1997. *Money: Who Has How Much and Why?* New York: Scribner.

Haley, Margaret. 1981 [1904]. "Why Teachers Should Organize." In Nancy Hoffman, ed., *Women's "True" Profession: Voices from the History of Teaching,* 289–95. Old Westbury, N.Y.: Feminist Press.

Hallinan, Maureen, and Michael Olneck, eds. 1982. Special issue on public and private schools. *Sociology of Education* 55, nos. 2/3.

Hanna, Paul. 1932. "The Need for Teacher Training." *Progressive Education* 9, no. 4 (Apr.): 273–74.

Hansot, Elisabeth. 1994. "Selves, Survival, and Resistance in *The Handmaid's Tale.*" *Utopian Studies* 5, no. 2: 56–69.

Harlan, Louis. 1958. *Separate and Unequal: Public School Campaigns and Racism in the Southern Seaboard States, 1901–1915.* Chapel Hill: University of North Carolina Press.

Harris, William C. 1962. *Leroy Pope Walker, Confederate Secretary of War.* Tuscaloosa, Ala.: Confederate.

Hartz, Louis. 1955. *The Liberal Political Tradition in America.* New York: Harcourt Brace.

Hausman, Daniel M. 1996. "Problems with Supply Side Egalitarianism." *Politics and Society* 24, no. 4 (Dec.): 343–52.

Hegel, G. W. F. 1942. *Hegel's Philosophy of Right.* Trans. T. M. Knox. Oxford: Clarendon Press.

———. 1961. *Phenomenology of Mind.* Trans. J. B. Baillie. London: George Allen and Unwin.

Held, Virginia. 1993. *Feminist Morality: Transforming Culture, Society, and Politics.* Chicago: University of Chicago Press.

Hess, G. Alfred, Jr. 1995. *Restructuring Urban Schools.* New York: Teachers College Press.

Hill, Paul. 1993. *High Schools with Character.* Santa Monica, Calif.: Rand Corporation.

Hill, Paul T., Lawrence C. Pierce, and James W. Guthrie. 1997. *Reinventing Public Education: How Contracting Can Transform America's Schools.* Chicago: University of Chicago Press.

Hirsch, E. D. 1987. *Cultural Literacy.* Boston: Houghton-Mifflin.

———. 1996. *The Schools That We Need and Why We Don't Have Them.* New York: Doubleday.

Hirschman, Albert O. 1970. *Exit, Voice, and Loyalty: Responses to Decline in Firms, Organizations, and States.* Cambridge, Mass.: Harvard University Press.

Hofstadter, Richard. 1979. *The Progressive Historians.* Chicago: University of Chicago Press.

Hollinger, David. 1975. "Ethnic Diversity, Cosmopolitanism, and the Emergence of the American Liberal Intelligentsia." *American Quarterly* 27, no. 2 (May): 144–45.

Hook, Sidney. 1963. *Education for Modern Man.* New York: Knopf.

———. 1991. Letter to Daniel Tanner. In Daniel Tanner, ed., *Crusade for Democracy: Progressive Education at the Crossroads,* 38. Albany: SUNY Press.

House, Ernest. 1978. "No Simple Answer: Critique of the Follow Through Evaluation." *Harvard Educational Review* 52, no. 4: 128–61.

Howe, Daniel Walker. 1979. *The Political Culture of the American Whigs.* Chicago: University of Chicago Press.

Hume, David. 1939. *A Treatise on Human Nature.* London: Oxford University Press.

Hutcheson, Francis. 1971. *Illustrations on the Moral Sense [by] Francis Hutcheson.* Ed. Bernard Peach. Cambridge, Mass.: Belknap Press, Harvard University.

Iversen, Robert. 1959. *The Communists and the Schools.* New York: Harcourt, Brace.

Jackson, Phillip. 1986. *The Practice of Teaching.* New York: Teachers College Press.

Jaramillo, Silver. 1955. "Organization, Establishment and Accreditation of Centennial Union High School." Master's thesis, Adams State College.

Jencks, Christopher. 1959. "Toward Public School Reform." *The New Republic* 141 (Nov. 9): 24.

―――. 1966. "Is the Public School Obsolete?" *The Public Interest* 2 (winter): 18–27.

Jones, Robin, John Portz, and Lana Stein. 1997. "The Nature of Civic Involvement in Pittsburgh, Boston and St. Louis." *Urban Affairs Review* 32, no. 6 (July): 871–91.

Jones, Thomas M. 1995. "Instrumental Stakeholder Theory: A Synthesis of Ethics and Economics." *Academy of Management Review* 20, no. 2 (Apr.): 404–37.

Kaestle, Carl F. 1983. *Pillars of the Republic: Common Schools and American Society, 1780–1860.* New York: Hill and Wang.

Kallen, Horace. 1934a. "Can We Be Saved By Indoctrination?" *Progressive Education* 11 (Jan.): 55–62.

―――. 1934b. *Education Versus Indoctrination*, Public Policy Pamphlet No. 13. Chicago: University of Chicago Press.

Kanigel, Robert. 1997. *The One Best Way: Frederick Winslow Taylor and the Enigma of Efficiency.* New York: Viking Press.

Kantor, Harvey, and Barbara Brenzel. 1993. "Urban Education and the 'Truly Disadvantaged': The Historical Roots of the Contemporary Crisis." In Michael B. Katz, ed., *The "Underclass" Debate: Views from History*, 366–402. Princeton, N.J.: Princeton University Press.

Kantor, Harvey, and David Tyack, eds. 1982. *Work, Youth, and Schooling: Historical Perspectives on Vocationalism in American Education.* Stanford, Calif.: Stanford University Press.

Karier, Clarence, Paul Violas, and Joel Spring. 1973. *Roots of Crisis: American Education in the Twentieth Century.* Chicago: Rand McNally.

Katz, Michael. 1966. "American History Textbooks and Social Reform in the 1930s." *Paedogogica Historica* 6, no. 1: 143–60.

―――. 1968. *The Irony of Early School Reform: Educational Innovation in Mid-Nineteenth Century Massachusetts.* Cambridge, Mass.: Harvard University Press.

―――. 1971. *Class, Bureaucracy and Schools: The Illusion of Educational Change in America.* New York: Praeger.

―――. 1987. *Reconstructing American Education.* Cambridge, Mass.: Harvard University Press.

―――. 1992. "Chicago School Reform as History." *Teachers College Record* 92, no. 1 (fall): 56–72.

Kearns, David T., and Denis P. Doyle. 1989. *Winning the Brain Race: A Bold Plan to Make Our Schools Competitive.* San Francisco: Institute for Contemporary Studies.

Kershner, Charles T., Julia E. Koppich, and Joseph G. Weeres. 1997. *United Mind Workers: Unions and Teaching in the Knowledge Society*. San Francisco: Jossey-Bass.

Kilpatrick, William Heard. 1935. "Freedom in the Schools." *New York Times* (July 14): Sec. 9, p. 9.

———. 1939. "The Promise of Education." *New Republic* (Nov. 8): 57–62.

Kingdon, John W. 1995. *Agendas, Alternatives and Public Policies*. 2d ed. New York: Harper Collins College Publishers.

Kirp, David L. 1982. "An Educational Tale." *Commentary* (Nov.): 74–78.

Kirst, Michael. 1988. "Recent State Education Reform in the U.S." *Educational Administration Quarterly* 24, no. 3: 21–29.

Kliebard, Herbert M. 1995. *The Struggle for the American Curriculum, 1893–1958*. New York: Routledge.

Kluger, Richard. 1977. *Simple Justice: The History of Brown v. Board of Education and Black America's Struggle for Equality*. New York: Vintage Books.

Knox, Paul L., and Peter J. Taylor, eds. 1995. *World Cities in a World System*. Cambridge, Engl.: Cambridge University Press.

Kohl, Herbert. 1967. *36 Children*. New York: New American Library.

———. 1980. "Can the Schools Build a New Social Order?" *Journal of Education* 162 (summer): 57–66.

Kozol, Jonathan. 1967. *Death at an Early Age*. New York: Bantam Books.

———. 1991. *Savage Inequalities*. New York: Crown Publishers.

Kraut, Richard. 1989. *Aristotle on the Human Good*. Princeton, N.J.: Princeton University Press.

Kristof, Nicholas D. 1999. "At This Rate, We'll Be Global in Another Hundred Years." *New York Times* (May 23): WK-5.

Krug, Edward. 1972. *The Shaping of the American High School, 1920–1941*, vol. 2. Madison: University of Wisconsin Press.

Labaree, David F. 1997a. *How to Succeed in School Without Really Learning: The Credentials Race in American Education*. New Haven, Conn.: Yale University Press.

———. 1997b. "Public Goods, Private Goods: The American Struggle over Educational Goals." *American Educational Research Journal* 34, no. 1: 39–81.

Ladson-Billings, Gloria. 1994. *Dreamkeepers*. San Francisco: Jossey-Bass.

Lagemann, Ellen Condliffe. 1992. "Prophesy or Profession? George S. Counts and the Social Study of Education." *American Journal of Education* 100 (Feb.): 137–65.

Lakoff, George. 1996. *Moral Politics*. Chicago: University of Chicago Press.

Lamore, James W. 1988. *What Rules America?* St. Paul, Minn.: West Publishing.

Lasch, Christopher. 1973. "Inequality and Education." *New York Review of Books* (May 17): 23.

Lawton, Millicent. 1996. "Three Business Groups Advocate Common Reform Agenda." *Education Week* (Oct. 2): 10.

Lazerson, Marvin. 1973. "Revisionism and American Educational History." *Harvard Educational Review* 43, no. 2: 278.

———. 1975. Review in *School Review* 83, no. 4 (Aug.): 722–25.

Lee, Valerie E., Anthony S. Bryk, and Julia A. Smith. 1993. "The Organization of Effective Secondary Schools." In Linda Darling-Hammond, ed., *Review of Educational Research*, 171–267. Washington, D.C.: American Educational Research Association.

Leidecker, Kurt F. 1946. *Yankee Teacher: The Life of William Torrey Harris*. New York: Philosophical Library.

Levin, Henry. 1998. "Educational Performance Standards and the Economy." *Educational Researcher* 27, no. 4: 4–10.

Levine, Daniel, and Lawrence Lezotte. 1990. *Unusually Effective Schools: A Review and Analysis of Research and Practice*. Madison, Wis.: National Center for Effective Schools Research and Development.

Lieberman, Myron. 1960. *The Future of American Education*. Chicago: University of Chicago Press.

———. 1989. *Privatization and Educational Choice*. New York: St. Martin's Press.

Liebow, Elliot. 1967. *Tally's Corner: A Study of Negro Streetcorner Men*. Boston: Little, Brown.

Lightfoot, Sara Lawrence. 1978. *Worlds Apart: Relationships Between Families and Schools*. New York: Basic Books.

———. 1983. *The Good High School*. New York: Basic Books.

Linn, Robert. 1994. "Assessment-Based Reform: Challenges to Educational Measurement." First Annual William Angoff Memorial Lecture. Princeton, N.J.: Educational Testing Service.

Lippke, Richard. 1995. *Radical Business Ethics*. Lanham, Md.: Rowman and Littlefield.

Lippmann, Walter. 1933. *A New Social Order*. New York: John Day.

Litwack, Leon. 1979. *Been in the Storm So Long*. New York: Knopf.

Loeb, Sophie Irene. 1916a. "No 'Charity' in Widows' Pensions or Child Welfare." *Evening World* (Mar. 24). Clippings in Community Service Society Collection, Columbia University, Box 97, Board of Child Welfare 1915–1929 folder.

———. 1916b. "Widows' Pension Law Lowers Public Charges in State Institutions." *Evening World* (Nov. 21). Clippings in Community Service Society Collection, Columbia University, Box 97, Board of Child Welfare 1915–1929 folder.

Los Angeles Times. 1998. "Language, Culture: How Schools Cope." Part 2 of "Public Education: California's Perilous Slide." *Los Angeles Times* (May 18): 1–6.

Loveless, Thomas. 1997. "The Second Great Math Rebellion." *Education Week* (Oct. 15): 48.

Lowe, Robert. 1992. "Choosing Inequality in the Schools." *Monthly Review* 44 (May): 21–34.

Lowe, Robert, and Barbara Miner, eds. 1996. *Selling Out Our Schools: Vouchers, Markets and the Future of Public Education*. Milwaukee, Wis.: Rethinking Schools.

Lubove, Roy. 1962. *The Progressives and the Slums*. Pittsburgh, Pa.: University of Pittsburgh Press.

Lukes, Steven. 1973. *Individualism: Key Concepts in the Social Sciences*. Oxford: Basil Blackwell.

Macedo, Stephen. 1999. *Deliberative Politics: Essays on Democracy and Disagreement*. New York: Oxford University Press.

MacIntyre, Alasdair. 1981. *After Virtue*. Notre Dame, Ind.: University of Notre Dame Press.

MacNair, John. 1864. *Report of the State Superintendent of Public Instruction to the General Assembly of the State of Louisiana*. New Orleans: W. R. Fish.

Mann, Mary. 1904. *Life of Horace Mann*, 5 vols. Boston: Lee and Shepard.

Manuel, Herschel T. 1930. *The Education of Mexican American and Spanish-Speaking Children in Texas*. Austin: University of Texas Press.

March, James G. 1994. *A Primer on Decision Making: How Decisions Happen*. New York: Free Press.

Martin, Cathie Jo. 2000. *Stuck in Neutral: Business and the Politics of Human Capital Investment Policy*. Princeton, N.J.: Princeton University Press.

Marty, Martin E. 1997. *The One and the Many: America's Struggle for the Common Good*. Cambridge, Mass.: Harvard University Press.

Mason, Gabriel. 1935. "Propaganda and Education." *High Points* 17 (Mar.): 37–42.

Mathews, David. 1995. *Is There a Public for Public Schools?* Dayton, Ohio: Kettering Institute.

Mattingly, Paul. 1976. Review in *American Educational Research Journal* 13, no. 1 (winter): 72–75.

Maynard, Robert. 1970. "Black Nationalism and Community Schools." In Henry Levin, ed., *Community Control of Schools*, 100–111. Washington, D.C.: Brookings Institution.

McCluskey, Neil J. 1958. *Public Schools and Moral Education: The Influence of Horace Mann, William T. Harris, and John Dewey*. New York: Columbia University Press.

McDonnell, Lorraine. 1994. "Assessment Policy as Persuasion and Regulation." *American Journal of Education* 102, no. 4: 394–420.

McEneaney, Elizabeth. 1998. "The Transformation of Primary School Science and Mathematics: A Cross-National Analysis, 1900–1995." Ph.D. diss., Stanford University.

McKean, Roland. 1975. "Economics of Trust, Altruism, and Corporate Behavior." In Edmund S. Phelps, ed., *Altruism, Morality and Economic Theory*, 202-32. New York: Russell Sage Foundation.

McLaughlin, Milbrey W. 1975. *Evaluation and Reform: The Elementary and Secondary Education Act of 1965/Title I*. Cambridge, Mass.: Ballinger.

McLean, Robert, and Charles Thomson. 1924. *Spanish and Mexican in Colorado: A Survey of the Spanish Americans and Mexicans in the State of Colorado*. New York: Board of National Missions of the Presbyterian Church in the U.S.A., Department of City, Immigrant, and Industrial Work.

Meier, Deborah. 1995. *The Power of Their Ideas: Lessons for America from a Small School in Harlem*. Boston: Beacon Press.

Mendus, Susan. 1992. "Strangers and Brothers: Liberalism, Socialism and the Concept of Autonomy." In David Milligan and William Watts Miller, eds., *Liberalism, Citizenship and Autonomy*, 26–42. Brookfield, Vt.: Avebury.

Mendus, Susan, and David Edwards, eds. 1987. *On Toleration*. Oxford: Clarendon Press.

Merriam, Charles. 1934. *Civic Education in the United States*. Report of the Commission on the Social Studies, American Historical Association. New York: Scribner's.

Messerli, Jonathan. 1972. *Horace Mann: A Biography*. New York: Knopf.

Meyer, John, and Ronald Jepperson. 2000. "The 'Actors' of Modern Society." *Sociological Theory*.

Meyer, John, David Kamens, Aaron Benavot, Yun-Kyung Cha, and Suk-Ying Wong. 1992. *School Knowledge for the Masses*. London: Falmer.

Meyer, John, Francisco Ramirez, and Yasemin Soysal. 1992. "World Expansion of Mass Education, 1870–1970." *Sociology of Education* 65, no. 2: 128–49.

Meyer, John, and Richard Scott. 1992. *Organizational Environments: Ritual and Rationality*. Newbury Park, Calif.: Sage.

Meyer, John, David Tyack, Joane Nagel, and Audrey Gordon. 1979. "Public Education as Nation-Building in America." *American Journal of Sociology* 85, no. 3: 591–613.

Mickelson, Roslyn Arlyn. 1999. "International Business Machinations: A Case Study of Corporate Involvement in Local Educational Reform." *Teachers College Record* 100, no. 3 (spring): 476–512.

Miller, Lina D. 1913. *New York Charities Directory*, 22d ed. New York: Charity Organization Society.

Mintz, Steven. 1995. *Moralizers and Modernizers: America's Pre-Civil War Reformers*. Baltimore, Md.: Johns Hopkins University Press.

Mirel, Jeffrey. 1993. *The Rise and Fall of an Urban School System: Detroit, 1907–81*. Ann Arbor: University of Michigan Press.

Mitchell, Broadus. 1934. "The Choice Before Us." *Social Frontier* (Nov.): 16.

Mitchell, Theodore. Forthcoming. *The Republic for Which It Stands: Citizenship, Schools, and the State in America.*

Mitchell, Theodore R., and Robert Lowe. 1983. "To Sow Contentment." *Journal of Social History* 24, no. 2: 318–40.

Mizruchi, Mark. 1992. *The Structure of Corporate Political Relations and Their Consequences*. Cambridge, Mass.: Harvard University Press.

Monroe, Kristen Renwick. 1994. "A Fat Lady in a Corset: Altruism and Social Theory." *American Journal of Political Science* 38, no. 4 (Nov.): 861–93.

Monte Vista High School. 1920. *Silver and Gold*. Monte Vista, Colo.: Monte Vista High School Library.

———. 1950. *The Pirateer*. Monte Vista, Colo.: Monte Vista High School Library.

Monte Vista School District. 1925. "Census List for School-aged Children Between Six and Twenty-one." Monte Vista, Colo.: School District Administration Building.

———. 1950. "Census List for School-aged Children Between Six and Twenty-one." Monte Vista, Colo.: School District Administration Building.

Moreo, Dominic. 1996. *Schools in the Great Depression*. New York: Garland.

Morlan, George. 1932. "The Paradox of Planning." *Progressive Education* 9, no. 5 (May): 341–43.

Morning Light. 1950. "Class of 93 to Graduate from Trinidad High School Tonight" (May 30). Denver, Colo.: Denver Historical Society, Trinidad Co.

Morrisey, George L. 1976. *Management by Objectives and Results in the Public Sector*. Reading, Mass.: Addison-Wesley.

Moulton, Samuel W. 1867. "Addresses and Ceremonies at the New Year's Festival to Freedmen, Arlington Heights." Washington, D.C.: Library of Congress, Daniel Murray Pamphlet Collection.

Murgatroyd, Stephen, and Colin Morgen. 1993. *Total Quality Management and the School*. Philadelphia, Pa.: Open University Press.

Murphy, Joseph, Phillip Hallinger, and Richard Mesa. 1985. "School Effectiveness: Checking Progress and Assumptions and Developing a Role for State and Federal Government." *Teachers College Record* 86, no. 4: 615–41.

Murphy, Marjorie. 1990. *Blackboard Unions: The AFT and the NEA, 1900–1980*. Ithaca, N.Y.: Cornell University Press.

Myrdal, Gunnar. 1944. *An American Dilemma*. New York: Harper.

Nagel, Thomas. 1970. *The Possibility of Altruism*. Oxford: Clarendon Press.

Nash, Achsa. 1949. "A Community School for Los Fuertes." Master's thesis, Adams State College.

National Alliance of Business. 1989. *A Blueprint for Business on Restructuring Education*. Washington, D.C.: National Alliance of Business.

———. 1990. *Business Strategies That Work: A Planning Guide for Education Restructuring*. Washington, D.C.: National Alliance of Business.

National Business Roundtable. 1990. "Essential Components of a Successful Education System: The Business Roundtable Education Policy Agenda." Sept. 11, unpublished document. Washington, D.C.

———. 1996. *A Business Leader's Guide to Setting Academic Standards*. Washington, D.C.: National Business Roundtable.

National Education Goals Panel. 1995. *Building a Nation of Learners*. Washington, D.C.: GPO.

———. 1997. *National Education Goals Report*. Washington, D.C.: GPO.

National Research Council. 1998. *Preventing Reading Difficulties in Young Children*. Washington, D.C.: National Research Council.

Nelson, William. 1982. *The Roots of American Bureaucracy*. Cambridge, Mass.: Harvard University Press.

New Republic. 1959. "Letters." *New Republic* 141 (Nov. 23): 23–24.

Niece, Richard, and Karen Viechnicki. 1987. "Recounting Counts: A Review of George S. Counts' Challenge and the Reactions to 'Dare Progressive Education Be Progressive?'" *Journal of Educational Thought* 21, no. 3 (Dec.): 149–54.

Noddings, Nel. 1984. *Caring: A Feminine Approach to Ethics*. Berkeley: University of California Press.

Novak, Michael. 1989. *The Spirit of Democratic Capitalism*. New York: American Enterprise Institute/Simon and Schuster.

Ober, Josiah. 1989. *Mass and Elites in Democratic Athens*. Princeton, N.J.: Princeton University Press.

Olneck, Michael. 1993. "Terms of Inclusion: Has Multiculturalism Redefined Equality in American Education?" *American Journal of Education* 101 (May): 234–60.

Olneck, Michael, and Marvin Lazerson. 1988. "The School Achievement of Immigrant Children: 1900–1930." In Edward McClellan and William Reese, eds., *The Social History of American Education*, 257–86. Urbana: University of Illinois Press.

Olson, Mancur. 1971. *The Logic of Collective Action: Public Goods and the Theory of Groups*. Cambridge, Mass.: Harvard University Press.

O'Neill, Tip. 1994. *All Politics Is Local and Other Rules of the Game*. Holbrook, Mass.: Bob Adams.

Orfield, Gary, and Susan E. Eaton. 1996. *Dismantling Desegregation: The Quiet Reversal of Brown v. Board of Education*. New York: New Press.

Osborne, David, and Ted Gaebler. 1992. *Reinventing Government: How the Entrepreneurial Spirit Is Transforming the Public Sector*. New York: Plume.

Paris, David. 1995. *Ideology and Educational Reform*. Boulder, Colo.: Westview Press.

Parks, Laurent Daloz, Cheryl Keen, James Keen, and Sharon Daloz-Parks. 1996. *Common Fire: Lives of Commitment in a Complex World*. Boston: Beacon Press.

Parlee, Mary Brown, et al. (the editors of *Psychology Today*). 1979. "The Friendship Bond: Psychology Today's Survey Report on Friendship in America." *Psychology Today* (Oct.): 43–114.

Pateman, Carole. 1989. *The Disorder of Women: Democracy, Feminism and Political Theory*. Stanford, Calif.: Stanford University Press.

Peccolo, Charles. 1949. "District Reorganization as Related to Transportation in the San Luis Valley." Master's thesis, Adams State College.

Pells, Richard H. 1985. *The Liberal Mind in a Conservative Age: American Intellectuals in the 1940s and 1950s*. New York: Harper and Row.

Perlstein, Daniel. 1996. "Community and Democracy in American Schools: Arthurdale and the Fate of Progressive Education." *Teachers College Record 97*, no. 4 (summer): 625–50.

Peters, Norman. 1988. "Saving the Schools: How Business Can Help." *Fortune* (Nov. 7): 42–56.

Peterson, Bob. 1996. "Total Decentralization: Too Much of a Good Thing?" In Robert Lowe and Barbara Miner, eds., *Selling Out Our Schools: Vouchers, Markets and the Future of Public Education*, 54–57. Milwaukee: Rethinking Schools.

Plato. 1961. "Republic." Trans. Paul Shorey. In Edith Hamilton and Huntington Cairns, eds., *Plato: The Collected Dialogues*, 575–844. New York: Pantheon Books.

Portz, John. 1997. *External Actors and the Boston Public Schools: The Courts, the Business Community and the Mayor*. Comparative Urban

Studies Occasional Paper, no. 12. Washington, D.C.: Woodrow Wilson International Center for Scholars.

Potter, David. 1968. *The South and the Sectional Conflict*. Baton Rouge: Louisiana State University Press.

Powell, Arthur G., Eleanor Farrar, and David Cohen. 1985. *The Shopping Mall High School*. Boston: Houghton-Mifflin.

Power, Sally. 1992. "Researching the Impact of Education Policy: Difficulties and Discontinuities." *Journal of Education Policy* 7, no. 5: 493–500.

Price, A. W. 1989. *Love and Friendship in Plato and Aristotle*. Oxford: Clarendon Press.

Progressive Education. 1932a. "The Association Faces Its Opportunities." *Progressive Education* 9, no. 5 (Apr.): 329–31.

———. 1932b. "Notes on the Convention." *Progressive Education* 9, no. 5 (Apr.): 288–91.

Public Agenda. 1994. *First Things First: What Americans Expect from Their Public Schools*. New York: Public Agenda.

———. 1998. *A Lot to Be Thankful For*. New York: Public Agenda.

Public Agenda Online. 1998. "Parents—African-American and White—Have Very Similar Definitions of Good Schooling," www.public-agenda.org (April).

Purcell, Jefferson. 1936. "The Dilemma of the Liberal Teacher," *High Points* 18 (Nov.): 47–50.

Putnam, Robert. 1993. *Making Democracy Work: Civic Traditions in Modern Italy*. Princeton, N.J.: Princeton University Press.

Rakove, Jack. 1996. *Original Meanings: Politics and Ideas in the Making of the Constitution*. New York: Knopf.

Ralph, James H., and John Fennessey. 1983. "Science or Reform: Some Questions About the Effective Schools Model." *Phi Delta Kappan* 64, no. 10: 689–94.

Ramirez, Francisco, and Marc Ventresca. 1992. "Building the Institutions of Mass Schooling." In Bruce Fuller and Richard Rubinson, eds., *The Political Construction of Education*, 47–60. New York: Praeger.

Ramirez, Francisco, and Yun-Kyung Cha. 1990. "Citizenship and Gender: Western Educational Developments in Comparative Perspective." *Research in Sociology of Education and Socialization* 9: 153–74.

Ramos-Zayas, Ana Y. 1998. "Nationalist Ideologies, Neighborhood-Based Activism, and Educational Spaces in Puerto Rican Chicago." *Harvard Educational Review* 68, no. 2 (summer): 164–92.

Raskin, Marcus G. 1986. *The Common Good: Its Politics, Policies, and Philosophy*. New York: Routledge and Kegan Paul.

Rauner, Mary. 1998. "The Worldwide Globalization of Civics Education Topics: 1955–1995." Ph.D. diss., Stanford University.

Ravitch, Diane. 1981. "Forgetting the Question: The Problem of Educational Reform." *The American Scholar* 50, no. 3 (summer): 329–40.

———. 1983. *The Troubled Crusade*. New York: Basic Books.

———. 1984. *The Schools We Deserve*. New York: Basic Books.

———. 1988. *The Great School Wars*, 2d ed. New York: Basic Books.

Rawls, John. 1973. *A Theory of Justice*. London: Oxford University Press.

Raywid, Maryann. 1985. "Family Choice Arrangements in Public Schools: A Review of the Literature." *Review of Educational Research* 55, no. 4: 435–67.

Reese, William J. 1995. *The Origins of the American High School*. New Haven, Conn.: Yale University Press.

Reich, Robert B. 1991. *The Work of Nations: Preparing Ourselves for 21st Century Capitalism*. New York: Knopf.

———. 1998. "When Naptime Is Over." *The New York Times Magazine* (Jan. 25): 32 (3 pp.).

———, ed. 1988. *The Power of Public Ideas*. Cambridge, Mass.: Harvard University Press.

Reynolds, Annie. 1933. *The Education of Mexican and Spanish-Speaking Children in Five Southwestern States*. U.S. Department of the Interior. Washington, D.C.: GPO.

Rich, Wilbur C. 1996. *Black Mayors and School Politics: The Failure of Reform in Detroit, Gary and Newark*. New York: Garland Publishing.

Rickoff, Andrew. 1864. "Freedmen as Citizens." *National Teachers' Association, Addresses and Proceedings*, 303–4. Madison, Wis.: National Education Association.

Riddle, Phyllis. 1993. "Political Authority and University Formation in Europe, 1200–1800." *Sociological Perspectives* 36: 45–62.

Rogers, David. 1968. *110 Livingston Street*. New York: Random House.

Rorty, Amelie, ed. 1980. *Essays on Aristotle's Ethics*. Berkeley: University of California Press.

Rose, Mike. 1995. *Possible Lives: The Promise of Public Education in America*. Boston: Houghton-Mifflin.

Rosenbaum, Robert. 1981. *Mexicano Resistance in the Southwest: The Sacred Right of Self-Preservation*. Austin: University of Texas Press.

Rotberg, Iris, and Jay Harvey. 1993. *Federal Policy Options for Improving the Education of Low-Income Students, Vol. 1: Findings and Recommendations*. Santa Monica, Calif.: Rand.

Rothstein, Richard. 1971. "Down the Up Staircase: Tracking in Schools." *This Magazine Is About Schools* 5 (summer): 103–40.

———. 1993. "The Myth of Public School Failure." *The American Prospect* 13 (spring): 20–34.

————. 1998a. "Charter Conundrum." *American Prospect* (July/Aug.): 46–
54.

————. 1998b. "Reply." *Dissent* 45 (winter): 95–97.

Ruenzel, David. 1995. "Two Schools of Thought." *Teacher Magazine* 6, no.
7: 1–5.

Rugg, Harold. 1941. *That Men May Understand: An American in the Long
Armistice.* New York: Doubleday.

Ruskin, John. 1967. *Unto This Last, and Traffic.* Ed. John Lewis Bradley.
New York: Appleton-Century-Crofts.

Sallis, Edward. 1992. *Total Quality Management in Education.* London:
Philz, Kogan, Page.

Sanchez, George. 1951. *Concerning Segregation of Spanish-Speaking Children in the Public Schools.* Inter-American Education Occasional Papers,
no. 9. Austin: University of Texas Press.

Sandel, Michael. 1978. *Liberalism and the Limits of Justice.* Cambridge,
Engl.: Cambridge University Press.

————. 1996. *Democracy's Discontent: America in Search of a Public Philosophy.* Cambridge, Mass.: Belknap Press.

San Juan Prospector. 1925. "Program for High School Commencement"
(Apr. 30). Denver, Colo.: Denver Historical Society, Del Norte Co.

San Luis School District. 1920–29. *Teachers Register.* San Luis, Colo.: Centennial High School.

————. 1953. *District Meeting* (Aug. 17). San Luis, Colo.: Centennial High
School.

San Miguel, Guadalupe. 1987. *"Let All of Them Take Heed": Mexican
Americans and the Campaign for Educational Equality in Texas, 1910–
1981.* Austin: University of Texas Press.

Sassen, Saskia. 1991. *The Global City: New York, London and Tokyo.*
Princeton, N.J.: Princeton University Press.

————. 1996. *Losing Control? Sovereignty in an Age of Globalization.* New
York: Columbia University Press.

————. 1998. *Globalization and Its Discontents: Essays on the New Mobility
of People and Money.* New York: New Press.

Schelling, Thomas. 1985. "The Mind as a Consuming Organ." In Jon Elster,
ed., *The Multiple Self,* 242–69. Cambridge, Engl.: Cambridge University
Press.

Schmidt, James. 1998. "Civility, Enlightenment, and Society: Conceptual
Confusions and Kantian Remedies." *American Political Science Review*
92, no. 2 (June): 419–27.

Schmuck, Richard A., and Patricia A. Schmuck. 1992. *Small Districts, Big
Problems: Making School Everybody's House.* Newbury Park, Calif.:
Corwin Press.

Schneewind, Jerome B. 1986. "The Uses of Autonomy in Ethical Theory." In Thomas Heller, Morton Sosna, and David Wellbery, eds., *Reconstructing Individualism: Autonomy, Individuality, and the Self in Western Thought,* 64–75. Stanford, Calif.: Stanford University Press.

Schollmeier, Paul. 1994. *Aristotle on Personal and Political Friendship.* Albany: SUNY Press.

Schrag, Peter. 1967. *Village School Downtown.* Boston: Beacon Press.

Schuker, Louis. 1934. "Indoctrination: Much Ado About Nothing." *High Points* 16 (Mar.): 5–17.

Schultz, Stanley. 1975. Review in *Harvard Education Review* 45, no. 3 (Aug.): 379.

Schwartz, Michael. 1998. "Peter Drucker and the Denial of Business Ethics." *Journal of Business Ethics* 17, no. 15 (Nov.): 1685–92.

Schwarzenbach, Sibyl A. 1996. "On Civic Friendship." *Ethics: An International Journal of Social, Political, and Legal Philosophy* 107 (Oct.): 97–128.

Scott, James C. 1990. *Domination and the Arts of Resistance: Hidden Transcripts.* New Haven, Conn.: Yale University Press.

Selznick, Philip. 1992. *The Moral Commonwealth: Social Theory and the Promise of Community.* Berkeley: University of California Press.

Sherman, Nancy. 1989. *The Fabric of Character: Aristotle's Theory of Virtue.* Oxford: Clarendon Press.

Shipps, Dorothy. 1997. "Invisible Hand: Big Business and Chicago School Reform." *Teachers College Press* 99, no. 1 (fall): 73–116.

Shipps, Dorothy, Joseph Kahne, and Mark Smylie. 1999. "The Politics of Urban School Reform: City Legitimacy, City Growth and School Improvement in Chicago." *Educational Policy* 13, no. 4 (Sept.): 518–45.

Shipps, Dorothy, and David Menefee-Libey. 1997. "The New Politics of Decentralization." Paper presented at the Annual Meeting of the American Educational Research Association, Chicago, Ill., Mar. 25.

Silberman, Charles. 1970. *Crisis in the Classroom.* New York: Random House.

Simmel, Georg. 1955. *Conflict.* Trans. Kurt H. Wolff. Glencoe, Ill.: Free Press.

Simmons, Virginia M. 1979. *The San Luis Valley: Land of the Six-Armed Cross.* Boulder, Colo.: Pruett Publishing.

Sizer, Theodore. 1984. *Horace's Compromise: The Dilemma of the American High School.* Boston: Houghton-Mifflin.

Slesinger, Zalmen. 1937. *Education and the Class Struggle: A Critical Examination of the Liberal Educator's Program for Social Reconstruction.* New York: Covici-Friede.

Smith, Adam. 1902. *The Theory of Moral Sentiments.* New York: Collier.

Smith, Eugene, and Ralph Tyler. 1942. *Adventure in American Education, vol. 3: Appraising and Recording Student Progress.* New York: Harper and Brothers.

Smith, Marshall S., and Jennifer O'Day. 1991. "Educational Equality: 1966 and Now." In D. Verstegen, ed., *Spheres of Justice in American Schools,* 105–32. New York: Harper and Row.

Smith, Timothy L. 1964. Review of *Education and the Cult of Efficiency* in *History of Education Quarterly* 4, no. 1: 76–77.

Snyder, Helen L. 1948. "Social and Cultural Aspects of the Spanish-American People in San Luis, Colorado." Master's thesis, Colorado Agricultural and Mechanical College.

Spragens, Thomas A. 1999. "Civic Friendship in Liberal Society." Paper presented at the Annual American Political Science Association Meeting, Washington, D.C., Sept. 1–3.

Spring, Joel H. 1972. *Education and the Rise of the Corporate State.* Boston, Mass.: Beacon Press.

Stedman, Lawrence. 1987. "It's Time We Changed the Effective Schools Formula." *Phi Delta Kappan* 69, no. 3: 215–24.

Stern-Gillet, Suzanne. 1995. *Aristotle's Philosophy of Friendship.* Albany: SUNY Press.

Stoddard, Ellwyn. 1973. *Mexican Americans.* New York: Random House.

Stone, Clarence N. 1989. *Regime Politics: Governing Atlanta, 1946–1988.* Lawrence: University Press of Kansas.

———. 1998. "Civic Capacity and Urban School Reform." In Clarence Stone, ed., *Changing Urban Education,* 12-14, 250–73. Lawrence: University Press of Kansas.

Strauss, Vivian. 1998. "D.C. Test Results Seen as 'Progress': Low Performers in Early Grades Show Biggest Gains." *Washington Post* (June 11): D1.

Tauber, Abraham. 1935. "New Aims for Debate." *High Points* 17 (June): 31.

Taylor, Charles. 1989. *Sources of the Self: The Making of Modern Identity.* Cambridge, Mass.: Harvard University Press.

Tenorio, Rita. 1998. "Charter System Hurts Public Schools." *The Shepherd Express* (Aug. 13): 17.

Thomas, George. 1986. *Christianity and Culture in the 19th-Century United States.* Berkeley: University of California Press.

Thomas, George, John Meyer, John Boli, and Francisco Ramirez. 1987. *Institutional Structure.* Beverly Hills, Calif.: Sage.

Threlkeld, Archie Loyd, et al. (Commission on Character Education, Department of Superintendence, National Education Association). 1932. *Character Education.* Washington, D.C.: American Association of School Administrators.

Tireman, L. S. 1948. *Teaching Spanish-Speaking Children.* Albuquerque: University of New Mexico Press.

Trinidad High School. 1925. *Commencement Program.* Trinidad, Colo.: Trinidad High School Library.

Trinidad School District. 1925. "Census List For School-aged Children Between Six and Twenty-One." Trinidad, Colo.: School District Administration Building.

———. 1950. "Census List For School-aged Children Between Six and Twenty-One." Trinidad, Colo.: School District Administration Building.

Troen, Selwyn B. 1974. "Strategies for Education in a Technological Society (Essay Review)." *History of Education Quarterly* 14, no. 1 (spring): 137–42.

———. 1975. *The Public and the Schools: Shaping the St. Louis System, 1838–1920.* Columbia: University of Missouri Press.

Tronto, Joan C. 1993. *Moral Boundaries: A Political Argument for an Ethic of Care.* New York: Routledge.

Tuveson, Ernest. 1968. *Redeemer Nation: The Idea of America's Millennial Role.* Chicago: University of Chicago Press.

Tyack, David B. 1966a. "Forming the National Character: Paradox in the Educational Thought of the Revolutionary Generation." *Harvard Educational Review* 36, no. 1 (winter): 29–41.

———. 1966b. "The Kingdom of God and the Common School." *Harvard Educational Review* 26, no. 4 (fall): 447–69.

———. 1967a. "Catholic Power, Black Power, and the Schools." *Educational Forum* 32 (Nov.): 27–29.

———. 1967b. *George Ticknor and the Boston Brahmins.* Cambridge, Mass.: Harvard University Press.

———. 1970. "Onward Christian Soldiers: Religion in the American Common School, 1870–1900." In Paul Nash, ed., *History and Education*, 212–55. New York: Random House.

———. 1971. "Religion and Public Education." In *Encyclopedia of Education.* New York: Macmillan.

———. 1974. *The One Best System: A History of American Urban Education.* Cambridge, Mass.: Harvard University Press.

———. 1976. "Ways of Seeing: An Essay on the History of Compulsory Schooling." *Harvard Education Review* 46, no. 3 (Aug.): 355–89.

———. 1978. "The Spread of Public Schooling in Victorian America." *History of Education* 7 (fall): 173–82.

———. 1981. "City Schools: Centralization and Control at the Turn of the Century." In Jerry Israel, ed., *Building the Organizational Society*, 57–72. New York: Free Press.

———. 1989. "Life in the 'Museum of Virtue': The Bleak Vision of Willard Waller." In Donald Willower and William Boyd, eds., *Willard Waller on Education and Schools*, 109–23. Berkeley, Calif.: McCutchan.

Tyack, David B., and Larry Cuban. 1995. *Tinkering Toward Utopia: A Century of Public School Reform.* Cambridge, Mass.: Harvard University Press.

Tyack, David B., and Elisabeth Hansot. 1982. *Managers of Virtue: Public School Leadership in America, 1820–1980.* New York: Basic Books.

———. 1990. *Learning Together: A History of Coeducation in American Public Schools.* New Haven, Conn.: Yale University Press.

Tyack, David B., and Thomas James. 1985. "Moral Majorities and the School Curriculum." *Teachers College Record* 86, no. 4 (summer): 513–37.

Tyack, David B., Thomas James, and Aaron Benavot. 1987. *Law and the Shaping of Public Education, 1785–1954.* Madison: University of Wisconsin Press.

Tyack, David B., and Robert Lowe. 1987. "The Constitutional Moment: Reconstruction and Black Education in the South." In David B. Tyack, Thomas James, and Aaron Benavot, *Law and the Shaping of Public Education 1785–1954*, 133–53. Madison: University of Wisconsin Press.

Tyler, Ralph. 1991. "The John Dewey Society's Early Activities as I Recall Them." In Daniel Tanner, ed., *Crusade for Democracy: Progressive Education at the Crossroads*, 35. Albany: SUNY Press.

U.S. Conference of Mayors. 1996. *Strengthening Public Schools in America's Cities: An Agenda for Action.* Washington, D.C.: U.S. Conference of Mayors.

U.S. Department of Education. 1997. *A Study of Charter Schools: First Year Report, 1997.* Washington, D.C.: Office of Educational Research and Improvement.

Urban, Wayne. 1978. Preface. In George Counts, *Dare the School Build a New Social Order?* Carbondale: Southern Illinois University Press.

Vinovskis, Maris A. 1995. *Education, Society and Economic Opportunity: Historical Perspective on Persistent Issues.* New Haven, Conn.: Yale University Press.

Violas, Paul. 1978. *The Training of the Urban Working Class.* Chicago: Rand McNally.

Vogel, David. 1989. *Fluctuating Fortunes: The Political Power of Business in America.* New York: Basic Books.

Walberg, Herbert J., Michael J. Bakalis, Joseph L. Bast, and Steven Baer. 1988. *We Can Rescue Our Children: The Cure for Chicago's Public School Crisis with Lessons for the Rest of America.* Chicago: Heartland Institute.

Wallach, Michael A., and Lise Wallach. 1990. *Rethinking Goodness.* Albany: SUNY Press.

Walzer, Michael. 1970. *Obligations*. Cambridge, Mass.: Harvard University Press.

Waring, Stephen P. 1991. *Taylorism Transformed: Scientific Management Theory Since 1945*. Chapel Hill: University of North Carolina Press.

Warner, W. Lloyd, Robert Havighurst, and Martin B. Loeb. 1944. *Who Shall Be Educated?* New York: Harper Brothers.

Washburne, Carlton. 1940. *A Living Philosophy of Education*. New York: John Day.

Wattenberg, William. 1936. *On the Educational Front: The Reactions of Teachers Associations in New York and Chicago*. New York: Columbia University Press.

Weber, George. 1971. *Inner-city Children Can Be Taught to Read: Four Successful Schools*. Washington, D.C.: Council for Basic Education.

Weiner, Lois. 1996. "Teachers, Unions, and School Reform: Examining Margaret Haley's Vision." *Educational Foundations* 10, no. 3 (summer): 85–96.

Wells, Amy S. 1993. *Time to Choose: America at the Crossroads of School Choice Policy*. New York: Hill and Wang.

Wells, Amy S., and Robert L. Crain. 1997. *Stepping Over the Color Line*. New Haven, Conn.: Yale University Press.

Westbrook, Robert. 1991. *John Dewey and American Democracy*. Ithaca, N.Y.: Cornell University Press.

Wickersham, James Pyle. 1865. "Education as an Element in Reconstruction." In *National Teachers' Association, Addresses and Proceedings*, 283–97. Hartford, Conn.: American Journal of Education.

Williams, Clifford. 1992. *On Love and Friendship: Philosophical Readings*. Boston: Jones and Bartlett Publishers.

Wilson, James Q. 1989. *What Agencies Do and Why They Do It*. New York: Basic Books.

———. 1993. *The Moral Sense*. New York: Free Press.

Wirt, Frederick, and Michael Kirst. 1989. *Schools in Conflict*. Berkeley, Calif.: McCutchan.

Wiseman, Frederick. 1994. *High School II*. Cambridge, Mass.: Zipporah Films.

Wishy, Bernard. 1968. *The Child and the Republic*. Philadelphia: University of Pennsylvania Press.

Wong, Suk-Ying. 1991. "The Evolution of Social Science Instruction, 1900–86." *Sociology of Education* 64, no. 1: 33–47.

Wood, George. 1992. *Schools That Work*. New York: Dutton.

Wood, Gordon. 1991. *The Radicalism of the American Revolution*. New York: Knopf.

Wuthnow, Robert. 1998. "The Foundations of Trust." *Report from the Institute for Philosophy and Public Policy* [www.puaf.umd.edu/ippp/summer-98/foundations_of_trust.html]: 1–8.

Yee, Gary. 1998. "School Governance: The Mayor's New Role in the Boston Public Schools." Research report prepared for Regime and Institutional Change Study. Stanford University: Consortium for Policy Research in Education.

Yergin, Daniel, and Joseph Stanislaw. 1998. *The Commanding Heights: The Battle Between Government and the Marketplace That Is Remaking the Modern World*. New York: Simon and Schuster.

INDEX

Library of Congress Cataloging-in-Publication Data

Reconstructing the common good in education : coping with
intractable American dilemmas / edited by Larry Cuban
and Dorothy Shipps.
    p. cm.
    ISBN 0-8047-3862-9 (cloth : alk. paper) — ISBN 0-8047-3863-7 (pbk. :
alk. paper)
    Includes bibliographical references and index.
    1. Education—United States. 2. Educational change—United States.
3. Education—Social aspects—United States. I. Cuban, Larry. II. Shipps,
Dorothy.
LA212.R42 2000
370'.973—dc21   00-027258

∞ This book is printed on acid-free, recycled paper.

Original printing 2000

Last figure below indicates year of this printing:

09 08 07 06 05 04 03 02 01 00